# LIVING GREATLY IN THE LAW

EMERITUS PROFESSOR DAVID DIXON worked at UNSW Law from 1989 to 2024, including as Dean 2006–2016. Of Hal, he writes: 'As 84-year-old Hal's kayak sped away from me across the estuary, I knew I had to try to keep up. That could have been an allegory of my years as Dean of UNSW Law, when we set out to renew Hal's vision of legal education in the context of the 21st century. Hal was my friend, mentor and role model for his integrity, bravery and humanity. We talked about his vision for UNSW Law, worked closely together on the Hal Wootten Lecture series, and collaborated on a project to bring Palestinian students to study in a law school imbued with commitment to democracy and the rule of law. Knowing Hal and learning from him was one of the best experiences of my life.'

PROFESSOR ANDREW LYNCH has been Dean of Law & Justice at UNSW since 2020 and a member of the Faculty since 2005. In his 20 years at UNSW he has shared in the appreciation of all that Hal Wootten achieved in his founding of the Law School, as well as the remarkable example he continues to set for the university's students of a life lived with commitment to both professional excellence and justice. Of Hal, he writes: 'It is very hard to look past Hal's many unforgettable turns at the lecture series named after him. But my fondest memory of Hal is a conversation at the time of the Faculty's 50th anniversary in which I shared with him my discovery in the minutes of the 1969 University Council meeting, which noted Hal's appointment as Foundation Dean, the provision of a $500 expense allowance. Hal's deadpan response was simply, "Well, this is the first I've heard of it."'

# LIVING GREATLY IN THE LAW

## HAL WOOTTEN'S SELECTED WRITING AND SPEECHES

Edited by DAVID DIXON and ANDREW LYNCH

UNSW PRESS

UNSW Press acknowledges the Bedegal people, the Traditional Owners of the unceded territory on which the Randwick and Kensington campuses of UNSW are situated, and recognises the continuing connection to Country and culture. We pay our respects to Bedegal Elders past and present.

**A UNSW Press book**

*Published by*
NewSouth Publishing
University of New South Wales Press Ltd
University of New South Wales
Sydney NSW 2052
AUSTRALIA
https://unsw.press/

Our authorised representative in the EU for product safety is Mare Nostrum Group B.V., Mauritskade 21D, 1091 GC Amsterdam, The Netherlands (gpsr@mare-nostrum.co.uk).

National Library of Australia
Cataloguing-in-Publication entry

A catalogue record for this book is available from the National Library of Australia

ISBN     9781761170409 (paperback)
         9781761179082 (ebook)
         9781761178528 (ePDF)

*Cover design* Luke Causby, Blue Cork
*Cover images* (front) Hal Wootten. Photo courtesy of UNSW; (back) portrait of Hal Wootten painted by Ted Markstein. Photo courtesy of UNSW
*Internal design* Josephine Pajor-Markus

All reasonable efforts were taken to obtain permission to use copyright material reproduced in this book, but in some cases copyright could not be traced. The editors welcome information in this regard.

UNSW
SYDNEY

Dedicated to Gillian Cowlishaw

*One thing that struck me was how basic the four values
of love, peace, justice and truth are for people of goodwill.*

— Hal Wootten

# CONTENTS

# FOREWORD

One always felt humbled and grateful working at a law school that had a close association with jurists such as Hal Wootten and Garth Nettheim who challenged you in every exchange to be a better thinker and a better lawyer. Hal would routinely attend law seminars and was visible and active in the intellectual life of the school. We would delight in his annual reply to his eponymous lecture. Aboriginal culture is a gerontocracy, and it teaches you to respect elders. Hal was revered in that way at UNSW Law & Justice. He did what most elders do: poke their nose into matters that defined the culture of a place and its people. He did that at UNSW, and he did that on a national level too, as lawyers should, on many legal issues but particularly Aboriginal people and the law.

We quarrelled on many Indigenous legal issues over the decades, but I am grateful that Hal never shied away from challenging me and questioning me. This formative experience, as a young Aboriginal legal scholar, is a world away from contemporary mores where so much goes unchallenged and there is a reticence to question. There was to be no 'Always was, always will be' grandstanding around Hal, because he would always press you about the utility of a grandstand with no plan. He would always interrogate the political imperative behind ideas for change. He came from a place of profound knowledge about Aboriginal law and culture and had witnessed over the course of his career the consequences of recognition and non-recognition of Aboriginal people in the legal system. He thought deeply about law reform and the strategy required for change. You needed to be well read and well prepared for a legal debate with Hal because he would not equivocate in challenging you, *just because you were Aboriginal*.

His writings on truth and courts and evidence in this collection are a testament to the careful way he thought about the impact of the intersection of the law and its procedures on Aboriginal people. His words about the native title regime, the failure of Keating-era politics to really grapple with the potential of *Mabo* and its detrimental impact on most communities today are accurate and not well understood in a profession that makes huge amounts of money from the crumbs being offered to impecunious and vulnerable communities. Hal was one of those distinguished legal minds who had the courage and care to publicly comment on injustice and unfairness in the law.

Hal's extraordinary contribution to the seminal Royal Commission into Aboriginal Deaths in Custody (RCIADIC), set out in fine detail in this collection, shines a light on the way the legal system and legal professionals grappled with the many manifestations of colonisation upon Aboriginal people from 1788 to the 1990s. But in reading this chapter in particular, it is distressing to reflect on how little has changed in 30 years since RCIADIC. One of the most important conclusions to be drawn from the RCIADIC report, which is poorly understood, is that no amount of reform to the criminal justice system can ever protect Aboriginal people. From sentencing circles to Aboriginal court lists, these are lipstick on a pig. The RCIADIC said that the only way to protect Aboriginal people is to not have them come into contact with the criminal justice system. But that side of the equation – the need for the relinquishing of bureaucracy's stifling control of Indigenous peoples and their empowerment through institutions of self-determination – is still lost on the Australian people and Australian politicians three decades later. There was no semblance of public memory of this in the 2023 referendum debate.

This foreword has singularly focused on Aboriginal matters, because 'unfinished business' remains, as it was for Hal's lifetime, one of the greatest unresolved legal and political issues for this country. And one of the contemporary issues delaying resolution of this is, I believe, the absenting of non-Indigenous lawyers and legal thinkers from this space. Self-determination is not about separatism; it is about entanglement. I was fortunate to learn from Hal and Garth about collaboration and I am fortunate in my life-long legal collaborations with Sean Brennan and Gabrielle Appleby at UNSW Law & Justice who, in that same tradition, have brought their minds and careers to bear on this big legal question and the many reforms attached to it that continue to evade resolution. On that, I conclude with Hal's words:

> Australia is not bound to mean-spiritedly hold its Indigenous people to the limited legal rights that ingenious lawyers can find surviving two hundred years of trampling on them. We seem to have forgotten that it is open to us to be generous and creative.[1]

Therein lies Hal's legacy to my people, and to the Australian legal profession and to my law school of 23 years: on exigent matters that face us domestically and internationally, let us not be cautious, let us be generous and creative, like Hal. It is open to all of us to create change, but especially lawyers in Australia who, no matter what specialisation or area of expertise, can and should turn their minds to the resolution of the original grievance. At least that is the hope for many First Nations people on whom the law always bears harshly.

**Professor Megan Davis** AC, PhD, FAAL, FASSA, FAHA holds the Whitlam and Fraser Chair in Australian Studies at Harvard University, and is a Visiting Professor at Harvard Law School and a Scientia Professor and Balnaves Chair in Constitutional Law at UNSW Sydney.

# 1
# INTRODUCING HAL

## DAVID DIXON AND ANDREW LYNCH

## JOHN HALDEN WOOTTEN AC QC

As an undergraduate at Sydney University during World War II, a young Hal Wootten read Oliver Wendell Holmes, the eminent American jurist, who taught him that it was possible to live greatly in the law. Hal's life went on to provide a vivid demonstration of such greatness. His formal appointments tell part of the story: Queen's Counsel; Dean of Law; Secretary-General of LAWASIA; Supreme Court judge; Royal Commissioner into Aboriginal Deaths in Custody; Companion of the Order of Australia; Deputy President of the Native Title Tribunal; rapporteur to the Minister for Aboriginal Affairs; Chair of the Australian Press Council; and President of the Australian Conservation Foundation. These sit alongside the paths *not* taken, for differing reasons: university lecturer in the 1940s; lawyer in and, later, Chief Justice of Papua New Guinea; and judge of the Court of Appeal of NSW.

But Hal was so much more than a holder of high offices; he had many passionate pursuits, as naturalist, conservationist, birdwatcher and farmer. He was also a lay anthropologist with a long association with the people of Papua New Guinea; friend, mentor and advocate for Indigenous Australians and the people of Palestine; husband to three wives, father to four children, and grandfather to four grandsons.

Finally, there is Hal's personal influence and friendships, from Indigenous people who credit him with transforming their lives, to the 'Originals' of UNSW Law School, to the Palestinian scholars whom he brought to UNSW to study successfully for PhDs, to Ali Gulzari, a talented 16-year-old Hazara whom he took under his wing, and his colleagues across the legal profession, government and beyond. We, current and past deans of UNSW Law School, are proud to be among so many in that final category.

# HAL'S WRITINGS
## The influence of Holmes, Stone and Kerr

Hal said that the primary and enduring influences on him were his grandmother's imparting of 'the moral and lifestyle teaching of the New Testament' and his Uncle Fred's lessons from his battlefield experiences in World War I, which had made him 'a great disrespecter of authority, and a great champion of the common man'.[1] While Hal lost religious faith before university, the combination of Christian values and unhoned socialism founded a commitment to justice which would last a lifetime.

Beyond childhood and through to middle age, there were three individuals whose impacts on Hal should be noted, for different reasons. The trio comprises American jurist, Oliver Wendell Holmes; Professor of Jurisprudence and International Law at the University of Sydney, Julius Stone; and the Chief Justice of NSW, later Governor-General, Sir John Kerr.

Holmes (1841–1935, US Supreme Court Justice 1902–32) was 'the most illustrious figure in the history of American law' whose work 'supplied the leading ideas for the legal-realist movement'.[2] Richard Posner emphasises Holmes's significance as a 'writer-philosopher [whose] distinction as a lawyer, judge, and legal theorist lies precisely in the infusion of literary skill and philosophical insight into his legal work'.[3] This combination both attracted and influenced Hal, as did Holmes's record as an undogmatic free-thinker.

Hal stumbled across Holmes's work and was influenced by both his life and his view of law. Like Hal's Uncle Fred, Holmes was deeply affected by the human experience of war, in his case the American Civil War. While he went on to be a lawyer, professor and judge, Holmes retained a critical distance from the regularities and norms of professional life, which Hal later shared. As an interpreter of the possibilities of being a lawyer, Holmes's impact can be seen in Hal's account in 'Living in the law' (see chapter 3). Reading Holmes convinced Hal, as a disenchanted student, that a worthwhile life in the law was possible.

As a legal theorist, Holmes is now best known for the first sentence of his great work, *The Common Law*: 'the life of the law has not been logic; it has been experience'. He went on from this aphorism, found in thousands of jurisprudence essay titles, to explain:

> The felt necessities of the time, the prevalent moral and political theories, intuitions of public policy, avowed or unconscious, even the prejudices which judges share with their fellow-men, have had a good deal more to do than the syllogism in determining the rules by which men should be governed. The law embodies the story of a nation's development through many centuries, and it cannot be dealt with as if it contained only the axioms and corollaries of a book of mathematics ...[4]

Holmes's words were as heretical to Australian lawyers in the 1940s as they had been to his American readers on their publication in 1881. Such realist revelations provided Hal with outlines of a new perspective on law. Julius Stone, Hal's lecturer in jurisprudence at the University of Sydney, would complete the picture.

Julius Stone (1907–1985) was Professor of Jurisprudence and International Law at the University of Sydney 1941–72 and Visiting Professor at UNSW 1972–85.[5] If Holmes opened Hal's eyes to the possibilities of law, it was Julius Stone who provided intellectual depth and breadth by introducing Hal to Holmes's successors in realist American legal theory. Stone's lectures showed Hal how to see law not just as black-letter doctrine, but as part of society and its structures of power. Judges were faced with an inescapable need to make choices and inevitably did so in social and historical contexts. Hal was Stone's research assistant on his classic work, *The Province and Function of Law*.[6] Hal expressed his appreciation of Stone by arranging for him to join UNSW on his retirement from the University of Sydney. Stone's influence was not just intellectual: he introduced Hal to John Kerr, who was looking for a talented young lawyer to work at the Australian School of Pacific Administration (ASOPA).

Sir John Kerr (1914–1991) influenced Hal's career from the mid-1940s to the mid-1960s. Kerr is irrevocably associated with the later dismissal of the Whitlam Government in the constitutional crisis of 1975, but is a far more substantial and interesting figure than accounts of him as a boozy Cassius to Whitlam's noble Caesar allow.[7] Before becoming Governor-General of Australia (1974–77), he had been an army officer, a barrister, a judge and Chief Justice of NSW, along with other significant appointments.

Kerr recruited Hal to ASOPA, to the Bar Council's committee on Papua New Guinea, and later to LAWASIA, all contributing to Hal's anti-colonialism, internationalism and commitment to regional cooperation. At ASOPA, a young Hal taught law to future New Guinea 'Kiaps' (district and patrol officers) and gained a taste for anthropology from Ian Hogbin.[8] As Hal recounts in 'Living in the law' in chapter 3, Kerr arranged Hal's naval extraction from Manus Island (where he was conducting fieldwork). They then shared chambers at the Sydney Bar, initially working closely together on trade union and industrial cases. Hal learnt from Kerr a problem-solving approach to legal disputes in which case law was a tool of subtle malleability, rather than a rigid determinant of outcomes. This would later influence Hal's vision for UNSW Law. They also collaborated in the Australian Association for Cultural Freedom. The friendship cooled when Kerr's first wife became ill and he cut back public activities, before becoming a judge in 1966. However, Hal remained loyal to Kerr (despite being critical of his role in the dismissal of Whitlam) and spoke often and at length about him in later years. He regretted that Kerr's quality and achievements were eclipsed by the decision that, for many, ruined his erstwhile mentor's reputation.

Kerr and Hal left the Australian Labor Party during the upheavals of the mid-1950s.[9] Despite seeing the worst side of organised labour during his legal practice and despite the Australian Association for Cultural Freedom's anti-communism, Hal never followed Kerr and James McAuley (see below) to the political right. He opposed the threat to civil liberties of all forms of totalitarianism, not just communism. While he could be close to old-school Liberals like Fred Chaney,[10] the modern Liberal Party of John Howard and his successors repulsed Hal for its political exploitation of issues relating to Indigenous policy, refugees and the environment.

## BEYOND INDIVIDUALS

Hal was influenced by groups as much as by individuals. He remained open to learning from experience throughout his life. An important early experience was living with the Usiai in the village of Kawaliap in the middle of Manus Island, where he spent six months when on leave from ASOPA. The villagers showed him a different way to live and to see the world and instilled in him 'an ability to feel at ease with people who were totally different to myself, different in culture, different in education, and different right through'.[11]

A different kind of influence came with Hal's immersion in the improbable intellectual hot-house of ASOPA, which included such intellectuals as the anthropologists Ian Hogbin,[12] Lucy Mair,[13] Camilla Wedgwood,[14] Charles Rowley,[15] and most of all the poet James McAuley[16] (before his conversion to Catholicism and conservatism), who shared Hal's love of nature and the land. Other significant work groups were his students and colleagues at the fledgling law school at UNSW in the early 1970s – Hal's 'band of brothers' (and a few sisters) to whom he pays tribute in chapter 4 – and the legal profession. While often disappointed by some of its members, Hal retained an abiding commitment to the ideal of a profession dedicated to justice and service.

Then there were Indigenous Australians, beginning with Redfern activists who appealed to Hal for help when he became Dean of the new law school and had announced that it was to meet the legal needs of *all* Australians. He assisted Gary Williams, Paul Coe, Gary Foley and others to establish the Aboriginal Legal Service in Redfern. His work with the Royal Commission into Aboriginal Deaths in Custody, and on sacred sites and on native title, extended the circle of Indigenous friends to people such as Richard Frankland, Noel Pearson and Riverbank Frank Doolan. His understanding of Indigenous people was also deeply influenced by his wife, the distinguished anthropologist Professor Gillian Cowlishaw.[17]

Finally, there were Hal's Palestinian and Israeli friends. As chapter 5 shows, Hal was deeply affected by his everyday experience living in Ramallah and his friendships with (and learning from) David Shulman,[18] Avishai Margalit[19] and Raja Shehadeh.[20]

As the following chapters will illustrate, these individuals and groups shaped Hal, but he was more than an amalgam of these influences. He was his own man, making up his own mind and following no party line. He was, he liked to say, a 'maverick'.

## CONTINUITIES AND CONNECTIONS

Hal explained his career in terms of his inability to turn down a job for which he was not qualified. Such self-deprecation obscured strong strands of continuity through his life. One thread was his concern for the underdog, memorably captured in a quotation still greeting all those entering the UNSW Law & Justice building: 'A Law School should have and communicate to its students a concern for those on whom the law bears harshly'. His character and personality allowed him to establish deep and lasting relationships with people outside circles usual for men of his race and class. Secondly, he breathed life into a traditional idea of legal professionalism. The duty to serve the excluded and marginalised was the corollary, not the antithesis, of serving the powerful in government, corporations and unions. Thirdly, Hal loved the law. He was a complete lawyer, one whose black-letter skills enabled him to serve on the Equity Division of the NSW Supreme Court, where abstruse, complex doctrine dominated. He knew that such skills were essential, but not enough: he also (as a student of Holmes and Julius Stone, and as a would-be anthropologist) knew that law had meaning only as one part of society. Fourthly, Hal was never satisfied with analysis: he demanded that it should lead to action. As Hal's friend, lawyer Andrew Chalk, explains in the following chapter, Hal would interrupt endless debate to ask, 'What is the plan?' As a reformer he was far-sighted, but also realistic and pragmatic. He was an exponent of 'nudging', never underestimating the impact and relevance of individual action. Examples included his role in establishing the Aboriginal Legal Service, in founding a scholarship scheme for Palestinian students, and, in a more personal initiative, befriending and supporting Ali Gulzari. Hal's mantra – analyse, plan, act – provides guidance to today's and tomorrow's reformers. He provides distinctive perspectives, driven by his insistence on straight talking, however uncomfortable for his audience.

## INTRODUCING THE CHAPTERS

Andrew Chalk's chapter 2 is followed by Hal's autobiographical account of 'Living in the law'. Hal often said that his proudest achievement was the establishment of a new (and, crucially, a new kind of) law school at UNSW. Chapter 4 explains his vision and its achievement, including a nationwide impact on legal education in Australia. It is particularly appropriate therefore that this collection of Wootten's writings should be published by NewSouth Publishing. A chapter on expert evidence provides insight into his experience as a judge and his knowledge of Indigenous history and cultures. His long association with Papua New Guinea is reflected in the chapter in which Hal discusses the importance and value of legal education there. Hal's reflection on his experience in Israel and Palestine – he lived there for several months in his late 80s – comes next in chapter 5. Then four chapters deal with the diverse areas of Indigenous experience in which Hal had official roles – as founder of the Aboriginal Legal Service, Commissioner on Aboriginal Deaths in Custody, Deputy President of the National Native Title Tribunal, and rapporteur on sacred sites under the Aboriginal and Torres Strait Islander Heritage Protection Act. The final chapter shows his commitment to conservation and the environment, both deeply founded in his love of the natural world and the Australian countryside.

As this collection shows, Hal was a fine public speaker and

writer (even when working under great time pressure, as at the Royal Commission). His sometimes-wicked wit and use of apt citations (whether from great poets, Law Lords or the Bible) made his speeches exhilarating, as well as demonstrating the breadth of his intellectual engagement and voracious, eclectic reading. He often quoted what he had learnt from Wavell to call 'other men's flowers',[21] whether they came from Shakespeare and Oliver Wendell Holmes or CJ Dennis[22] and James Thurber.[23] Gillian Cowlishaw remembers him passing on Thurber's advice: 'You might as well fall flat on your face as lean over too far backwards.'[24]

Although he was a Supreme Court judge, a Queens Counsel and a Companion of the Order of Australia, Wootten was at ease with people from all walks of life, whether they were ministers of the Crown and judges, or Papuan villagers, imprisoned Indigenous people, and Palestinians on the streets of the West Bank. From that flowed empathy and an ability to speak and write impressively and authentically on the experience of others. A fine example, included in this collection, is his account of the death (and life) of an Indigenous prisoner, Malcolm Smith.

This book is not just a homage to Hal or a resource for a long overdue biography of this remarkable Australian. It seeks to bring his wisdom and many insights borne of his experience in the law and in his public engagements to contemporary and future audiences. As we have sorted through Hal's papers and pored over his words – some written more than five decades ago – we have been struck by the clarity of his vision and its crisp relevance to our own times. In part, this is because Hal reached for the large problems, those that are fundamental and enduring, and he did so with an unwavering faith that they were not insoluble. There was *always* some way forward – a 'nudge' to be made towards a better, more just, tomorrow. But in saying that, Hal never pretended that problems of entrenched antagonism or inequality were easily resolved – or even understood. A steady theme in these chapters is Hal's questing search for better understanding, his humility and fairness in doing so, and his aversion to simplistic and dogmatic thinking.

We have edited his writings quite intensively, for example cutting material which referred to controversies and actors that have dated. While some papers are reproduced almost in full, others are presented more selectively with commentaries linking key sections from different papers. However, in all editorial decisions we have been keen to ensure Hal's voice comes through clearly, unaltered from when these speeches were made and articles published. An aspect of this has been our decision to retain Hal's use of the terms 'Aboriginals' and (less often) 'Aborigines', as well as other occasional examples of language that we recognise do not accord with contemporary usage.

We draw not only on published work, but on an archive of unpublished work made available to us by Hal's widow, Professor Gillian Cowlishaw, to whom the book is dedicated. We are deeply grateful to Gillian for allowing us this opportunity and for being so involved in the project. Her comments on Hal's involvement in Indigenous affairs have been essential. We also draw on a series of informal interviews and conversations with Hal by David Dixon (material from these is identified as 'personal communication'). We are grateful, too, to Andrew Chalk for allowing us to include his biographical essay on his dear friend and to our colleague and UNSW Balnaves Professor of Constitutional Law Megan Davis AC for her Foreword. The National Library of Australia completed its archiving of a collection of Hal's personal and working papers too late for us to access for this collection: see <https://catalogue. nla.gov.au/catalog/8633074>. This begs the attention of a biographer.

We have cut, edited and supplemented Hal's notes and references. When we have done more than add a reference, this is identified by ending with 'Eds'. Most chapters include extracts from more than one published piece. The exception is the chapter on Israel and Palestine. Hal published little on this but left a mass of drafts and often overlapping fragments. We have edited these into one essay.

Our research assistants have been invaluable. Kate Jackson extracted and sorted Hal's computer files. Oscar Iredale helped in editing the manuscript, not least in pointing out people who or events which may be unfamiliar to younger readers and where the addition of explanatory references might be helpful. Kate and Oscar are UNSW lawyers of whom Hal would have been proud.

Hal's life was not just long, it was uniquely rich in the breadth of his contributions towards a more just society. His vision was expansive, and he was courageous in acting on his convictions. At each stage of his remarkable career, Hal reflected on the challenges to be faced and the ways through which they might be most effectively met. His writings remain fresh and intensely relevant today. This is not only because they focus on areas in which justice continues to prove elusive – relations between Australia's Indigenous peoples and the post-1788 newcomers, the environment, the Middle East and, of course, the role of law and the legal profession. It is also because as a man and as a writer, Hal displayed such remarkable foresight and principle. These chapters are testament to a life lived greatly.

# 2

# PRINCIPLES, VISION AND ACTION

## ANDREW CHALK

A few weeks before he died at 98 years and in the middle of a COVID lockdown, I received a call from Hal Wootten's wife, the anthropologist Professor Gillian Cowlishaw, who was very concerned about him. We knew that he mightn't have long, so I went over to see him. He was sound asleep when I arrived, but Gillian thought that I should wait to see him nonetheless.[1]

Hal woke up, a bit dazed and groggy and then smiled, said hello, looked at me quizzically and asked, 'And to what paragraph of the Public Health Order do I owe the pleasure of this visit?' I didn't want to plead civil disobedience and I didn't have the heart to tell him that it was a care visit for a dying friend. Sensing that I didn't have an answer, he looked at me, smiled again, and said, 'I suppose it could be a care visit for a dying friend.' I smiled back.

For around two decades, I would catch up with Hal regularly, often every month, and we would sit down over lunch and discuss the state of the world. We discussed the law and Indigenous policy, and what George W Bush or Donald Trump were up to. And we – though more him than me – would reminisce. Sometimes he told stories that I had heard before, but usually they were new. Each time they were wonderful and were told with generosity, humanity and sheer goodwill that said so much about the teller. Indeed, Hal had said, 'One thing that struck me was how basic the four values of love, peace, justice and truth are for people of goodwill.' The guiding influence of those values on him were evident everywhere.

But that afternoon, with Hal well aware that death was finally coming, I had the unique privilege of telling his stories back to him, reminding him of why his life was one of great meaning, why he had lived out his motto – 'to thine own self be true' – and why, in his own humble way, he had had an immeasurable impact on this country.

For a man with such a keen sense of humour, and who led such a reflective life, irony sometimes escaped him. I remember having lunch with him when he was 87 and living at Hawks Nest, 230 kilometres north of Sydney. He was complaining that he was feeling a bit sore. I raised a curious eyebrow, but privately thought it was just an old person complaining about his ailments. However, he went on to say that earlier in the week he had used a wheelbarrow to move 10 tonnes of soil from the front of the house, where it had been delivered, to the back. I asked him why on earth he would do that. His response: 'I want to build up the garden beds so that when I get old, I won't have to bend over so far.'

There was always a certain restlessness to Hal, one that would cause him to spend two months walking the untracked reaches of the Snowy Mountains as a student; or to leave a prestigious city law firm, now MinterEllison, to join the Australian School of Pacific Administration and then head to Manus Island in New Guinea to undertake fieldwork; or to leave a lucrative practice at the Bar and sell up his fledgling cattle enterprise in order to establish a law school; or to leave Australia in his late eighties to spend three months living in Ramallah in order to get a deeper understanding of the Palestinian situation. Hal certainly gave licence to his curiosity, and the more any learning experience involved an element of adventure, the keener he was.

He once told me how he would continually ask his colleagues at the Australian School of Pacific Administration – poets, historians, anthropologists and experienced Kiaps (New Guinea field officers), many of whom had spent years working in very challenging environments – 'Why?'; 'Why do you say that?'; 'Why is that the case?' He genuinely wanted to know the answer, but they came to think of him as the true intellectual among them for doing no more than constantly asking 'Why?' That was something that amused Hal, and he continued to make good use of the technique throughout his life, often to the discomfort of his hyperbolic friends.

People often speak of Hal as a figure on the left of politics. Certainly, in his early days as a lawyer he was briefly a member of the Communist Party. It did not trouble the senior partner who employed him as his personal brains trust. But then Hal would later be the industrial lawyer of choice for the Packers (that was Frank and Kerry, not the storemen) and the pastoralists. He was also the unionists' lawyer of choice on occasion. Whether he was for capital or labour, he was respected by and independent of both. He was not just open to the arguments but determined to test his own assumptions and preferences. He liked to see himself as a maverick, bearing nobody's brand. His compassion was never in doubt, but his intellect was always his guide. No one owned Hal Wootten, but he was loyal to people and causes.

Despite John Kerr's[2] very public shortcomings, Hal remained loyal to him. Kerr had taken Hal up as a protégé and was one of Hal's early mentors, although never in the league of Hal's mother and grandparents. But Hal was also one of the first to privately signal his disapproval after Sir John's dismissal of Gough Whitlam as prime minister in 1975. When Sir John rang him on the day it happened to seek affirmation of what he had done, Hal's response – 'I'm sure you must have had a very good reason' – delivered in his sceptical tone, would not have been the one Kerr was seeking.

Like all of us, Hal was not without his contradictions. He could show enormous patience and sympathy in some situations, especially in dealing with those who were struggling, and yet be short and even cantankerous in others. As his son Richard put it at Hal's funeral,

Dad had a … complex character which still has us wondering even after all these years. To those nearest and dearest to him he had an acerbic side which could be quite unnerving. As children we remember his quick temper and thin patience and we were on the end of many a scolding perhaps we didn't think we deserved.

One of the few times I encountered Hal in a professional capacity was in the early days of the *Native Title Act 1993*, when he was conducting a mediation as Deputy President of the National Native Title Tribunal.

The parties were a group of native title claimants at Peak Hill, for whom I acted, a gold-mining company wanting to mine the old town reserve, the local council, and the NSW Government. Peak Hill is south of Dubbo and the history of the Aboriginal people there, like elsewhere, had been one of dispossession, discrimination, suffering and exclusion.

In listening to each party speak, Hal was unrushed and very attentive. Occasionally he would ask an open question for clarification, but there was no judgment in his manner. He was there to listen and learn. Importantly, no lawyer spoke. It was the people at the heart of the dispute talking directly to one another, airing, in the case of the claimants, grievances that were generations old. The mayor acknowledged the wrongs but spoke of what the mine would do for the town; the miner's CEO, confronted with a situation that he hadn't experienced before, promised that they would be respectful of the community's concerns and interests.

It was a genuine and moving exchange – until the state government, through its barrister and senior lawyers, delivered its legalistic position, which gave no scope for compromise or agreement. In an instant, Hal, the gentle grandfather, transformed into the very grumpy, acutely attuned judge. But there are limits to what a mediator can achieve in the face of intransigence, and with the state unwilling to shift, Hal terminated the mediation. Unlike so many of his successors on the tribunal, who kept matters in fruitless suspension for years, Hal knew there was no value in flogging a dead horse.

Never content with talking about a project or problem, Hal would insist on planning, then acting. This is well illustrated by Richard Wootten's memory of his childhood, given in his eulogy at Hal's funeral:

> If we casually mentioned an interest, he would enthusiastically find us a reference book from his vast and varied library. An interest in a couple of goldfish would lead to tanks of tropical fish which would then lead to saltwater aquariums with seahorses, which would then lead to Mexican walking fish. When my brother Lindsay and I convinced him a 16 feet fishing boat would be a good idea, it appeared as an 18 feet half cabin with

a 100 horsepower motor. Not content with us just fishing we soon found ourselves members of the Volunteer Coastal Patrol plying the seas looking for unfortunates to save. Once he got the bit between his teeth, he generally took a project to new extremes both in his personal and professional lives.

This enthusiasm for a project was never more evident than in his love of hobby farms. Dad always told us being a lawyer was not his preferred occupation. He always wanted to be a farmer. He maintained working on the land was the only way he could turn off his mind from his legal work. It was his relaxation therapy. It almost killed his children several times over.

As with all his projects he supercharged it. His properties grew and he filled them with bigger and more dangerous creatures. A few rough looking Devon cattle became a breeding herd of Red Polls. A few ponies became a herd of quarter horses complete with a pure bloodline stallion. It was Sir Laurence Street who inspired dad to breed quarter horses, which nearly resulted in his early demise when a young horse he was breaking-in kicked him in the stomach perforating his bowel. It was only his strong constitution and very good luck that saved him.

Dad always insisted that given a book with clear instructions on how to do something he could master it. This is no more evident than in a memory I have of being about 10 years old and looking over my older brother's shoulder and watching dad armed with a bottle of Dettol, a razor blade, and an open book laying on the ground, castrating calves. This was a man who the following morning would be in an industrial courtroom arguing over points of law that would affect the lives of millions of Australian workers. I know Dad would be disappointed in me if I didn't mention the fact that out of the dozens of calves we operated on, we only lost one patient. It was not all child slavery down on the farm and there was plenty of time for Dad to instil in us his great love of the outdoors. He taught us many things about the natural history of Australia and especially about birdlife, which was one of his passions.

Hal had a number of important personal friendships with people 'on whom the law bears harshly'. Frank Doolan, a renowned senior Wiradjuri man who is known across the state as 'Riverbank Frank', would introduce Hal to friends as 'Gill's legal aid boyfriend'. Frank, who always had a very deep affection and respect for Hal, remembers him as 'a kind, gentle man with enormous strength of character'. He goes on:

> Although I often argued (or tried to argue) about Black issues with him I can't recall a single time when I won the argument. Hal would sigh, look at me, with the patience of Job and say, 'Frank, you've got to have a plan.' The Aboriginal Legal Service, which was born in Redfern, actually came into being because Hal (and people like Neville Wran, Frank Walker and Paul Landa)[3] supported Indigenous Australians and saw their great need for proper representation in the legal world.

For some years until he was well into his nineties, Hal and Gillian would join Frank in quiet protest at Villawood Detention Centre each Australia Day. Hal was concerned for the plight of refugees in Australia, especially those arriving by boat. One was Ali Gulzari, a Hazara refugee who became Hal's friend when Ali's remarkable success as a new arrival at high school in western Sydney led to them being put in touch. The friendship between these two flourished and they both learnt much about the world from sharing stories with one another, sometimes on long exploratory drives across the country, including visits to Richard Frankland, a respected Aboriginal leader from western Victoria who assisted Hal in the landmark work of the Royal Commission into Aboriginal Deaths in Custody.

Richard Frankland recalls that he first met Hal when he was about 25:

We investigated First Nation deaths in custody together. It was a hard job, and we covered many miles together, over a period of about four years. As I watched Hal work, I was astounded at his ability to listen and actually hear what people had to say. We heard stories from many people who had lost a friend or family member in custody, stories about grief, injustice, systemic discrimination. Hal humanised what had been dehumanised. I once asked Hal what advice he would give a young man, meaning myself. He said, 'Love with an open hand, have humility and give of yourself generously.'

During the first decade of the 21st century, Hal was disturbed by events in the Middle East and the tensions between Islam and the West, so he decided to develop a deeper understanding of the roots of the conflict. In particular, he was concerned at the demonisation of Muslims. He returned to university, this time as an undergraduate student in Arabic studies. But this was not enough, and he decided to spend three months living in Ramallah, on the West Bank. It was a time in which he formed friendships on both sides of the border and made links that led to a program of Palestinian lawyers undertaking doctoral studies at UNSW. It also led to close friendships with the students as well as with Naser Shakhtour, the founder and director of the Palestinian Film Festival in Australia.

Hal was arrested among a group of Israelis defending Palestinian farmers from Israeli settlers in the West Bank. He insisted on the soldiers telling him under what law he was being detained. Eventually they released him without charge, but he refused to leave until all of the protesters were let go. After hours and hours of waiting around, the whole group was released.

Hal cherished his time as a barrister and a judge, but establishing the law school at UNSW was, for him, the highlight of his career and the source of his greatest professional pride. How a country trains its lawyers is no small thing. In setting out to change legal education, Hal was conscious of the impact that it could have on changing the country.

By the time I came to study law in the early 1980s, UNSW had already marked itself out as a progressive and highly innovative law school that broke with century-old methods of how lawyers were to be trained. Importantly, the UNSW Law School took seriously its duty to engage students actively in their training, while inculcating a strong sense of professionalism and the responsibilities to society as a whole, especially 'those on whom the law bore harshly'. This was the inherent obligation for the privileges of practice. The pedagogy designed by Hal was based on the simple but effective principle of avoiding all that he had found miserable and useless in his own legal education. As time goes on, elements of Hal's approach have been adopted in every law school in the country, and many overseas institutions have explored UNSW's approach.

No brief reflection like this can ever do justice to such a rich, purposeful and long life as Hal's. Brought up by his widowed mother and her parents, he studied law part-time while working as a government clerk and went on to become a leading law student, adviser to the senior partner of a leading commercial firm as a graduate lawyer, New Guinea field worker, lecturer in law for colonial government administrators, leading industrial barrister, Secretary-General of LAWASIA, found- ation Dean of a law school offering a new mode of legal education, founding Chair of the first Aboriginal Legal Service, adviser to the government of the newly independent Papua New Guinea, Supreme Court judge, Chairman of the NSW Law Reform Commission, Chairman of the Australian Press Council, Chancellor of the NSW Institute of Technology (now the University of Technology, Sydney), President of the Australian Conservation Foundation, Royal Commissioner into Aboriginal Deaths in Custody, Deputy President of the National Native Title Tribunal, Patron of the Environmental Defenders Office, Queen's Counsel, Companion of the Order of Australia, farmer, activist, conservationist, humanitarian, friend of the downtrodden.

Hal was intellectually brilliant, warm, quick-witted, generous and humble. But of all his many wonderful qualities, three made him stand out. The first was his vision of what could be achieved. He was so often the johnny-on-the-spot, trusting his instincts and judgment; he saw what others couldn't but which in hindsight was so often blindingly obvious.

The second was his practicality. He didn't hesitate in taking the first, often simple, step and seeing where it would lead. He was courageous and tenacious in doing what needed doing. And lastly, he was principled. One friend has said that he held a mirror up to the country, which he did, but not before he held it up to himself.

**Andrew Chalk** is an alumnus of UNSW Law who founded the firm that is now Chalk & Behrendt, which focuses 'on meeting the needs of Indigenous Australians and their organisations'. He is now a Strategic Consultant to the firm. Andrew was the founding Chair of Gawad Kalinga Australia Limited, the regional arm of the international community development organisation, and is also a former Chair of the Environmental Defender's Office Ltd, a director of the Mark Tonga Relief Fund, former Secretary of the NSW Chapter of the Australian Institute of Administrative Law, and former Chair of the NSW Law Society's Public Law Committee. He was one of Hal's closest friends.

# 3
# LIVING GREATLY
# IN THE LAW

*In 2006, UNSW Law began a process of reform which sought to renew Hal Wootten's vision in the different circumstances of the early 21st century. Happily, this led to Hal being more engaged with the Faculty than he had been for some time, as he became an invaluable mentor and adviser for the Dean, David Dixon.*

*An important expression of this process was the establishment of the Hal Wootten Lecture as the Faculty's premier public event. The lecture series had a particular purpose: it was to celebrate Hal's founding vision for the Law School by inviting a speaker*

> *to discover in their lives in the law personal and social meanings and connections with the history of the times. In that way, the lectures might accumulate, not a pattern for a life in the law, but examples of the varied opportunities that a life in the law can provide, and the varied ways in which people respond to its challenges.*

*In 2008, Hal gave the lecture himself: it is reproduced below. He examines Oliver Wendell Holmes's insistence that it is possible 'to live greatly in the law' and outlines his own life, showing how right Holmes was.[1]*

*The Hal Wootten Lecture has been delivered by a diverse group of prominent national and international lawyers, judges and academics. Speakers in the series include José Ramos-Horta, Michael McHugh, Hina Jilani, Albie Sachs, Martha Nussbaum, Sir Gerard Brennan, Richard Abel, Julian Burnside, Bret Walker, Elizabeth Broderick, Noel Pearson, Jennifer Robinson, Susan Kiefel and David Heilpern.[2] While he was well enough to do so, Hal gave the vote of thanks, always enjoying making the point that the lecture was eponymous rather than posthumous.*

*In 2015, he went further in commenting on the founding vision:*

*As always, I stress that my name is not only an eponym but a metonym. In contrast to a static creed, a vision is organic, and my name stands in for all those – staff, students, administrators and benefactors – who as time goes by contribute to developing, shaping and nurturing the vision cherished in this Law School.*[3]

## LIVING IN THE LAW:
## THE 2008 HAL WOOTTEN LECTURE

The Law School prepares students for a life in the law, and I saw the lecture series as an opportunity for lawyers to reflect on what living in the law has meant. Consciously or not, everyone seeks meaning in their lives, although they find it in a great variety of ways; aware of it or not, everyone has a role, however small, in the historical changes that inexorably sweep through and shape our world. In 1944, when I was still at an impressionable age, Lord Wavell published an anthology of verses entitled *Other Men's Flowers.*[4] I too have gained much comfort, insight and help in expressing my thoughts by appropriating other men's flowers. For me, one unwitting florist was Lord Diplock, who remarked that a judge seldom has the opportunity to say, like Lord Mansfield, 'The air of England is too free for any slave to breathe, let the black go free',[5] but every now and then there is the opportunity to give a little nudge that sends the law along the direction it ought to go.[6] I believe it is not just judges, but every man and woman who, in everything they do, can give the world little nudges that, in conjunction with all its other little nudges, can affect where the world goes.

One role of the Hal Wootten Lecture could be to invite, occasionally perhaps, a Lord Mansfield, but more often a little nudger like myself, to discover in their lives in the law personal and social meanings, and

'The 2008 Hal Wootten Lecture' (2009) 32(1) *University of New South Wales Law Journal* 198–212.

connections with the history of the times. In that way the lectures might accumulate, not a pattern for a life in the law, but examples of the varied opportunities that a life in the law can provide, and the varied ways in which people respond to its challenges.

One of those challenges often comes to law students or young graduates, who are beset by doubt whether the law is for them, whether indeed it can provide a worthwhile life for anyone. There is no lack of generic criticism of lawyers. It flows through the classics – Shakespeare, Burke, Dickens, Thackeray to name a few – through the great social critics like Marx, through the realists and ultimately into postmodernism where the critical legal theorists deconstruct us from within. Equally there is no lack of evidence of the agonies suffered in wrestling with the choice of such a profession. For long it was a literature of personal anecdote and rhetorical affirmation, then from the 1980s and 1990s it was subjected to largely subjective theoretical analysis, followed more recently by statistical collection and analysis so that it increasingly merges with epidemiological study of mental illness and depression, where lawyers head the tables.

The challenge was, for me, an intensely personal matter to be resolved within me. There were no counsellors or mentors, or kindly souls to manipulate my learning or working environment. As so often in my life I turned to other men's flowers, taking comfort in William Henley's 'Invictus':

> Out of the night that covers me,
> Black as the Pit from pole to pole,
> I thank whatever gods may be
> For my unconquerable soul.[7]

As a star to steer by, I had Polonius's advice to Laertes, hackneyed to the point of derision but still meaningful to me:

> This above all: to thine own self be true,
> And it must follow, as the night the day,
> Thou canst not then be false to any man.[8]

The world in which we live has changed mightily, and I applaud those who use the new techniques of science to identify and solve or ameliorate problems that have taken a serious, even deadly, form. But tonight, I will revert to anecdote and rhetoric to tell of my youthful wrestling with such issues and my early life in the law that did much to shape not only my career but the vision of the Law School that these lectures are intended to commemorate.

It is 66 years since I entered law school, found a job in the State Crown Solicitor's Office, and began a life in the law. I became a lawyer by accident. Growing up as a lower-middle-class boy in the Great Depression, law was not within my horizons. I owed two things to the widowed mother who saw me through Sydney Boys High School by working long hours as a dressmaker. One was to obtain a 'safe' job. The other was to 'improve' myself by further study. The pursuit of these objects landed me in the NSW Public Service attending the only university in the state as an evening student in Arts and then a part-time student in Law. I did Law because the alternative was Economics, about which I knew even less.

My arrival at the Law School coincided with that of Professors [James] Williams and [Julius] Stone, to each of whom I successively became a protégé. My departure coincided with that of Professor Williams, following bitter conflict between the two professors in which my brief participation as a student activist was to shape my subsequent life.[9] All I did was move an amendment at a student meeting adding the words 'and Professor Stone' to a motion that would otherwise have expressed appreciation only of Professor Williams, thus neutralising the resolution as a potential weapon in a struggle of which most students were unaware. My action led Professor Williams to block a then rare opportunity for me to enter an academic career,[10] but attracted the favourable attention of John Kerr, whose subsequent influence on me, as well as on the country, was considerable.[11]

My legal education left me torn. From Professor Williams I acquired a respect, even fondness, for the scholastic, black-letter law tradition, a world of the intellect albeit narrowly confined. It was a world where the common law was still found, not made. From Professor Stone, with whom I worked on the production of the first gargantuan edition of *The Province and Function of Law*,[12] I learnt that law was an evolving part of society, accountable to it. From many of the other lecturers, busy practitioners who rushed in to read out issued notes before or after court, I absorbed a different message. Law was a tightly controlled profession, ruled by a narrow clique mainly concerned with the welfare of the profession, enforcing its restrictive practices. Anybody else's welfare was not really its business. What Professor Williams taught us was harmless enough, even admirable if you liked that sort of thing, but what Stone taught was beyond the pale – a not inappropriate metaphor for what some may have felt. Baffled by the intensity with which part-time lecturers rallied behind the outraged Professor Williams when Professor Stone sought a voice in the running of the Law School, I approached a senior barrister in whose subject I had won the prize. What, I asked, were the issues? 'My lips are sealed', he said, 'but there is one thing I can say: Professor Stone is not a gentleman.' There was no irony; I am sure that, unlike me, the barrister had not read Harold Laski's recently published book, *The Danger of Being a Gentleman*.[13] However, it was this barrister, not Professor Stone, who was for me the face of the profession for which I was preparing. Browsing in the library in the depths of my gloom, I stumbled on an address by Justice Oliver Wendell Holmes to the doubtless all-male Harvard undergraduates of 1886:

> I know that some spirit of fire will say that his main question has not been answered. He will ask, what is all this to my soul? You did not bid me sell my birthright for a mess of pottage; what have you said to show that I can reach my own spiritual possibilities through a door such as this? How can the laborious study of a dry and technical system, the greedy watch for clients and the practice of shopkeepers' arts, the mannerless conflicts over often sordid interests, make out a life? Gentlemen, I admit at once that these questions are not futile, that they may prove unanswerable, that they have often seemed to me unanswerable. Yet I believe there is an answer … I say – and I say no longer with any doubt – that a man may live greatly in the law as

elsewhere; that there as well as elsewhere his thought may find its unity in an infinite perspective; that there as well as elsewhere he may wreak himself upon life, may drink the bitter cup of heroism, may wear his heart out after the unattainable …

Although he emphasised the role of scholar, which is not for all of us, the inspiration was irresistible. He went on:

Thus only can you enjoy the secret, isolated joy of the thinker, who knows that, a hundred years after he is dead and forgotten, men who never heard of him will be moving to the measure of his thought – the subtle rapture of a postponed power, which the world knows not because it has no external trappings, but which to his prophetic vision is more real than that which commands an army. And if this joy should not be yours, still it is only thus that you can know that you have done what it lay in you to do, can say that you have lived and be ready for the end.[14]

An American wag has translated these last words into the proposition that 'those of us to whom it is not given to "live greatly in the law" are surely called upon to fail in the attempt'.[15] Perhaps that was how I felt – but it was enough. Life in the law was what you made it, not what some miserable lecturer in Legal Ethics reduced it to. It was not about achieving eminence or wealth but realising oneself. It was the antithesis of the life Leonardo da Vinci decried as leaving behind nothing but full privies, an image that haunted my darker moments.[16]

Today I can detect in Holmes's language the voice of the veteran of the Civil War, speaking to restless young men who had never known the challenge and adventure of any similar experience. I could identify with them because medical rejection from military service had excluded me from the wartime experience of most of my peers, many of whom might have reacted to Holmes by saying they had had more than their fill of wreaking themselves upon life and drinking the bitter cup of heroism.

Holmes offered neither argument nor authority, apart from his own. It was pure inspiration. He claimed no magic for a career in law, only the negative virtue that it did not prevent the good life: that you 'can live greatly in the law *as well as elsewhere*'. It was up to you. He made no moral claim for a life in the law; I was to discover that he was the protagonist of the bad man's theory of the law[17] and supported eugenics[18] and capital punishment. Although his affirmation of the power of the human spirit to survive a life in the law buttressed me against despair, he did not draw me away from my existing values. When Holmes said 'I think "Whatsoever thy hand findeth to do, do it with thy might" infinitely more important than the vain attempt to love one's neighbour as one's self,'[19] for me he posed a false choice.

Between the ages of two and nine I was largely brought up by my mother's parents, who taught me to read and write and share the homely values that had brought them the life of pioneer dairy farmers on the North Coast. My grandmother communicated to me her love of nature, often expressed in poetry, and her love of the Jesus of the Gospels. As a small child myself I was captivated by the man who welcomed little children; stood up for the poor, the meek and the peacemakers; admired the lilies of the field above Solomon in all his glory; showed his suspicion of the corrupting effect of wealth by likening the rich man trying to enter the good life to the camel passing through the eye of the needle; silenced the self-appointed custodians of other people's morals by inviting the one without sin to cast the first stone; and provided a simple basis for morality and sociality: do unto others as you would they do unto you.

Happily, my grandmother did not suffer the besetting vice of the religious – self-righteousness: she often quoted Burns's plea for 'the gift to see ourselves as others see us'.[20] Her message was simply about making the most of life on earth. Those who made the pursuit of riches the purpose of life would find that they did not bring content and happiness in the here and now.

Everyone seemed to share this view. While few of us managed to live up to it, we saw that as our own shortcoming. The relatively wealthy seemed more embarrassed by their wealth than boastful of it; those who acted otherwise were seen as having been corrupted by it. You were judged not by what you had, but by what you were and how you treated your fellows.

As my world expanded, I found these basic assumptions were shared by Christians, Jews, Muslims, Hindus, Buddhists, Aboriginals, Melanesians, or those who like myself found no foothold in divine revelation or human doctrine, and did their best with the critical powers with which they were endowed and the experience and shared wisdom that life brought. I don't remember a religion or philosophy that taught that the chief end of man was the pursuit of wealth, and I still feel shocked by the legitimacy that this view has acquired in recent times.

This outlook was supported by the other great influence in my youth, an atheistic uncle, the only one of four uncles to survive the Great War. Brought up in the sheltered world of strictly Methodist dairy farmers, he found himself as a very young man in the trenches in France, often dependent on men he had once looked down on. He returned a champion of the common man, contemptuous of those who thought themselves superior, and impatient with rank, pretence or what he called 'humbug'.

I grew up with a love of nature and books, interest in social and political issues, a short fuse in the face of what I felt to be injustice, a belief that the world could and should be improved, and identification with the underdog. Some of these led me to a brief membership of the then pro-war Communist Party, which turned out to be a very boring institution in which dissent from the party line was not so much discouraged as simply unimaginable. I found more interest when a kindly older colleague let me try my hand at drafting Crown Solicitor's opinions and I spent many contented hours among the musty volumes of the Crown Law Library, including the old digests and the then current but unwieldy English and Empire and Australian Digests, our anticipation of computerised law.

Looking back, I see that the young man who left the Law School and the Crown Solicitor's Office in 1945 had some ideas about the right directions in which to nudge the world. However bad one's legal education, one could not spend four years reading cases and common law classics, daily imbibing the embedded ethics of a government law office, and briefing barristers without some things rubbing off. There was a passion for truth and justice but no illusions about the difficulties in attaining them. The rule of law was a given: no person was above the law, no person could be deprived of life, liberty or property without due process; every power and discretion, however wide, was given for a purpose and had to be exercised honestly for that purpose. Natural justice required that no one should be condemned without a fair hearing, no one should be judge in their own cause, judges should give reasons for their decisions, the burden of proof was on the accuser. Society depended on freedom of contract, but it should not be used unconscionably. Words could have many meanings and should be used with care and precision. Scratch a lawyer worth his or her salt and you will soon start to discover these things. Whether I liked it or not, by my 23rd birthday I was a lawyer. But could this make a life?

My legal career, having begun by accident, continued by a series of accidents. On the few occasions I have had a plan for my future, even a plan to abandon the law, it has foundered on some unexpected opportunity I could not resist. I sometimes say that my career has been built on my inability to say no when invited to do something I was not qualified to do.

My first job after graduation was a 'brains trust' position advising the senior partner in one of Sydney's largest and most powerful firms, a position for which Professor Williams had nominated me before I showed my true colours. It carried a promise of a career in the firm or a good start at the Bar after a year in the job. I was a young man who liked to murmur John Masefield's 'A Consecration', in which he warned his readers that he would sing 'not of the princes and prelates with periwigged charioteers / Riding triumphantly laurelled to lap the fat of the years', or of 'the portly presence of potentates goodly in girth', but rather of 'the scorned – the rejected – the men hemmed in with the spears', 'the slave with the sack on his shoulders pricked on with the goad / The man with too weighty a burden, too weary a load'.[21] I found myself serving the princes and prelates and potentates of business and industry, who not infrequently seemed to ask what was the least they were obliged to do for the man with too weary a load, or the government trying to improve his lot. It was a legitimate question that I could answer to their satisfaction. But Holmes came back to haunt me: 'You did not bid me sell my birthright for a mess of pottage'. Was this living greatly in the law?

In retrospect, the problem was that I had no direct contact with clients – just abstract questions filtered through the senior partner. Not many years later, I found myself working happily as a barrister with representatives of some of the most powerful commercial and industrial interests, finding that more often than not they were ready to be fair to the man with too weary a load; some even shared my taste for Masefield.

My frustration was greater because 1946 was a time of hope and optimism before the chill of the Cold War. The troops were home; post-war reconstruction was under way; the five freedoms of the Atlantic Charter[22] were revered; Germany and Japan were being rebuilt as democracies; decolonisation was in the air.

One day the phone rang and Colonel John Kerr introduced himself as Principal of ASOPA, the newly founded Australian School of Pacific Administration, which would train staff for the civil administration of Papua and New Guinea, particularly patrol officers and district officers who would be administrators and magistrates.

The charismatic colonel painted an inspiring picture of the part ASOPA would play, through teaching, research and policy influence, in the decolonisation of New Guinea. I accepted a tutorship, giving no thought to the fact that I was sacrificing my powerful employer's promise to give me a good start at the Bar at the end of the year. The five years I spent at ASOPA, mostly as Senior Lecturer in Law, were rewarding in many ways, but I will speak of only one formative experience.

I was attracted to anthropology, which seemed to offer more scope than law for understanding and getting close to New Guineans and helping to improve their lot. The senior anthropologist at ASOPA, Ian Hogbin, devised a plan for me to switch to anthropology by under-taking a doctorate based on a field study of what was then called 'Primitive Law'. In 1947, I found myself in the village of Kawaliap, among the Usiai in the middle of Manus, three days' walk from the nearest European. No one spoke English, but having studied Melanesian Pidgin at ASOPA, I rapidly became fluent. I started collecting information about the people and their culture, observing the meagre living extracted by the arduous work of shifting subsistence agriculture in rugged muddy rainforest.

I was 24 and men of my age would spend hours each evening yarning in my hut. They told me of the humiliating racism they had suffered at the hands of whites who, administrators, planters or missionaries, were always the 'mastas' and they the 'bois'. We got close, but they could not bring themselves to sit down and eat with me. One tried but was unable to eat. I asked him why. He pondered and said with great bitterness: 'Yu masta; mi boi.' I learnt the power of humiliation, its ubiquitous and corrosive effect where one group of people believe they are superior to another, the 'others'.

An older man, Kompen, would sometimes come, and contradict the young men, saying that people were very happy with the government and whites. Thinking him a hypocrite, I treated him with increasing impatience. One evening he stayed behind. He had thought I was a government spy; now he believed I was a friend and would tell me what the people of Kawaliap really thought.

He took me through the serial invasions from an unknown outside world that had shattered traditional Manus. First Japanese, then German governors and planters, Catholic missionaries, Australian forces in World War I, Australian administrators between the wars, an occupying Japanese army, a technologically overpowering recapture by Americans, followed by Australian servicemen, the Australian New Guinea Administrative Unit (the military government) and now a post-war civil administration and returning missionaries. One thing never changed: the Usiai were the 'bois', the invaders the 'mastas'. The bois always loved the mastas, Kompen said, [because] 'the mastas had guns'.

The Usiai were never admitted to the secrets of wealth and power. They knew there must be a key but it was hidden, and every time they thought they found it they were disappointed. Perhaps the key was Pidgin, but learning it changed nothing. Nor did working on the plantations, going to school, or converting to Christianity. They knew that it was not the colour of their skins because, although they were not allowed inside the American naval base, they could see from afar that black Americans shared its fabulous wealth. If only the white man had shared the key, today we would be able to sit down as brothers and eat at one table.

That night changed my relationship with Kawaliap. For the first time in my life, I felt the warmth of acceptance into a small community. But it was no longer possible to play the detached academic studying these people. I could not remain a hider of the key. How could I find a way to help these people gain access to the world they envied? Perhaps as a patrol officer.

I tried to explain in a letter to John Kerr. Concluding that I was 'troppo', he sent the Australian navy to get me out. A runner brought word that in three days I was to board a frigate which would take me to Rabaul, where the Administrator of Papua New Guinea was joining the vessel. JK Murray was a wise and kindly man. He said that if on reflection I still wanted to be a patrol officer, it could be arranged, but he urged me to return to Sydney and get things in perspective. In my heart I knew he was right. I was a very immature young man, far from ready to be anyone's saviour. I returned to ASOPA, researched and taught law, grew up, handed out how-to-vote-no cards in the Communist Party referendum,[23] saw Humphrey Bogart in [the 1948 film] *Key Largo*, got married and started a family. I could feel that in teaching law to those who governed New Guinea at the local level I was giving a little nudge towards an enlightened rule of law that would be no less important for the realisation of Kompen's aspirations than the agriculture, education, and tropical medicine that others taught. My commitment remained, but I knew I could only fulfil it as a lawyer. There was then only one private lawyer practising in Papua New Guinea. At the end of 1951 I contacted him, he invited me to join his practice, and I resigned from ASOPA.

Not for the first or last time, John Kerr intervened. He had returned to the Bar in Sydney and urged me to join it, one argument being that I could do more for New Guinea as a lawyer in Australia than in the Territory. I yielded and opportunities came.

On the Council on New Guinea Affairs, I could give little nudges to New Guinea policy. As a member of a Law Council committee in 1962 I was able to give a nudge to the establishment of a university law school in New Guinea, and in subsequent years I initiated and ran a successful scheme to encourage Indigenous students to study law by bringing them to Australia as guests of the Law Council. As a leader of the industrial Bar in the 1960s,[24] I was briefed by the Commonwealth to oppose a claim for equal pay for Indigenous public servants, represented by a rising trade union star, Bob Hawke.[25] Professionally trained New Guineans were few and were rapidly pushed into senior positions on New Guinea rates of pay, where they were often senior to Australians enticed to serve in New Guinea by loadings on top of much higher Australian rates of pay. I knew the painful side of this racial dilemma, having stayed in the homes of New Guinea friends and written about it in *The Bulletin*.[26] Discovering this, Bob Hawke, without notice, called me as his opening witness. The arbitrator upheld his right to do so, and the Bar Council ruled that it was my duty to remain as advocate if my client so wished. As a witness I felt no embarrassment in defending the proposition that, deplorable as the discrimination was, the solution lay not in saddling a country on the eve of independence with Australian rates of pay for public servants but in getting rid of the Australians by training Indigenous replacements as quickly as possible. Bob suggested that independence was at least a hundred years away. I disagreed and we bargained it down to ten. In upholding our case, the arbitrator said he had been much assisted by my evidence.

Almost exactly ten years later, I attended a celebration of New Guinea's independence in Sydney, hosted by Prime Minister Michael Somare and Minister for Education Ebia Olewale. I wondered how I would be received, for both had been among the angry young witnesses I had cross-examined. Guests were assembled on a large open floor; the lift door opened and out stepped Somare and Olewale. They surveyed the crowd and walked directly to me. With a puckish grin, Somare sought my sympathy on the problems of balancing a budget when public servants wanted higher pay. It was for me one of many lessons that conflict is often not between good and bad, but between competing goods, in this case racial equality and the viability of an independent state. Much legal work is resolving conflicting claims, each of which has some legitimacy. When I left the Bar, I had completed without shame the trifecta of opposing equal pay for New Guineans, equal pay for Aboriginals,[27] and equal pay for women.[28]

Four years after independence, the Supreme Court sentenced the Minister for Justice to eight months gaol for contempt, Somare released her, and the Supreme Court judges (all expatriates) resigned. The Opposition accused Somare of wrecking the system; no reputable lawyer would accept appointment as a judge in New Guinea again. He asked me to be Chief Justice, no doubt calculating that if an Australian Supreme Court judge was willing to accept office, the crisis would be over.[29] New Guinea still tugged my heartstrings, and I was sympathetic because I felt the judges may have over-reacted, but in any event Somare had been taught his lesson and the important thing was to get the legal system back on the rails. However, for personal reasons, the last thing I wanted was to be away from Sydney in the next few years.

I agreed to go to New Guinea at the end of the year and stay 12 months, calculating that with a grateful government supporting me I would be able in a year to do a lot to rebuild the Court and develop the profession. My appointment was announced, I found some immediate appointees, and the crisis passed. However, before I took up office Somare was defeated on a vote of confidence over other issues, and I had no wish to spend a year overcoming the suspicions of the new government. I helped persuade a young Indigenous lawyer to take the Chief Justiceship, where he performed admirably. Both the Court and the legal profession developed, I understand, as institutions of integrity supporting the rule of law in a country where corruption and chaos have been rife. Perhaps my little nudges in developing an Indigenous legal profession, supporting debate on New Guinea's future, deflecting a major fiscal issue and assisting the Supreme Court over a constitutional crisis went some way to vindicating John Kerr's prediction and Holmes's affirmation, as well as redeeming my commitment to Kampen and the Usiai.

In persuading me to come to the Bar in 1951, when chambers were unavailable, John Kerr generously offered me a desk in his spacious room. The close professional association that continued till he became a judge in 1966 shaped my career at the Bar. Briefed by Jim McClelland,[30] he was appearing for Laurie Short to wrest the Federated Ironworkers Union from communist control. I spent much of my early years at the Bar acting for clients fighting thuggery, conspiracy and undemocratic manipulation of unions and took part in developing a jurisprudence of union government that brought more effective rule of law to institutions that I consider vital to a liberal democracy. There was a political side, reflecting a bitter Cold War struggle between Communists and anti-Communists. I became entwined in the affairs of the Labor Party, and when the great split came in 1955,[31] I vowed never again to join a political party. I like to be a maverick, a word coined by American cattlemen for the animal that bears nobody's brand.

Successful clients who had learnt to rely on me were suddenly in charge of big unions, with all the business of industrial regulation in Higgins's 'new province for law and order'[32], and turned to me for advice and representation. What started as a trade union practice soon broadened. I was the first to transcend a fairly rigid division between employers' and union barristers, acting not only for major unions, but governments, employers like BHP, CSR and newspaper and television proprietors, and industry groups like meat exporters, stevedoring companies and retail traders. This made real for me the vaunted independence of the Bar. I had no connections with employers; they sought my services and there were plenty of others in the queue.

A great value of independent lawyers is that they can tell clients what they may not want to hear. Clients often come to lawyers wrapped in their own self-righteousness, unable to recognise any merit in their opponent's case. The best service of the lawyer is often not just to explain the law but to make clients see how their case looks to others, not only to the party on the other side, but to the judge who will hear it, perhaps to the journalists who will report it. Intelligent clients appreciate this and some use lawyers as sounding boards on a wide range of issues.

Despite my youthful misgivings about acting for the big end of town, I found that most big employers were motivated at least by enlightened self-interest. Like Edmund Burke, they were interested not only in 'what a lawyer tells me I *may* do; but what humanity, reason, and justice, tell me I ought to do'[33] and expected their lawyer to share that interest. Unenlightened policies were more often the result of short-sightedness than malevolence and, by the time I explained the problems of defending such policies, clients would either gratefully change their position or realise that I was not the best barrister for them.

Not many barristers ventured into the industrial jurisdiction; those in more conventional practice often regarded it as mysterious or inferior, not 'real' law. But there was plenty of real law, and judicial and quasi-judicial process. That one often had to take more explicit account of Burke's humanity, reason and justice went along with working on great social, political and economic issues. One recurring theme in my practice was the conflict between workers seeking to retain purpose and sociality in their work or defend treasured practices, and those who sought to override them in the pursuit of maximum efficiency and profitability. Charlie Chaplin long ago satirised this conflict in *Modern Times,* but I participated in its re-enactment as bulk-loading and containerisation took over the waterfront, computers took over newspaper production, division of labour spread in the meat industry, and tradesmen resisted the unpicking of their trades. Along with automation and the incipient information revolution went conflict between egalitarian ideals and claims of a new elite.

I needed ways to switch off from practice. My refuge was a small weekend farm, where I personally did the fencing and pasture improvement and managed cattle and horse breeding. Each of my portrait painters, commissioned to paint the Dean of Law at UNSW and the Chancellor of the NSW Institute of Technology,[34] decided that the real me was a Kangaroo Valley farmer. I took part in public debate, for example over Barwick's amendments of the Crimes Act,[35] against the campaign for a Royal Commission into the Professor Orr case,[36] and about the conviction and death sentence of the Aboriginal Max Stuart in South Australia.[37] From 1967, I put much time, including most of the Law vacations, into the role of Secretary General of LAWASIA, an organisation initiated by the Law Council of Australia to develop cooperation between the varied legal professions of Asian and Pacific countries. Founded in 1966, it was virtually defunct a year later, when John Kerr, then President of the Law Council, asked me if I could revive it. Over the next few years, I engaged most of the professional organisations in the region, enrolled thousands of individual members and held successful conferences in Kuala Lumpur, Djakarta and Manila.[38]

My values did not change. A comfortable income was a by-product of my practice, not its purpose. When my services were in great demand, I did not feel tempted to charge high fees. I had a client who wanted me to charge more, but never one who thought my charges excessive.

On two occasions, I rejected opportunities to take up what would have been more lucrative work. Jim McClelland was known as the 'kingmaker' because of his power to make the fortunes of barristers from the vast pool of common law negligence claims available when our once struggling clients gained control of unions. 'Nello', as it was affectionately known, was immoderately lucrative to barristers because they received not only well-paid briefs for the largely formulaic work in drafting pre-trial documents but a brief on hearing, carrying a fee for the preparation of the case and the first day's hearing, paid even when the case was settled, as it usually was. Jim was insistent that I, who had done so much to help the clients win control of the unions, should participate. He would allot me all the work from the great steel city of Wollongong; it did not matter that I was busy doing the industrial work for the unions – indeed, this was all the more reason why I should benefit. I would have the fees from all the cases that were settled, and if I was not available when the odd one went to trial, another barrister would take the brief. It was perfectly legal, the way the system worked: what did I have to lose? I was tempted to quote: 'What shall it profit a man if he shall gain the whole world but lose his own soul?'[39] I never regretted or even thought about the very considerable wealth I rejected because I felt that my most precious possession, the one thing I could not surrender without destroying myself, was my self-respect. This above all, as Polonius had said.

The other opportunity I rejected had no ethical problems and many attractions. After a forensic triumph of great importance to the stevedoring industry, my instructing solicitor, a senior partner in the largest Melbourne firm, made an offer hard to refuse: if I would abandon my specialisation in industrial law he would brief me across the whole range of his diverse practice. It would have given a young barrister great prestige, high income, and the kind of practice that could lead to appellate judicial appointment. The downside was greatly increased pressure and hours and the risk of becoming a slave to practice.

I also declined two offers of [judicial] appointment, one state, one federal.[40] That the drop in income was not the major reason for refusal is shown by the fact that shortly afterwards I found irresistible an offer to become foundation Dean of Law at UNSW at about half the judicial salary. There was a limited right of private practice, but I did not expect to make much use of it as I thought the Law School would be all absorbing. It turned out to be not altogether all absorbing as I became involved in the establishment and running of the first Aboriginal Legal Service.[41] This cut into other activities, as I was forcibly reminded when my teenage daughter greeted me late one evening with 'Daddy, it's not our fault we're not black.'

Another who thought my time could be better spent was a client who offered to pay for a full-time manager for the Aboriginal Legal Service, as well as whatever fees I liked to charge, if I would give the time saved to his companies' work. I declined, feeling that it would be too difficult to explain to my new Aboriginal friends why an arm of Lord Vestey's empire[42] was paying for the manager of their Legal Service. More importantly, it would have meant limiting one of the most rewarding experiences of my life, my entree to the Aboriginal community with all its warmth, humour, wisdom and generosity of spirit that were to mean so much to me and to engage much of my subsequent life.

Those later years have been rewarding and rich in experience in other ways, but I have outlined my life in the law up to the time I was, out of the blue, asked to become founding Dean of [UNSW] Law School in 1969.[43] As things worked out, I enjoyed a very free hand in distilling out of that life a vision of what a law school should be and selecting the initial staff to implement it. However, I left early in the third year of operation, going back briefly to the Bar and then to the Supreme Court.

Other hands have nurtured and built the Law School and I feel at once humble and proud that nearly four decades later they value and honour the vision.

Their achievement has been remarkable because for many years government funding has been hostile to the vision and geared to the old view that students are receptacles into which the law should be poured, rather than minds and personalities to be developed into lawyers who can accept the responsibilities of a profession critical to the functioning of an economically complex liberal democratic society ...

The vision saw lawyers as a socially important and honourable profession, the purpose of which was not to maximise the income of lawyers or the GNP, but to serve society and those who lived in it in an enlightened, honourable and socially responsible way. This was the accepted view when I entered the profession, and I could still articulate it without fear of challenge when the Law School was established. Making an income was a by-product of practising a profession, not its rationale. One continually sees evidence that the professional spirit endures, as integrity, the rule of law and human rights are defended by a profession which, dare I say, is now overwhelmingly composed of graduates of this and like-minded law schools.

In recent decades, however, the concept of a profession has been increasingly rejected or ignored in the prevailing wisdom that individuals and societies are to be judged by their economic achievement. The chief end of man is the production of wealth. A profession is just another business or job, whether you are a lawyer, a doctor, an architect, an engineer or a journalist – all callings where integrity and independence are vital.

My life is now far from practice, and I must rely on others to explain how the profession is being affected. Bret Walker, a former President of the Bar Council, gave a detailed account in the 2005 Lawyers' Lecture at the St James Ethics Centre.[44] One major change has been the appearance of large firms, some employing 1000 lawyers and structured on a business model to generate income for equity partners. Old conflicts that bedevilled the factory floor in Chaplin's day, and brought other industries to my chambers in the 1960s, are now being worked through in the law.

Another big challenge is the incidence of depression, a growing scourge in the whole community, but particularly high in law, across students, solicitors and barristers. Research as to causes is in early stages but is looking at the type of personality attracted to law, the nature of legal work and the way it is organised.

Against this changing backdrop, a review of my own experience as a young lawyer seems almost antiquarian. Have I anything to say to young lawyers of today? Much of what life taught me is not peculiar to law. Holmes himself said that the questions he raised were the same as those that meet you in any form of practical life. 'If a man has the soul of Sancho Panza, the world to him will be Sancho Panza's world.'[45] As a fan of the common man, I dislike Holmes's elitist dismissal of Don Quixote's earthy servant but the point is clear and you can substitute a name of your choice – Donald Rumsfeld perhaps,[46] or one of the Australian equivalents that spring to mind.

For want of a better word, much of the inspirational literature, like Holmes, uses the word 'soul' to refer to whatever it is that encapsulates one's precious individuality, the indomitable thing that remained in the central character of *The Diving Bell and the Butterfly* when he lost all capacity to move or communicate except the fluttering of one eyelid, through which he yet managed to write a book.[47] I prefer the word 'self', the self of self-respect, the self to which Polonius told Laertes he should be true. For me the most important thing in life is to retain my self-respect. I have felt that if I lost that I would lose everything, I would have no ground on which to stand.

I remain convinced of the perennial wisdom that it is more important to be than to have, that the pursuit of wealth is not the road to the good life, to happiness and satisfaction. I am not opposed to wealth. I would love to have the power of George Soros or Bill Gates to do some of the things they do. On a more modest scale, I sometimes regret that I did not take wealth more seriously when I had the opportunity to accumulate so that I would now be able to do some of the things I would like to do – endow the Law School in its hour of need, or provide scholarships and fellowships to students and staff of the law schools of Nablus and Jenin that I got to know during my recent three months on the West Bank,[48] men and women who are isolated by the checkpoints and travel controls of the Occupation, the obscene wrangling between Fatah and Hamas, and the lack of access to English language scholarship, yet aspire to help build in Palestine a liberal democratic state that respects the rule of law and human rights. It would be like rain in the desert, a Jewish friend said, when I mentioned my dream that these Palestinians might have opportunities to spend time in Australian law schools.

It is destructive when the pursuit of wealth becomes an end in itself, to which the good life must be sacrificed, or redefined as simply 'more' – more assets, more palatial houses, more luxurious holidays, more powerful or ornate boats and cars, more ostentation. One of my most powerful film memories goes back to 1948; in *Key Largo,* Humphrey Bogart and Lauren Bacall become the hostages of a gangster, Edward G Robinson, in a house battened down for a hurricane. As the tension builds, Bogart says to Robinson: 'I know what you want; you want more'. Robinson thinks about this and chuckles: 'Yes, that's right, that's good'. 'Will you ever have enough?' responds Bogart.

The consequences of rejecting the perennial wisdom, of always wanting more, are clear not just in threats to the legal profession but in the crumbling world around us, spectacularly in climate change and the collapse of the market, which has had to turn to its old enemy the state to avert complete catastrophe resulting from the pursuit of more.[49] In climate change, our inability to abandon the pursuit of more is leading us to re-enact two great parables – the tragedy of the commons and the boiling frog. Amid mounting evidence that climate change is much faster than predicted, no government has had the courage to give the lead in reducing a country's carbon input into the stratospheric commons because it might impinge on the pursuit of wealth. And for a decade we belittled the idea of an international authority that is needed to protect a global commons. Meanwhile, we sit like the frog awaiting our fate as temperatures slowly rise. By contrast, when the water boiled and actual money, not just the future of the world, was at stake in a market collapse, frogs leapt everywhere. Billions that could not be found to tackle climate change appeared from nowhere to bail out delinquent banks.

What I say is not original; I learnt it from my grandmother who probably learnt it from hers. Life is not about the pursuit of wealth, of GNP, of getting more. It is about nurturing and respecting that precious self, and realising its potential to do worthwhile things, however small the nudges you give to the world may seem. Always be true to that self, never surrender it to greed or a cause or creed or ideology. Don't enter law if you really want to do something else. Don't be slow to seek or give help. Don't be afraid to take comfort from other men's flowers, however worn the cliches, whether from the New Testament or Shakespeare or Humphrey Bogart, or Henley's concluding lines:

> I am the master of my fate:
> I am the captain of my soul.[50]

In conclusion, let me say to the students and young lawyers, 'Don't let the bastards get you down, and don't forget about climate change', and to all of you, thank you for coming and listening.

## 'JUSTICE IS FOR EVERYBODY'

*Hal's responses to other lectures in the series were always a highlight. As an example, what follows is an extract from Hal's response to Richard Abel's 2014 lecture, 'How to Be a "Good Lawyer" – Lessons from the American "War on Terror"'.[51]*

Like inconvenient groups everywhere, asylum seekers have suffered serial vilification: we have been told they threatened piracy on the *Tampa*,[52] they threw their children overboard, they were secret terrorists, they destroyed their papers to conceal their criminal records, they were wealthy people buying access that others could not afford, they were queue jumpers, they were not genuine refugees but economic

'Response to Lecture Delivered by Professor Richard Abel' (Hal Wootten Lecture, UNSW, 13 March 2014).

migrants, they were disorderly and violent people who destroyed the accommodation we generously provided, they insulted and provoked the local population in their host country. We, in contrast, have been patient and forbearing, and, oh, so humane. Naturally, we had to defend our borders against invasion and stand up for genuine refugees. But our real concern has always been to save the lives of the poor boat people who were drowning in leaky boats; at one stage we even planned to buy up all the leaky boats in Indonesia. If preventing drowning were our real aim, it would have been much cheaper to provide some boats that didn't leak or some storm-proof capsules. Our Navy could then have played 'turn the boats back' without fear of anyone drowning. We did not think of that; instead we humanely set out to make the lives of those who did get through so painful, bleak and hopeless that no one else would even try. We did not intend Reza Barati's death, but it really made our point.[53]

This absurd farce has left the motivation of Australian policy nakedly exposed for all to see. We are a privileged, wealthy country in a world where nearly everyone else is poorer and less privileged, often undernourished and distressed, but we are not prepared to share what we have in any significant degree, not even with persecuted refugees or people who are prepared to work hard and take extreme risks to give their families a chance to live in a world like ours. We do not even acknowledge a problem. The world is not for everybody; this part at least is for us. There is a parallel with climate change. We are not prepared to curb our greedy consumption even a little to share the world with future generations. It will last us out. The world is not for everybody, but for us, here and now.

I am not seeking to cast the first or any stone; I am as implicated as everyone else, and I have no easy answers to what are difficult problems. But it is essential that we first see clearly what we are doing, acknowledge that it is not acceptable and be open to working with people of goodwill throughout the world in the search for solutions. A whole new world order awaits imagination and negotiation, one that takes account of changing patterns of aspiration, expectation, need, consumption and technical capacity. We may have left it all too late, but we must retrieve what we can. If we can take something away from this evening, perhaps it may be this: if humanity's problems are to be solved, they will be solved only by people who start their thinking and their negotiation from the premise that justice is for everybody; not only procedural justice for the wretched inmates of Guantanamo, Manus and Nauru, but substantial justice for all who have a claim on the world and its resources. We cannot go on pretending that nothing is wrong or that we are not responsible.

# 4

# A NEW LAW SCHOOL

**Peter Thompson:** *In your long public life, can you single out a few things, or maybe one thing, which has given you most satisfaction?*

**Hal Wootten:** *Well, I think undoubtedly, I would find most satisfaction in the establishment of the new Law School at the University of New South Wales ... I really had a wonderful time there, and I feel very proud of the result in the present Law School.*[1]

*Hal Wootten's interest and involvement in legal education went back to drafting an alternative curriculum while a student at the University of Sydney*[2] *and an unsuccessful application for a university lectureship in the 1940s.*[3] *He taught law at the Australian School of Pacific Administration and in Papua New Guinea – among his papers is a proposal for a PNG law school (see chapter 7) – and tutored and lectured at the University of Sydney while at the Bar in the 1950s and early 1960s. His appointment in 1969 to establish a new law school at UNSW gave him the opportunity to revolutionise legal education in Australia.*[4]

*Hal's vision not only reacted against the deep faults of traditional legal education, but also had a strong, positive direction that remains inspirational today. At its centre is a distinctive conception of the role of a lawyer as a professional dedicated to serving all sections of the community. This involves no downgrading of lawyers' traditional commitments to serving business, corporations and government. It does mean that such commitment should be extended to serving the rest of society: those excluded from using the law and those who usually have the law used against them. In the entrance hall of the Law & Justice Building, a banner carries Hal's words: 'A Law School should have and communicate to its students a keen concern for those on whom the law bears harshly.' Black-letter law is necessary, but not enough: the society in which law operates must be understood, and other disciplines are needed in order to do so. Equally significant was rejection of traditional didactic teaching methods in favour of contextual analysis and discussion between teachers and students, long before such methods became fashionable. Teachers and students were seen as partners in this new venture.*

*The extracts from Hal's letter to the first law class, followed by speeches looking back on the early days, explain and illustrate Hal's vision and his relationships with those involved, both colleagues and students.⁵ While proud of the vision, Hal neither claimed that he was solely responsible nor that it was fully formed when the Law School opened. As he indicates below, Hal was uncomfortable with references to the 'vision' if it suggested a finalised project designed in advance by him alone. Rather, it was the product of a process over the years to which many colleagues and students contributed – and continue to contribute.⁶ The dynamic adaptability of this vision has been an important reason for its durability.*

## DEAN'S LETTER TO NEW STUDENTS, 1971

It is easy in compiling a handbook to set out the formal courses and requirements of a faculty, but harder to convey the objectives it seeks to achieve. It is easy to set out the impersonal rules that everyone must obey, but harder to suggest the more important personal relationships that can make a good Law School. The rest of the Handbook is formal and impersonal; this section is personal.

On behalf of the members of the Law School staff, I extend a warm welcome to the students of 1971. We have come here attracted by the challenge of establishing a new and, if we can, a better Law School. We look forward to meeting you, the foundation year of students, because together we will establish an atmosphere and pattern of relations that

'Faculty of Law: 1971 Handbook' (UNSW, 1971) 5–8 <legacy.handbook.unsw. edu.au/archive/historical/UNSWLawHandbook1971.pdf>.

may shape the Law School for many years to come. You, as much as the staff, share the rare opportunity of coming into an important institution without having to step into a mould created by your predecessors. On the other hand, what we do together in 1971 will create an environment into which future students will enter.[7]

The members of the staff share a number of attitudes. One is that our first obligation is to our students. Individually and collectively we hope to make worthwhile contributions to scholarship, and to the solution of social problems. But as teachers we are to be judged primarily by the extent to which we make your stay in the Law School a worthwhile experience and send you out better equipped to face the great challenges that your generation of lawyers will meet.

We accept the need to have a big Law School, but we are determined that we will not allow it to become an impersonal factory in which we mass-produce graduates we barely know. In the first place we simply would not enjoy it. In the second place we do not think that we would give you a meaningful legal education in that way. We will be striving to keep our classes as small as possible. We will use them mostly not to tell you things you can learn from textbooks, or notes, or in the Law Library, but to help you develop your understanding of the law, and the skills a lawyer needs, by active discussion with your teachers and with each other. Much of a lawyer's work is concerned with peacefully resolving particular disputes, so the study of law lends itself to the discussion of cases and problems. This will, we hope, make your legal studies more interesting and more fruitful, but it will not make them lighter. For every hour in class you will have to spend several in the library or in private preparation. You will also take part in a number of special programs to develop your legal skills.

We share the belief, too, that law is not an end in itself. It is to be judged by the extent to which it promotes the well-being of the people living in society. We believe that the study of the law should never lose sight of the social problems that law exists to deal with, and that lawyers should always be ready to criticise and reform the law. We believe that a Law School should not exist in an ivory tower. Staff and students should build and maintain contacts with the practising profession, and with the real world in which lawyers work. On the other hand, the Law School should be a good vantage point from which to stand off and look at the law and the profession with a detachment the practitioner can seldom enjoy. One of the advantages of a Law School on campus is that the staff and students can mix and work with those of other faculties. We would like to see this interdisciplinary contact manifest itself in a meaningful way within the Law School, as well as in the varied societies and activities of a great university.

The worlds of the profession and of the wider university are important in a Law School, but there are other worlds with which it should have contact. Some of these worlds – business, industry, trade unions, governments – supply much of the work and income of the legal profession and are not likely to be overlooked. But we believe that a Law School should have and communicate to its students a keen concern for those on whom the law may bear harshly, either because they cannot afford its services, or because it does not sufficiently recognise their needs, or because they are in some way alienated from the rest of society. The poor, the Aborigines, the handicapped, the deviants, all need their champions in the law as elsewhere.

We admire the social concern that so many of today's students bring to the University. We hope that when these students emerge from the Law School these qualities will have been sharpened, not blunted. We hope they will feel not frustrated, but better equipped, through soundly developed professional knowledge and skills, to express their concern in constructive contributions and lead satisfying lives.

Every student will encounter a variety of problems and uncertainties. The staff are here to see that you get the most out of your stay at the University, so do not hesitate to seek their help. If you cannot find an answer to a question ... make an inquiry at the Faculty Office. If there is any special difficulty, the Senior Administrative Officer, Mr Wildblood, will see you personally. If you have any question about the use of the Law Library, ask the Library staff. Again, if you have a special difficulty, the Law Librarian, Mr Brian, will see you personally. If you have any difficulty about your law studies, raise it in class or approach one of the staff who teaches the subject.

Sometimes, however, you may have a problem that does not fit into any of these categories, or that is too complex or personal to take to someone you do not know well. The staff of the Law School feel that every student should have 'a friend at court', so that there is someone in particular in whom he can confide and to whom he can take his problems. Early in first year every student will be given the name of a member of staff who will make it his business to get to know him.[8] Every member of staff will be assigned a small group of students. Treat this member of staff as a friend whose door is always open. He will give a sympathetic ear to any problem that is worrying you, and if he cannot help you himself will try to refer you to someone who can. This of course can be a two-way traffic. Most teachers could improve their technique or their relations with students, and you may be able to give him some friendly advice.[9] Finally, you have only to tell Miss McCartney, the Dean's Secretary, that you have something important you would like to discuss and she will make an appointment for you to see me.

Sometimes students may feel that they would like to work out a collective point of view and present it to the Faculty. This is one of many useful functions that a Law Students Society could perform. If there are any suggestions for making this a better Law School, the Faculty will be keen to listen. ... There will be student representatives elected to the Law Faculty, and an active and representative society can help them to remain in touch with their electorate.[10]

A law student's life to a large extent revolves around the Law Library ... Recognising the importance of the Law Library, the University has established it as a separate branch of the main library. Mr RF Brian, who until his appointment was High Court Librarian, is engaged in rapidly building up a first-class collection. ... In first year, students will be trained in the use of the Law Library in the Legal Research and Writing Programme. The Library staff will always be willing to help you learn to use the Library. ... The Law Library is temporarily located in Hut C[11] on the lower campus.

We wish you every success.

JH Wootten, Dean.

## 'THE VISION'

I may be wrong, but I cannot recollect that [in 1971] any of us who were there thought or spoke in terms of a vision, let alone tried to write one down. We were too busy starting a Law School. From the beginning the Law School was conceived neither as an intangible vision nor as a mere organisation, but as an institution. As our own Martin Krygier[12] reminded us recently, his mentor Philip Selznick identified the difference between organisations and institutions as being that institutions are organisations that have become 'infuse[d] with value beyond the technical requirements of the task at hand'.[13] This usually happens as a result of the working of spontaneous social processes over time or as the result of a deliberate project of institutionalisation. It seems to me that what is different about this Law School is that it was never conceived as a mere organisation, an impersonal bureaucracy as it were. From the beginning, it was conceived and established as an institution with infused values, and the values embodied in it are what is referred to the 'founding vision'.

I came to the Law School with an embryonic vision of the kind of law school I wanted to emerge at UNSW. It was in part a negative reaction against my own unrewarding experience as a student, and in part a desire to express the things I had learnt to value in 20 years of professional practice. But I knew it had to be fleshed out and realised by teachers who had experience and talents that I did not have. I was by temperament and skills a practitioner of the law, not a scholar or teacher. So, I was looking for staff who shared the basic vision and had the personal qualities and skills to develop it and put it into practice. Two things bulked large for me. One thing was the capacity and desire to engage students in a rich, rewarding and maturing experience. The other was to present law not as a fixed body of rules but as an ongoing social process that should strive to meet the needs of all sections of society

---

The first paragraph is from Hal Wootten's Response to Elizabeth Broderick's 2017 Hal Wootten Lecture. What follows is from personal correspondence from Hal to David Dixon (23 November 2011).

in a just manner, a process in which lawyers played a professional role with all that that implied.

The academic staff who were at UNSW Law School when teaching began in 1971 were Curt Garbesi, Garth Nettheim, Tony Blackshield and Bob Hayes. There were two other people I think of as part of the original academic team who shared the vision and made a major and essential contribution. They were Fred Katz and Susan Hayes of the UNSW Tertiary Education Research Centre (TERC). We thought TERC shared our vision; it thought it had at last found a faculty that shared its vision of education. It was a very productive relationship ...

We did not talk of or copy the 'Socratic method'. There were certain objectives everyone shared, but there was much experimentation in teaching methods guided by Fred Katz and Susan Hayes, neither of whom were lawyers or influenced by legal experiments in case method or Socratic method. We all had a very intense relation with TERC ... [T]he possibility that all the work and imagination the combined team put into developing teaching practice might be written off as merely the adoption of the Socratic method ... would greatly understate its achievement, and tie it to one very narrow and often authoritarian and unpleasant way of realising its objectives.[14] What I brought to the table was essentially a problem stated in negative terms, to which the combined team responded creatively and positively. My very unrewarding legal education had been based on the didactic and usually boring mass lecture, in which the lecturer imparted information usually easily available elsewhere, sometimes by reading out the issued notes. For the most part students were expected to absorb this information and reproduce it in exams.

I was determined to eliminate lectures, and have a system of participatory learning, in which information was available beforehand to students, all of whom were expected to be ready to discuss it in classes small enough to make participation the norm. Instead of being passive receptacles for information, students would learn to analyse, argue, and challenge and be challenged about their thought processes and the values brought to bear. This vision, which came to be taken for granted, left wide open the question of what techniques could be used to achieve these results. This was the subject of open-ended discussion between TERC and the team, and remains a matter of ongoing discussion today. Ideas (positive and negative) could be gained from the case method or the Socratic method, but the limits of neither were acceptable, and there was always a lot of flexibility in the way individuals applied the broad principles that emerged from discussion.

---

*In speeches reproduced below, Hal complained about his university education that 'Law was taught to me as essentially a closed static system' and that 'lawyers thought too much in terms of cases and too little in terms of clients, too much in terms of the law as a closed system and too little of its role in shaping a more just or even a more functional society'. Prospective employers of law graduates often say nowadays that they seek young lawyers who are 'solution focused', who think 'outside the box'. In the 1970s, such thinking was rare. In this respect, US experience did influence Hal. He was impressed by Willard H Pedrick, founding Dean of Arizona State University's law school,[15] who contrasted Australian lawyers' narrow search for relevant cases with American lawyers' broader search for solutions in advising clients. Hal also brought a problem-solving approach to UNSW from his experience at the Bar, working with 'an imaginative and unconventional lawyer'. This demonstrates how black-letter law is made the tool of a wider approach.*

## PROBLEM-SOLVING, CASE LAW AND CREATIVITY

As a young barrister, I shared the chambers of a very creative man. He used to say he went back to 'first principles'. What he did was to take up his client's problem and apply all the energy of his powerful and restless mind to analysing, shaping it, looking at it from every possible

---

'Creativity in the Law' (1972) 4(3) *Australian Journal of Forensic Sciences* 107–20.

angle, turning it inside out and upside down, and asking how it might be affected by some yet unknown fact. At the end he would know what the case really was about – which might be different from what everyone up to that time had assumed it was about. At that stage he would say from a deep feeling for the law, 'There must be a case somewhere that says so and so.' Invariably a little research would show that here was such a case, although once again imagination and experience might be necessary to locate the appropriate analogy under a different heading in the digests or encyclopedias. So the case was won, or at least presented with its strongest aspect, which a less creative mind might never have discovered. So, too, are opportunities to develop the law seized or lost ... The difference between a good teacher and a bad teacher is essentially a difference in creativity. The good teacher does not treat his students as blotting paper to absorb what he says. He treats them as whole human beings to be stimulated and led into using their own creative resources to make themselves lawyers.[16]

## THE FIRST LAW GRADUATION CEREMONY

Mr Chancellor, I thank you for the kind things you have said about the Law School. I thank you not just on my own behalf, but on behalf of all who have taken part in shaping it – academic staff, administrative staff and students. This is the last time so many of us from the inaugural years will be gathered together, and I am quite incapable of treating it as a formal occasion. To me it is as much a personal occasion as it is to each of you who have received your degrees today, and I share with each of you the joy and pride of the day. For me, as for each of you, today marks the culmination of an important part of my life. For many of you it began in 1971, for some in 1972 or 1973. For me it began towards the

'Occasional Address Given by the Honourable Justice Wootten, Foundation Professor and Dean of the Faculty of Law, University of New South Wales, at the First Conferring of Degrees for the Faculty, April 1976' (1976) 1(3) *University of New South Wales Law Journal* 189–92.

end of 1969, when Professor Myers,[17] the Vice-Chancellor, asked me to come to the University and establish the Law Faculty.

In the ensuing year we gathered that happy band of misty-eyed idealists who were the foundation staff.[18] With the exception of Professor Garbesi, they all remain, still recognisable to the familiar eye beneath the burden of years, new titles, degrees, letters to the editor and other less well-known publications. In that year we developed the basic program of the Law Faculty and had it accepted by the professional bodies. Everyone agreed that it was a good program, shaking off a lot of dead wood and finding new ways of looking at the law and developing professional skills. But, alas, to the making of curricula there is no end. An American Dean once maintained to me that there is a predictable ten-year cycle in curricula, staff turnover being sufficient to ensure that few remain to recognise the return of old patterns. That the curriculum continues to change is a healthy sign. It is due less to changes in the law than to the continual quest of active scholars and teachers to find new meanings in their studies, new ways of looking at them, and new ways of presenting them. Show me a Law School that does not have a bristling Curriculum Review Committee, and I won't bother to look at it.

In 1970 the foundations of a good Law Library were laid, a first-class Law Librarian recruited and the administrative staff that did so much to give a warm and human touch to the Law School. The much-loved huts were reclaimed to house the School for two years. I am glad to see that the horrors that followed in the huts have been left behind this year with a move to more adequate accommodation. Those who bemoan the lack of a Law School building should ponder the Parkinson's Law which states that an institution obtains a building worthy of it only at the point of its decline.

When I was invited to start the Law School, I said that all that I knew about legal education was how bad my own had been. Fortunately, other members of the Faculty were more experienced, but TERC and Professor Katz[19] opened to all of us new understandings of educational processes. Professor Freund of Harvard[20] on his recent visit told the story of a boy doing his homework. 'Dad,' asked the boy, 'What is the population of Paris?' 'I've no idea,' was the reply. A few minutes later: 'Which is further north, Venice or Vladivostok?' 'I'm afraid I don't know, son.' Silence. 'I hope you don't mind me asking you these questions, Dad.' 'Of course not, son. How are you ever going to learn if you don't ask?' I suspect many of you felt a bit like that boy after your first few weeks at the Law School. At all events, I hope you did, because the teachers were not there to tell you the answers to questions, but to stimulate you to ask questions and help you to learn how to answer them for yourself.

One gets the feeling that parts of some universities could go on functioning happily for years after the last students had disappeared, scarcely noticing their absence. The frustration of students who felt virtually ignored as passive counters in the educational process had, I am sure, something to do with the widespread student unrest of a few years ago. From the beginning, the Law School stated and practised a very different policy, and the students responded enthusiastically to the discovery that they had a major role to play in shaping the Law School. Ivan Illich had not published *Deschooling Society*, or we might have adapted his words and said that we were seeking not to create an 'educational funnel', but an 'educational web' which would 'heighten the opportunity for each one to transform each moment of his living into one of learning, sharing and caring'. Growth in numbers – that great subverter of human values – has made it harder to maintain this atmosphere, but I sense that there is still a lot of it around in the Law School …

Many of these things have been recalled to me by re-reading the first Dean's letter to new students, which endeavoured to state the common attitudes of the foundation staff. Among other things, it sought to link the Law School not only with the profession and the rest of the University, but with other worlds outside – not only with business, industry, trade unions and governments, which supplied most of the income of the legal profession, but with those on whom the law might bear harshly – the poor, the Aborigines, the handicapped, the deviants. That these were not empty phrases is shown by the great contribution this Law School has already made, in a few short years, to the study of law and poverty, to legal aid, civil liberties, the welfare of children and Aboriginal rights. It is no accident that among today's graduates is the first Aboriginal lawyer in Australia.[21]

All this has not been done without making mistakes, or without raising a few hackles in the legal profession and elsewhere. As in every profession, there are lawyers who are smug and conservative, and some who are exceptionally sensitive and defensive. A law school which displeased nobody would be doing very little.

In that first letter we said:

> We admire the social concern that so many of today's students bring to the University. We hope that when these students emerge from the Law School these qualities will have been sharpened, not blunted. We hope that they will feel, not frustrated, but better equipped, through soundly developed professional knowledge and skills, to express their concerns in constructive contributions and lead satisfying lives.

It is too early to ask whether this hope has been realised. You have not had time to test yourselves on the world, and you graduate in a time of widespread disillusionment. Hopes of a continued concerted attack on social problems have been raised in recent years only to be disappointed. Many feel frustrated, and the pursuit of scapegoats has not yet given place to the hard work of understanding what went wrong, and the rebuilding of new bases from which to attack the old problems, most of which still remain.

There is emerging, I believe, a realisation that many problems will be solved only by much more fundamental social change than has yet been attempted, and that the ever-increasing application of old remedies often becomes counter-productive ... Resort to law over an ever-increasing range of disputes does nothing for social harmony. More importantly, the ever-increasing dependence on institutions prevents the development of self-reliance and mutual community reliance. People no longer think of educating themselves and each other, as they once did so fruitfully. Care of one's own health, or mutual care in a family or community context, is disdained. The social fabric that once enabled much disputation to be settled by the mediation of friends, relatives, neighbours or respected citizens, has been destroyed, and turning the other cheek to a minor wrong is no longer regarded as a virtue.

I think that, on my record, I need not fear an accusation of hostility to legal aid or of insensitiveness to the need for the underprivileged to have equal access to the law. But when one finds legal aid invoked for the purpose of financing an inquiry over several days by two barristers and two solicitors before a Supreme Court judge to decide whether someone in a country town has turned his radio up to annoy his neighbour, something is wrong. It is not a condemnation of legal aid, any more than excessive pathological tests are a condemnation of Medibank. But it does show a neurotic reliance on institutionalised dispute settlement to the exclusion of the natural processes that should operate within neighbourhood and community. With all its faults, it would be a pity to see the affluent society disappear into the maw of the hypochondriac and litigious society, and to see individual and community self-reliance quite displaced by institutional dependence.

Like lawyers of every generation, you will face the dual challenge of keeping the substantive law responsive to changes in other areas of society, and of preventing the institutions of the law itself from being exploitative, burdensome, and destructive of the social fabric. I have some hope that this Law School may have prepared you well.

Former students, now fellow lawyers, the reputation of this Law School is now in your hands. But whatever happens, it was a great privilege to have worked with you.

# ON BEING AWARDED AN HONORARY DOCTORATE OF LAWS

I am proud to have received today an honorary degree from what I can say without any pretence of impartiality is a great university with a great Law School ...

When it has been decided to award an honorary degree, it is necessary to construct an *ex post facto* justification in the form of a citation, listing supposed achievements, which is read out while its embarrassed subject stands exposed to the sceptical eyes of the Chancellor and the Faculty. The older the recipient, the longer the list. As I listened to the lengthy list read out today, it seemed more like a random series of events that had befallen me – a monument, not to my purpose and determination, but to my inability to say no when someone has asked me to do something for which I am not qualified.

The invitation to be Foundation Dean of the Law School was no exception, but it was irresistible. It was at the end of the glorious 1960s, and although I had never actually been a hippie ... many of the hippie tenets had struck responsive chords in me. I was reacting against many of the same things, although not in the same way. I believed, as I still do, that universities should encourage the mind and personalities of students to flower rather than press them into conformity; that what you were was more important than what you had, and that love and justice needed restoring to a primary place in public values. I believed that lawyers thought too much in terms of cases and too little in terms of clients, too much in terms of the law as a closed system and too little of its role in shaping a more just or even a more functional society. I believed that law schools thought too much in terms of academic publications and formal qualifications and too little about what students got out of their time at law school, in developing their skills, maturing their personalities, increasing their understanding of social processes, and simply enjoying some of the most important years of their lives.

---

'Occasional Address, 14 October 1994' (1995) 18(2) *University of New South Wales Law Journal* 232–36.

I was fortunate to be able to gather a young faculty who shared these beliefs and could realise them far more effectively than I could ever have done, and with them I spent four rewarding years. One of the things that happened to me and to the embryonic Faculty during that period was the Aboriginal Legal Service, which was the first in Australia, and had its home in the Law School for the first months of its existence.[22] This fitted well with my belief that the law paid too little attention to the rights of the poor and underprivileged and to glaring injustices in society.

This association led to the University adopting, operative from 1971, what I suspect was the first program of special Aboriginal admission to an Australian university. The Law School became the leading centre for Aboriginal legal education in Australia, and for study and teaching about Aboriginals and the law. In the 80-odd law graduates today, I was delighted to see three Aboriginals.

# CELEBRATING THE 30TH ANNIVERSARY OF THE FIRST STUDENTS' GRADUATION

I was a silk at the NSW Bar, where I had practised for nearly 20 years, when, 37 years ago, the Vice-Chancellor, Professor Myers, gave me the unexpected invitation to start the Law School. My mind went back to the time, 60 years ago this year, when I sat as you graduates do now, listening to someone pontificating about something I have long forgotten. I recalled my barren experience as a student in the previous four years in a law school that had no vision, in which students simply didn't matter, and in which law was treated as an end in itself, and I saw that it had done little of significance to prepare me for the 20 years of practice that now lay behind me, or to produce lawyers equipped and committed to discharge the responsibilities that go with membership of a privileged profession enjoying monopoly rights.

'Occasional Address at a Graduation Ceremony on 6 October 2006, the 30th Anniversary of the First Graduation Ceremony', unpublished.

I began to form a vision of a Law School in which students did matter, in which they would find the three or four years they spent in the School an enriching, maturing and rewarding experience that prepared them for a potential 50 years of practice in which nothing was certain but change, a School from which they would go out with a strong sense that the law existed to serve the well-being of society, and that they had qualified for an honourable and worthwhile profession committed to playing a constructive role. For staff it would be a School in which they felt satisfaction in securing such an outcome for students whom they had come to know, a place where civility and collegiality ruled so that people of widely differing views could cooperate in a shared enterprise, and where critical scholarship appropriate both to a university and a learned profession could flourish.

In Australia, university legal education had been seen primarily as a certifying process, an alternative to the qualifying examinations administered by the judges and professional bodies, who jealously policed this way around the examinations they controlled. I was warned by well-wishers that it would be impossible to innovate. But I was buoyed by support from within the University itself, not only Professor Myers but the deans of other professional faculties, and from the executive of the reputedly conservative Law Society, under the leadership of solicitors who acted primarily for the big end of town.

Their professional experience, like my own, had shown them that the world and its expectations of lawyers were changing, and that traditional concepts of legal education were no longer adequate. Clients didn't just want lawyers who could, whether from memory or after looking it up, tell them what the law said. They wanted people who could bring independent, educated minds to their affairs, as well as a deep appreciation of the law, and help them decide what to do.

The vision was never intended or treated as a blueprint; the submission to Council stressed the desirability of constant innovation and experiment in legal education. Much of the proposal was couched in deliberately broad and vague terms, to leave room for the expertise and creativity of yet-to-be appointed staff, who in the event jettisoned some of my proposals. An insightful speech by Professor David Brown at the School's 30th anniversary, warning against the reification of the founding vision as part of the mythology of the Law School, has itself become part of that mythology.

I left in 1973 and have had no part in any decision made in the last 33 years. However, I feel great pride in what my successors achieved. The School rapidly became, and has remained, competitive in attracting the highest-rated students and has scored highly in teaching performance and student and graduate satisfaction. It attracted and continues to attract very impressive staff, not least because the aspiration for civility and collegiality among people of widely different views has been realised. A staff member[23] was invited to give the Boyer Lectures. Another, in collaboration with a student, has carved out a place in the legal history not only of Australia, but of the world, in making freely available on searchable databases on the Internet all the basic legal materials first of Australia, then successively of the Pacific, Great Britain and Ireland, the countries of the Commonwealth of Nations and, most recently, Asia.[24]

The School has reason to be proud of its Centres, including the renowned Kingsford Legal Centre. The Indigenous Law Centre was a trailblazer. The Gilbert + Tobin Centre is today the pre-eminent venue for the discussion of Australian constitutional issues. They are but some of the Centres housed in the Centres Precinct. Publications by staff have achieved great respect and are widely used in the profession. The interactive small-group teaching method developed in collaboration with Professor Katz's Tertiary Education Research Centre achieved its central aim of producing graduates with a highly developed understanding of the law and legal processes, and lawyerly skills of analysis, argument and judgment appreciated by employers. Rejecting both the lecture and the case method models, it was highly demanding of both teachers and students, but found rewarding by both.

In the only authoritative review, the 1987 Pearce Committee adjudged the Law School the best in Australia. At the 25th anniversary, the then Chief Justice of Australia collated and endorsed this and other accolades.[25]

This year, it at last attained a building worthy of it, an event not without its embarrassment for me. I was known for comforting those unhappy with the old building by citing what I believed to be a Parkinson's Law that an institution only obtains a building worthy of it at the point of its decline. I had relied on memory for this version and was dismayed to find yesterday that the only source Google could find for it was myself. The real Parkinson's Law has an emphasis that I missed – it refers to the decline that is signalled when an institution builds an ostentatiously grand building for itself, Louis XIV's Palace of Versailles being an example. As the new Law Building was built not by the Faculty but for it by the University, I would contend that the law has no application …

Today I believe more strongly than ever that students matter, law schools matter and the legal profession matters – they all matter both in their own right and because the law matters. Everywhere we look in a turbulent and depressing global landscape reinforces the lesson that without those fundamentals of the law, the rule of law and human rights, humanity has no future. For all its faults, I think that we have a pretty good legal profession in Australia today, as good as at any time in the 65 years I have known it. We have an incorrupt judiciary; powerful people are brought to book for criminal acts, including white collar crimes; even when they are isolated in Nauru the boat people have lawyers taking up their cause; lawyers from the Law Council down speak out against the disgraceful treatment of David Hicks by his own government[26] and the belittling of international law in many ways. I believe that the relatively healthy legal profession is partly due to the hefty leaven provided over the last 30 years by this Law School and other law schools that share its vision in greater or lesser degree. I believe that the vision, reworked as it has been by many hands, is worth fighting for.

## REMINISCING WITH THE 'ORIGINALS'

Words cannot convey my pleasure to be with so many graduates – not least our present Chancellor[27] – who in 1971 and 1972 were among the students I invited to join with the foundation staff – 'we few, we happy few, we band of brothers'[28] – in laying the foundations of a new and, we hoped, one day great law school.[29] The importance I attached to your role was not empty words. It was part of the vision that we build a law school in which a rewarding student experience was of central concern, and I believed that the atmosphere of student response and orientation developed in the early years would be critical, and for better or worse would become a tradition handed on to later students.

Your response was all that could be desired: goodwill; open minds; intellectual curiosity; willingness to give things a go, to interact with staff with mutual respect and friendship, to enjoy yourselves and your time at the Law School, to argue, to challenge yourselves and each other and staff, to stand up to Curt Garbesi, to encourage Garth Nettheim, to cheer up Bob Hayes, to understand Krishna Sharma's accent, to care for young Richard Chisholm, to follow Tony Blackshield's imaginative flights, to share my dreams (even if in your enthusiasm you dented the roof of my Kombi van transporting a public telephone box, an attempt to win the University treasure hunt for the faculty unfortunately eclipsed by the two elephants produced by another faculty).

The late Paddy McGuiness[30] once accused the staff of radicalising you; it felt more like you were radicalising us, although viewing the pillars of the establishment before me, it is hard to believe that anyone was radicalised. When I think back to those almost mythical days in the huts, a phrase from one of Justice Holmes's speeches rushes to my lips: 'in our youth, our hearts were touched with fire …'.[31]

Honesty rears its ugly head and compels me to acknowledge that it wasn't *our* youth – it was *your* youth and *my* middle age – and to ask:

---

'An Address to a Gathering of Foundation Students, 27 February 2008', unpublished.

who am I to speak for your hearts? But although it would be safer to say that in *your* youth *my* heart was touched by fire, it would do less than justice to the way we jointly embarked on our project all those years ago. So if you will once again permit me, as you did so generously then, to share vicariously in your youth, I will make bold to say that in *our* youth *our* hearts *were* touched by fire, and a flame was lit which, although passed on through many hands, has not gone out.

A flame is an unfortunate metaphor in days of climate change, but it has been fuelled by remarkably renewable energy. Nor has the Law School mined and consumed the inheritance of the past, but learnt from it, leaving it undiminished, indeed enriched by new contributions to be woven into the fabric of thought and knowledge, of insight and inspiration; that is the human and the legal heritage.

Our flame – and I include succeeding generations of students and staff who have tended it, some of them here today – our flame has not only lit and warmed and stimulated the life of the Law School in which we meet, but, I dare to hope, has through it made an important and positive contribution to the wider societies of which we are part. This is not a claim of exceptionalism for this Law School, but only that it has made honourable and worthwhile contributions in many fields of social endeavour – education, scholarship, professional service, politics, administration, business, international cooperation, social inclusion, law and justice, to name some.

A venerable dean/professor of today, but one of your most junior teachers, finding himself at the head of another great law school, asked me to address his staff on how to make it the best in Australia. I liked the implication that I had some expertise in that subject. However, the burden of my talk was that he had posed the wrong question: that a law school should not have the Pharisee's concern to be thought better than others. Every law school exists in different circumstances, each with its own distinctive location, history, opportunities, resources, traditions, myths, intellectual foci, social commitments, staff and student mixes. Although ours fares well in attempts to rank law schools,[32] the better question is whether a law school, given its specificities, is making the best use of its talents in contributing to the collective responsibilities that law schools have to the local, regional, national and international communities that they serve.

I say 'serve' advisedly because I passionately believe that law schools exist in a professional context. 'Serve' implies no subservience. As the motto of the NSW Bar Association has it, lawyers are 'servants of all, yet of none'. The [UNSW] Law School emerged among conflicting claims as to whether legal education should be 'practical' or 'academic'. I rejected this dichotomy in favour of 'professional'.

In return for the individual and corporate privileges and independence a profession enjoys, it undertakes a measure of responsibility for society's needs in its field: a responsibility to provide needed services with skill and integrity, to conserve and enlarge scholarship, and to maintain standards. A law school contributes to all three responsibilities. There need be no conflict between its role as part of the profession and its role as part of a university, with common commitments to excellence and integrity in scholarship and professional practice, and a common tradition of responsible independence.

For me a law school is important, very important, because of its role in maintaining and shaping the law and the legal profession, both of which are fundamental to the liberal, democratic, secular society under the rule of law, which I treasure for its potential to provide its members with justice, liberty and opportunities for individual self-realisation. The challenge is to ensure that a law school worthily fulfils its role.

It is part of the mythology of this Law School that when the Vice-Chancellor invited me to be founding Dean, I replied that all I knew about legal education was how bad my own had been. Professor Myers, always a great friend of the Law School, is, to my delight, here tonight, and I hope that his recollection accords with mine, which is that he replied, with his customary mix of courtesy, courage and prescience, that this was a good starting point.

Part of what I had in mind was the ineffective and demeaning teaching process my generation had endured, and which we decisively rejected, but another part was the substance of what was taught. With the great exception of Julius Stone,[33] law was taught to me as an introverted discipline administered within its own parameters by an inward-looking profession.

In first year, we were solemnly taught Dicey's version of the Austinian doctrine of sovereignty, not as political theory but as the law. If parliament decreed that all blue-eyed (or was it red-haired?) babies should be killed, there was nothing lawyers could or, it seemed, even should, do about it. Yet at the same time we were taught smugly that the Australian Constitution was superior to that of the United States because it did not contain a Bill of Rights. Who needed a Bill of Rights when we had the common law to protect us? Babies, blue-eyed or red-haired, could not be allowed to compromise the purity of the law.

It was part of the revolution in legal education, in which this Law School played its part, that lawyers came to look at the law from outside as well as inside, to ask how it was actually working, and to feel some responsibility for the outcome.

Law was taught to me as essentially a closed static system, not a process of sometimes rapid response to a changing society. For many, the common law was still discovered rather than made by the courts, and legislation, other than deliberate reform of the common law, was largely ignored. Rather than making students experts in the law in force when they happened to do a subject, the new law schools sought to give them basic concepts and tools to manage the legal change that would continue throughout their lives.

A third major defect was the non-inclusive character of law unconsciously taught as something catering for white middle-class males, the reasonable men in the Clapham omnibus, in the days before it was filled by Pakistanis and professional women on their way to work. Even corporations did not get treatment commensurate with their importance, and government departments, women and other deviants from the norm got none.

You have probably noticed that the Law School still likes to quote words I addressed to you all those years ago:

> [W]e believe that a Law School should have and communicate
> to its students a keen concern for those on whom the law may
> bear harshly, either because they cannot afford its services, or
> because it does not sufficiently recognise their needs, or because
> they are in some way alienated from the rest of society. The poor,
> the Aborigines, the handicapped, the deviants, all need their
> champions in the law as elsewhere.

I am proud to be so quoted, but I like to add that I was affirming the responsibility of the law to serve the whole of society and singling out certain groups as those whose needs were too easily overlooked.

I hope that I am not smug and complacent when I look with some satisfaction at the profession produced by our revolution. If one looks for faults and areas in need of improvement, they are not hard to find, nor are they ever likely to be. But overall, I think our legal profession is in reasonably good shape, given the challenges of recent decades. These include extraordinary technological, economic, social and demographic change, globalisation, racial conflicts, the decline of family and church authority, the corruptions of consumerism and national prosperity, the commercialisation and commodification of nearly everything, growing inequality of wealth and power, tensions over national and international security, the constant invitation by advertisers and some politicians to be relaxed, comfortable and greedy.

To a very high degree the rule of law has been maintained, the judiciary has remained incorrupt and accessible, a free democracy has survived, the legal position of women, children and most minorities and the legal protection of the environment have greatly improved, and a rapidly growing market economy has thrived under legal regulation. Whether speaking through their professional organisations or responding individually as advocates or judges to the needs of citizens, not least Aboriginals, prematurely accused 'terrorists', victimised migrants and the desperate flotsam of humanity washing up on our shores, our lawyers have maintained a readiness to speak truth to power, or at least to tell power what it doesn't want to hear, and to insist on the fundamental legal right to a fair hearing for all. Although we do not always achieve our aspirations, law graduates have with few exceptions been among those who care about the rule of law, about integrity in public office, about justice, fairness, equality and liberty, and about the protection of the vulnerable.

Through its teaching, its scholarship, its contribution to public debate, and above all the graduates it has produced, this Law School has played an honourable and distinguished part in producing this result. We may be justly proud of what we started in your youth, so many years ago, and are justly entitled to celebrate it joyfully tonight. But not only does much remain to be done; with the wisdom of those years, we know that the things we value in our society are never finally won; old threats and challenges take different forms and new ones arise. Technology has brought us to a level of wealth undreamt of in human history, and with it great unsolved problems: how that technology is to be curbed and channelled so that it does not destroy the very conditions of life on earth; how both that wealth and the burdens that accompany its production can be shared fairly between individual and social purposes, between managers, investors, workers and those not in the workforce, between generations, between nations; how people can find new ways to give meaning to their lives as old ways erode; how our cherished values of the just, liberal, democratic society under the rule of law can be preserved as people of different faiths and assumptions and identities increasingly rub shoulders and live together in a globalising world.

The role of the Law School and its graduates will be no less important in the present and future than it was in the past, and I hope that you who gave it so much in your youth will stand ready to support it in whatever ways are open to you now and in the years to come.

I offer you a toast. Let us all drink to what was, is, and will always remain 'our Law School'.

# 5

# IN AN ANCIENT LAND: PALESTINE AND ISRAEL

*In 2008, David Dixon was commiserating with Hal Wootten about the death of Hal's daughter Victoria after an illness. 'It's very sad,' Hal said, 'but it means I am able to carry out a plan I had to postpone.'*

*What was this 86-year-old planning? A holiday? Spending time with grandchildren? Working on an autobiography? No – he was going to Palestine to learn. Second only to climate change, Hal believed the relationship between Israel and Palestine was the most urgent global issue of our time, and he wanted to understand it from close quarters and see whether he could do something about it. His experience of observing and talking to people in Israel and the West Bank is recounted in this chapter. The 'little nudge' that he eventually settled on was helping Palestinian law schools to produce lawyers familiar with Western legal ideas and liberal democratic principles so that they would be ready to negotiate and then contribute leadership to a Palestinian state. This echoes his work, decades earlier, on the role of legal education and the profession in supporting the development of an independent Papua New Guinea (see chapter 7).*

*Hal only received his permit to visit Gaza after he returned to Australia from the West Bank in 2008. When he went back to visit three law schools in Gaza, all were welcoming and at least one was a secular, progressive institution interested in working with Australian law schools. Seeing from afar the 2014 war in Gaza, Hal wrote 'events there wrench my heart'. A decade later in a new catastrophe, following the Hamas attacks on Israel on 7 October 2023 and Israel's response, all Gaza's universities are in ruins and many faculty and students have been killed. The West Bank, East Jerusalem and Lebanon are in crisis. The current conflict makes Hal's analysis more relevant than ever.*

*Hal only finished two short pieces for publication. He accepted one invitation to speak publicly, but incessant heckling from a member of the audience and ad hominem attacks in response to his articles discouraged him from further talks or publications (see 'Australian Jewry and "The Promise"', below). Most of this chapter is a compilation of drafts and notes from 2008 to 2014, reflecting his own experience, research and conversations with Israelis and Palestinians in that period. All the words are Hal's, but we have edited his writings into one text and added occasional references to explain or update as needed.*

# IN ISRAEL AND PALESTINE
## Getting to Palestine

In 2008, I spent three months based in Ramallah on the West Bank. It was a private, unfunded, unsponsored trip, and I lived alone in a rented apartment, with no function except to enlarge my own understanding and experience. What finally hooked me was the great human drama unfolding in Israel and Palestine, and the responses of people of conscience and humanity who found themselves on one side or another of a complex conflict that, despite a great deal of international effort to end it, continued to escalate, always festering painfully and periodically breaking out in episodes of extraordinary suffering, destruction and slaughter. After reading *Dark Hope*,[1] in which David Shulman, a Jewish Professor of Humanistic Studies at the Hebrew University of Jerusalem, told how he had responded, I felt there was only one place to go. Much of *Dark Hope* was about the persecution of impoverished Palestinian villagers in the South Hebron Hills by Israeli settlers protected by Israeli police and soldiers. I was horrified by the callousness, cruelty and arrogance with which some human beings, in this case Israeli Jews, could treat fellow human beings. I was humbled by the courage and moral clarity with which other human beings, in this case also Israeli Jews, could confront and challenge their own countrymen.

## In Israel

As a foreigner, I could do something my Palestinian friends could not: pass freely through the dominating 8-metre-high concrete wall that segregated them (on all but rare, permit-ridden occasions) from face-to-face meeting with their Israeli counterparts.[2] In nearby Jerusalem, I found a remarkable number of Jewish Israelis working tirelessly for Palestinian rights. Along with ordinary Israeli citizens were some of Israel's most distinguished scholars, journalists and creative writers, and numerous lawyers. Not only did I come to know and admire these Jewish Israelis, but with them I could enter Jewish settlements in the West Bank, using the network of Israeli-only roads, visit Bedouin villages in the Negev,[3] explore Jerusalem, experience Israeli police at work, and engage in activities with Jewish dissidents, among them the author of *Dark Hope*, with whom I spent a memorable day locked up in the police station of a West Bank settlement. We had been on our way to a peaceful demonstration in the South Hebron Hills when we were detained on a specious pretext that was maintained just long enough to stop us getting to the demonstration.

Beyond the wall, I found a different Israel to the one that dominates the minds and confines the lives of Palestinians – not a confident, oppressive military monolith, but a complex society, divided along fault lines of race, history, culture and religious sectarianism, a democracy hobbled by a voting system that guarantees extremist minorities a disproportionate influence, sometimes a veto. Nor was it the romantic early Israel that lingers in the minds of many Westerners – the Israel of the kibbutz[4] where selfless community members worked to make the desert bloom and willingly donned the uniform of a citizen army of heroic, but peace-loving warriors. In many ways, it had become another Western society, consumerist, individualist, pleasure-loving, urban, high-tech, but with an albatross around its neck – the Occupied Palestinian Territories (OPT), the land to which it is attached by 3000 years of history, by delusions of economic and political advantage, by extremist settlers and by fear of a perceived enemy to which it is bound by mutual misperceptions.

I had long talks with Zionists, often themselves pro-Palestinian activists who, precisely because they so passionately want their own country, understand how Palestinians want theirs. On a tour of West Bank settlements conducted in Hebrew by the Jewish organisation Peace Now, a man near my own age translated for me. He had come from America as a young man to work on a kibbutz, became a teacher, and was proud that he had fought for Israel and lost a son in its wars, and worked many years for the World Zionist Organization. After seeing him argue heatedly with a settler, I asked how he reconciled his present activities with his Zionism. He said simply, 'We want this country, but the Palestinians want it too. We have to share it.' I realised that most of the Jews with me were Zionists in his sense, and ever since I bridle when I hear the term used loosely in a denigratory way.

## In Palestine

Palestine, the best educated and most secular of Arab societies, with an influential Christian minority, is also unique and diverse, not part of a monolithic and hostile Arab world. There are secularists, Christians, Islamists and the moderate Muslim majority; generational divisions, the old and new guard in the Palestinian Liberation Organization; Arab nationalists and jealous Palestinians; and some like Hamas, still tugged in opposing directions. Although united in the desire to end the Occupation, Palestinians are no more a society of rabid Islamists bent on destroying Israel than Israel is a society of fanatical settlers bent on eliminating Arabs in Eretz Israel.[5] Yet each group has a disproportionate influence on the lives of ordinary people in the other country and the images they form of 'the Other'. I saw how the Occupation at once locks Jews and Arabs in the deadly embrace of enemies and denies them the possibility of normal human friendship and cooperation.

Israel and its lobbies make sure the world knows of the genuine human rights violations its citizens suffer in the form of terrorism, something always newsworthy in the Western press. There is no equal publicity for the massive daily human rights violations against the population of the OPT, despite the thorough documentation by Israeli and Palestinian human rights organisations. It takes the extreme killing and devastation of the invasion of Gaza or Lebanon to make the world's headlines.

A lasting impression was my reception among ordinary, usually poor, Palestinians. To them, I was a lone stranger, an old, vulnerable, relatively affluent European who turned up in their midst, of unknown provenance and with unknown intentions. Universally, they treated me with respect, more often friendly warmth, and with generous hospitality and scrupulous honesty. I was left feeling that shopkeepers and taxi drivers would rather serve me free than overcharge me. Losing my way one night in a poor, ill-lit suburb of Ramallah, I realised that I felt no fear at all, but confidence that I could accost any shadowy figure and find someone who would be anxious to see I got home safely.

Ordinary Palestinians had suffered deeply from the Occupation for 40 years, but seemed surprisingly free of antisemitic prejudice. I found most were prepared to be sympathetic to the suffering of Jews in the Holocaust, but not to the world salving its conscience by imposing a state for Jews in their own long-standing homeland, Arab Palestine. They tolerated the delays and humiliation at the ubiquitous checkpoints or arbitrary accosting with quiet dignity.

Bitterness, sometimes hatred, there certainly was, usually just below the surface but easily aroused. How could Palestinians live, day in day out, with the Occupation without cracking? Some did so,[6] but most carried on. What was the secret of their resistance? I felt I had some clue when I read Raja Shehadeh's *The Third Way*.[7] Taking wisdom attributed to Jewish inmates of the Treblinka concentration camp, Shehadeh wrote: 'Faced with two alternatives, always choose the third. Between mute submission and blind hate, I choose the third way.' For Shehadeh, taking the third way is to practise *sumud*, usually translated as persevering steadfastness, and manifested as a determination not to give in, to stick it out, not to yield to what was universally believed to be Israel's intention to make their lives so miserable that they would one by one, family by family, go abroad and leave the country to the Zionists. The Palestinians I got to know well see their life as one of endurance: enduring the Occupation, practising *sumud*. James Prineas defined *sumud* as 'steadfastness, the non-violent resistance of Palestinians against land confiscation and ethnic cleansing. Like an old olive tree deeply rooted to the ground, those practising *sumud* refuse to move away despite political, economic and physical injustices committed against them.'[8] A rough Australian translation might be: 'Don't let the bastards get you down …'.

## The past lives on

Reading the history of Palestine and Israel with an eye on its continuing influence on the present, one notices ideas, aspirations, myths that are never fully embraced, but never fully rejected (except by a radical minority), yet never go away. They are there waiting to surface if their moment comes, and in the meantime they have subterranean influences on events that are hard to identify or quantify.

On the Palestinian side, most such ideas would stem from the premise that the Israeli presence is not legitimate, that the whole idea of a Jewish state or even a Jewish homeland was an invention of Western imperialism unlawfully and unjustly imposed on Arabs, and on Palestinian Arabs in particular, to salve consciences of the West, embarrassed by European antisemitism and later the overwhelming horror of the Holocaust. From this premise, it is a short step to the view that Israel should be no more, and its Jewish population sent back to where they came from or forced to become citizens of a state with an Arab – and Muslim – majority. Hamas is not alone in treating this as the proper starting point for bargaining. It surfaces in a more acceptable form in the idealistic idea, intermittently espoused by both Palestinians and Jews, of a single state based on full human rights and toleration.

My judgment, both from extensive reading and living among Palestinians, is that while nearly all would accept the premise, a large majority would, however grudgingly, accept that the corollary is not a tenable policy. Israel, with its Jewish population, is there to stay, and Palestinians will have to make do with a state based on a partition of historic Palestine in which they will not get even the portion allocated by the United Nations in 1948, but only that which survived the fighting in 1948 and was taken by Israel in 1967. The problem is that Israel has never been willing to return to the 1967 borders, not even in the allegedly 'generous offer' of Prime Minister Ehud Barak at Camp David in 2000,[9] but the possibility of turning back the clock still lingers on in ghostly or subterranean form in Arab consciousness or subconsciousness.

But a more complex place to study ideas that roll around, neither embraced nor abandoned, but tugging at people's hearts and constituting obstacles to rational solutions, is on the Jewish Israeli side. After all, there it is in the Torah, in Chapter 15 of Genesis, that God gave the descendants of Abraham all the land between the Nile and the Euphrates. At a less ambitious level, the West Bank's Judea and Samaria were the heartland of the ancient Jewish kingdom, yet they have ended up mostly in the OPT, not Israel. Many Jews saw 1967 not as the conquest of Arab land, but as the divine restoration of land to its true owners. Most Jews have grown up with the words 'next year in Jerusalem', with its evocation of return to the ancient kingdom, frequently on their lips. Many who accepted the partition that created Israel (Prime Minister David Ben-Gurion, for example) saw it only as a first step; the rest would come in the fullness of time.

Cleansing the Jewish homeland – whatever its borders – of Arabs, by fair means or foul, is another idea of extraordinary resilience. Canvassed by Theodor Herzl[10] in the 19th century, it has never gone away. Many Palestinians see it as the rationale underlying policies of the Occupation that subject them to constant frustrations, humiliations, restrictions, discomfort, delays and denial of permits that have no other rational explanation than trying to make Palestinians give up and leave.

Ideas such as these may not be embraced, but nor are they fully put to rest, and their tug is a factor making it difficult for Israelis to take what some of their leaders cryptically refer to as 'painful decisions'. Colliding with each other, and with a reality that denies the possibility of some or all of them, they may explain opinion polls in which incompatibly large majorities were both peace-loving *and* extreme nationalist, or supported expelling all Arabs west of the Jordan *and* supported withdrawal from the OPT.[11] Contradictions in Israeli policy may be a result. For example, in 1967, government policy was not to annex the OPT but to retain them to use as bargaining chips, yet it could not bring itself to say 'no' to those who wanted to settle in Etzion and Hebron, and other settlements that followed. Centre and Labor-based governments did not support the expansion of settlements, but they could not bring themselves to dismantle them, or stop their expansion, which went on irrespective of the government in power. After Prime Minister Menachem Begin was elected in 1977, such haphazard development hardened into a government strategy of using the settlements to undermine hopes of a Palestinian state by breaking up the contiguity of Palestinian communities and establishing 'facts on the ground'.[12]

The Israeli philosopher Avishai Margalit has described how the addition of small numbers of settlers to settlements scattered through the West Bank – by the construction of illegal outposts, their defence by the Israel Defense Forces (IDF), the construction of service roads, the declaration of security zones, and the cutting off of access to villages – steadily expands Israeli control of land in the West Bank 'and gets rid of the Palestinians living on it by making their lives intolerable'.[13] He stressed to me his concern that Palestinians did not appreciate that this often-overlooked process was undermining their position far more than the large numbers of settlers in the concentrated towns around Jerusalem.

## Al-Haq and the limits of human rights

By chance, I ended up in close association with human rights organisations. The Australian Section of the International Commission of Jurists introduced me to its West Bank affiliate, Al-Haq, which generously took me into the 'family' made up of its interns, several expatriate and many local staff. Al-Haq's director, Sha'wan Jabarin, proved his independence of spirit by enduring over seven years of administrative detention without charge at the hands of the governing IDF.[14]

Al-Haq, pre-eminent among many human rights organisations in Palestine, documents violations of the individual and collective rights of Palestinians in the OPT, irrespective of the perpetrator.[15] Affidavits taken by staff located around the OPT are used by researchers working in a collegiate atmosphere of constant peer review to produce studies that can rarely be challenged by the well-resourced monitoring organisations dedicated to faulting critics of Israel. The advocacy effect of these published studies, all available on Al-Haq's website,[16] is supplemented by representations to international agencies, national governments and local authorities, and by making documentary films that bring to life the human dramas underlying the factual reporting, statistics and argument. Sometimes legal action is initiated, although scope for effective litigation is very limited.

The number of Jewish Israelis who work tirelessly for Palestinian rights is remarkable, and their many organisations cover the whole spectrum from the highly professional to the aggressively activist, often combining a range of approaches. Al-Haq's outstanding Israeli counterpart, B'Tselem,[17] the Israeli Center for Human Rights in the Occupied Territories, documents all human rights violations in the OPT, whoever commits or suffers them. B'Tselem is an organisation of outstanding integrity, thoroughness, reliability and independence, whose website is a rich mine of authoritative reference covering many subjects. An innovative step was the distribution of video cameras to Palestinian families who live near settlements, to military bases or at the sites of frequent army incursions. Many such Palestinians had long reported assaults and damage to their property, with complaints resulting in their own arrest, not that of the wrongdoers. The cameras are doing something to level that playing field.

Another type of predominantly Jewish activist organisation is represented by Ta'ayush, a grassroots movement of Arab and Jewish Israelis working 'to break down the walls of racism and segregation by constructing a true Arab–Jewish partnership' working 'through concrete, daily actions of solidarity to end the Israeli occupation of the Palestinian territories and to achieve full civil equality for all Israeli citizens'.[18] David Shulman's *Dark Hope* describes and reflects on many years of non-violent activity with this organisation, mostly supporting Palestinians in West Bank villages or East Jerusalem against aggression and harassment by settlers, and often against Israeli police and army who regard it as their role to support settlers against Palestinians, or who have the task of enforcing programs aimed at Judaising East Jerusalem and parts of the West Bank.

For those who focus on human rights as an engine of progress in justice and liberty, the extensive network of strong organisations, reinforcing each other's findings from opposite sides of the conflict, should give satisfaction and comfort, particularly when contrasted with the weakness and suppression of such institutions in other places of concern – China or Myanmar, for example. But it raises disturbing questions. Why does this work continue to be necessary, facing similar daily issues and periodic catastrophes, and offering similar condemnations and recommendations to a deaf world over decades? What is all this scrupulous, dedicated and heroic work achieving?

In a politically stable country such as Australia, the practical purpose of documenting human rights violations is to bring those particular violations to an end. But in less fortunate contexts, there may be a wider need: to challenge the legitimacy of the political system and bring about fundamental change. In South Africa, the purpose was not to make apartheid more benign, but to eliminate it. So, it seems to me, must be the attitude to the Occupation, for two reasons: first, the continuation of the 40-year-old Occupation is itself a breach of Israel's obligations as an occupying power and a violation of the Palestinian right of self-determination; and second, and most important, it is the very nature of the Occupation that calls into being a self-perpetuating cycle of reciprocal human rights violations with fearsome effects.

The potency of human rights depends on legal enforcement, ultimately by the courts. Much is made by Israeli apologists of the role of the Supreme Court of Israel as an agent for the rule of law. There is well-merited international admiration for the way the Court has developed constitutional and administrative law, and its own function within Israel itself, but its role in relation to the OPT has been extremely limited and one might say opportunistic. Certainly, Palestinians have been left with no sense that the Supreme Court is their court, or even a neutral court. It is definitely the court of a hostile occupying power, which gives priority to 'security' issues as asserted and interpreted by the army that bears oppressively on Palestinians from every direction. The Court's emphasis on security is reiterated in its judgments to the point of monotony and is reflected in the very metaphors it chooses. When Peace Now asked it to rule on the legality of the politically controversial Israeli settlements in the OPT, one judge ended his opinion with the words: 'The petitioners have the right to place a "legal mine" on the Court's threshold, but the Court does not have to step on a mine that may destroy its foundations, which are the public trust in it.'[19]

Occasionally, and not very predictably, a ray of light from the admirable principles of administrative law, through which the Court may review the legality of military decisions, pierces the barriers imposed by the non-justiciability of political and security issues. It is enough to keep a small stream of usually unsuccessful applications flowing to the Court, thanks in no small measure to the tireless dedication of a small group of Israeli lawyers who seem to be motivated less by the remote possibility of success than by the shared conviction that it is the duty of lawyers everywhere to stand up for justice, however unpopular the case may be in their own community. Equally praiseworthy is the work of Israeli legal scholars like David Kretzmer whose book, *The Occupation of Justice*,[20] judiciously appraises the work of the Court.

## Living the Occupation

From Raja Shehadeh's books, one gets something that one also gets by living in Palestine, but which is lost in the accepted narration of the Israeli–Palestine conflict current in Australia and most of the Western world.[21] That is the all-pervasive effect of the Occupation in which all Palestinians live and into which most have been born. This historical context, so fundamental to the understanding of every Palestinian, barely surfaces in standard Western reporting and discussion.

The 2008 Gaza conflict, for example, was treated as starting with Hamas firing rockets into the innocent city of Ashkelon, damaging the homes and threatening the lives of its peace-loving Israeli citizens. For Palestinians, any account that ignores the period since 1948 makes no sense at all. Take the Gazans firing those rockets. It is quite possible that they or their parents or grandparents came from Ashkelon, which was in 1948 the Arabic town of Majdal, with about 11 000 residents and a large weaving industry. It was bitterly fought over by Egypt and Israel and most of the inhabitants fled. Those who remained when Israel took the city were induced to leave or expelled, and most ended up in the refugee camps of Gaza, where they and their descendants remain. They were not allowed to return to their former homes which were given to Jewish immigrants as the town was developed as the regional urban centre of Ashkelon.

Hamas did not exist in 1948 or before the 1967 war. If Israel had returned Palestine to the Palestinians in the first 20 years of the Occupation, instead of succumbing to the temptation to seek permanent control by settlement building, Hamas would probably have never come into existence. It was formed in December 1987 because its parent organisation, the Palestinian Muslim Brotherhood, which believed in strengthening religion before engaging in armed struggle, was losing out to its more militant and nationalistic competitor, Islamic Jihad. Hamas was formed specifically to be a resistance movement – its very name means Islamic Resistance Movement. Its *raison d'être* is to resist the Occupation, and its refusal to ever abandon resistance and submit helps explain the persistence of the largely futile fusillades that seemed so illogical to outsiders. Even if largely symbolic, the rockets were continuing resistance, and moreover they had an extraordinary impact on Israel and placed Palestine in the headlines of a world that would rather forget it. I mention this not to justify Hamas's conduct, but to bring out how the world of the Palestinians is framed by the Occupation.

Inevitably human rights violations arise from the Occupation. In what they consider their country, Palestinians face demands, backed by unilateral military force and ruthless collective punishment, for complete submission and watertight security. They experience manipulation of the economy and resources to their disadvantage, restricted opportunities and mobility, privileges for abusive settlers and daily humiliation. Inevitably they seek ways to resist. Non-violent resistance and all but the most random violent methods are efficiently suppressed. When a people face denial of self-determination some will resort to terrorism, as both Jews and Arabs did under the British Mandate.[22]

## The Occupied Territories and the settlements

There is now[23] wide support in Israel for a two-state solution because it is realised that in the long run the alternative would be one state, with an inevitable Arab majority and an end to the Zionist dream of a Jewish state. However, this does not mean return to the 1967 borders, which Israel has never accepted. Palestinians believe the most Israel would ever concede is a truncated, balkanised Palestinian state, dependent on Israel and formed on the principle of concentrating as many Arabs on the smallest area possible, isolated from East Jerusalem. They see the foundations laid in the second Oslo Accord and reflected in the withdrawal of settlers from the densely populated Gaza strip and an otherwise inexplicable route for the wall/security barrier.

Discussion of the OPT takes place in the context of the international law of belligerent occupation, comprising the regulations annexed to the Hague Convention of 1907 and the Fourth Geneva Convention of 1949. Israel could not *lawfully* acquire land by conquest as a result of the 1967 war, and as an occupying power could not *lawfully* change the status of the territories. It was obliged to administer public property as a usufructuary; that is, it could use the product of public land but was obliged to be ready to return it in undiminished state. However, the military government not only took control of public land for long-term purposes, but greatly increased its quantity at the expense of private owners by placing the onus on them to prove that uncultivated land was not public land. This could only be discharged in ways that were procedurally and evidentially very difficult. The settlement program not only involved the unlawful taking of Palestinian land but was in breach of the Fourth Geneva Convention, which prohibits the occupying power from transferring its own citizens into the occupied territory.

The settlements in the OPT are often portrayed as the work of extremists out of control of the Israeli Government. This disguises the reality that the settlements have become geographically and politically essential to Israeli Government policy. If a two-state solution is ever to be acceptable to Israel, then the Palestinian state must present no threat to Israel. Consequently, the West Bank is riddled with settlements which separate and isolate Palestinian areas.[24]

Soon after the 1967 War, Mossad officers reported that the vast majority of West Bank leaders, including the most extreme among them, were prepared to reach a permanent peace agreement based on 'an independent existence for Palestine … without an army'.[25] From early on, the establishment of settlements was envisioned as an obstacle to Israel giving up the territories as part of such an agreement. Immediately after the 1967 war, Ariel Sharon – then a senior army officer and later Israel's Prime Minister 2001–06 – reasoned that 'facts on the ground' would fortify Israeli leaders in their hours of weakness, allowing them to stand firm in the face of inevitable pressure to cede the West Bank. In the Begin Government elected in 1977, Sharon became Minister of Agriculture and Chairman of the Ministerial Committee for Settlement Affairs. These two posts put him in the position to implement his plan, the purpose of which, he said, was to take hold of as much West Bank territory as possible and block the establishment of a viable Palestinian state.[26] While Israel's supporters bridle at the application of the term 'apartheid', it was Ariel Sharon who, as early as 2000, was using the word 'bantustans'[27] in relation to a possible Palestinian state.[28]

The foundations for such a solution were laid in the Oslo Accords of 1993 and 1995 which, as interpreted by Israel, put 90 per cent of the West Bank's Arab population in only 30 per cent of the land under limited Palestinian administration designated as Areas A and B, while Israel controlled the remaining 70 per cent in Area C. In this area, it is virtually impossible for a Palestinian to get permission to build. From 2000 until September 2007, for every construction permit granted to a Palestinian by the Civil Administration, 18 other buildings were destroyed and 55 demolition orders issued. Nor can permission be obtained for infrastructure or development projects. The Israeli organisation Peace Now sees the denial of permits for Palestinians on such a large scale as a specific policy to encourage a 'silent transfer' of the Palestinian population from Area C.[29] The objective appears to be the eventual absorption of Area C into Israel and the concentration of Palestinians into Areas A and B for which Israel could deny responsibility as it did regarding Gaza in 2005.[30] Israel stumbled on what Uri Avnery called 'the brilliant idea of an eternal military occupation', which allows the occupier to maintain control of a territory but 'abstain from conferring citizenship on the occupied population'.[31] Given the state of international law and opinion, eternal occupation cannot be an avowed goal, it must be cloaked by what Tanya Reinhart described as 'eternal negotiations'.[32]

In the Jerusalem area, Israel went further, illegally annexing the Old City in 1967 and 105 square kilometres of the West Bank in 1980 as East Jerusalem. East Jerusalem has always been desired and seen as the potential capital of a Palestinian state: Israel has pursued a range of policies to make this difficult or impossible in any peace settlement. These include isolating East Jerusalem from the Palestinian population of the West Bank by concentrating Israeli settlements, by constructing the Separation Barrier or 'Wall', by using discriminatory policies in land expropriation, planning, building, demolition of houses, residency permission, social benefits and budgetary allocations for infrastructure and services, all of which are calculated to discourage or deny Arab residency and facilitate Jewish settlement.[33] Moreover, the Oslo Accords provided for a network of Israeli controlled roads, which have been developed to cut off from each other many of the areas containing the nine large population areas and 450 smaller towns or villages. Meanwhile, roads servicing Palestinian villages are routinely blocked.[34]

The illegal settlements on the West Bank and the discriminatory manipulations of the illegally annexed East Jerusalem have placed about half a million Jewish settlers[35] in residence on the potential Palestinian state, intentionally presenting a formidable obstacle to any meaningful two-state solution. Facilitating settlements, and building secure roads servicing them, was less about pandering to religious extremists than about ensuring that a potential Palestinian state would be weak and divided.

I did not meet a Palestinian who believed that Israel, for all its talk of negotiated peace, would accept a return to the 1967 borders. For them the proof is in the settlement policy that Israel has pursued for over 40 years, despite repeated UN condemnation. This policy is in breach of its obligations as an occupying power to respect the status quo, to make only a usufructuary use of public land, to respect the rights of private landholders, and to refrain from transferring parts of its population into the occupied territory. Israel's continuing settlement building over the long years of professed negotiation to end the Occupation has convinced Palestinians that – irrespective of the party in power – the Israeli Government will never abandon the dream of Eretz Israel that includes the West Bank and Gaza, leaving Palestinians at best with a chain of 'bantustans'.

## The problem of Palestinian leadership

There is no Palestinian government in waiting with legitimacy to negotiate and assume power. Historically, there never was a Palestinian government and no credible one is likely to develop under the conditions of the Occupation. While Hamas is grudgingly respected by Palestinians as honest and dedicated, even supported if the choice is a bankrupt Fatah, it is not seen as having solutions to contemporary problems and its Islamist convictions sit uncomfortably with a remarkably secular, albeit basically religious, wider Palestinian community. Hamas was spawned in reaction to the Occupation and has won support, far less for religious dogmatism than for its lack of corruption, its extensive provision of social services, its refusal to bend the knee to the occupying power, and the many indications that, despite its constitution, it will pragmatically accept, not the legitimacy, but the hard fact of Israel's existence and military power.

Coming from a free community, one is tempted to ask why more impressive or effective Palestinian leadership has not emerged. How naive and patronising this must sound to Palestinians! How many potential leaders are among the convicted prisoners in Israeli gaols? How many more are among the thousands in administrative detention? How many were among those who have been killed without trial or charge? How many among the targeted assassinations? How many were burnt out among those who spent years in administrative detention during the Occupation? How many are silenced or frustrated by rigorous controls or threats or concern for their families? Few men could spend 25 years in prison as a terrorist and emerge, like Nelson Mandela, apparently unscathed.

In the absence of effective political leadership, many Palestinians think of *sumud* as a practical non-violent way to strengthen the community and civil institutions to prepare for the day when something changes; even after 40 years, they hope it must. Most are not attracted to violent means, and in any event the ruthless and all-encompassing controls imposed by the Israeli army largely rule out such action. As construction of the Wall and the network of Israeli-only roads show, Israel will spare no expense to defend itself. Even non-violent expression of opposition or hostility to the IDF comes at a high price, including risks of denial of the many permits required for ordinary activities such as extending one's house or travelling to family functions. There are threats of detention without charge or trial; of missed educational opportunities; of public humiliation at checkpoints; of closed access to one's village or lands; of demolished housing; even of extra-judicial execution or targeted assassination. In a society where so much depends on the grace and favour of an occupying army, the scope for recruiting informers is great and one has no way of knowing what an informer is saying about you.

Particularly during the Second Intifada,[36] suicide bombing reached a level of cruelty and horror that won the world's sympathy for Israel and did great harm to the Palestinian cause. But the question is whether such attacks should be seen as justification and cause for the continuation of the Occupation or instead as predictable consequences of the Occupation. It is a bit rich to occupy a peoples' land for 40 years in denial of their right to self-determination, subjecting them to a brutal security regime and unrelentingly taking and populating their land in a way calculated to make its return difficult or impossible, and then condemn their hostility as explicable only as mindless addiction to terrorism, antisemitism or Islamic fundamentalism. Far from terrorism being an invention of Islam, it has long been practised by people denied self-determination by military force, as it was by both Jews and Arabs under the British Mandate. To say this does not in the least justify terrorism, or reduce its horror, but it does point to the absurdity of denying its causal factors. The Second Intifada arose in a period when the enormous hopes of an end to the Occupation raised by the Oslo Accords collapsed into a despairing perception that the 'Accords' had laid the ground to weaken and dismember any possible Palestinian state.

## Ending the Occupation: An international responsibility

I am not concerned to be an advocate for Palestine or for Israel, or for Jews or for Palestinians, but for a solution that offers each the opportunity to live their lives in a state with which they can identify.

I will not be more prescriptive or ambitious than that. I certainly have my own strong preferences for states with certain secular, liberal, democratic characteristics, including universal equal citizenship, but I would not deny the right of Israel to remain a Jewish state or for Palestinians to work out their own particular compromise between secularism and its competitors. Nor would I seek to close the door on a one-state or two-state solution, although the former seems utopian to me.

So far, I have said nothing very controversial. However, the accepted wisdom has been that one must negotiate a solution, one-state or two-state, in order to end the Israeli Occupation. My view, on the contrary is that one must end the Israeli Occupation in order to negotiate a solution. Put another way, I do not believe it will ever be possible to negotiate a solution while the IDF remain in control of Palestine. The idea that the Occupation can be ended by peace negotiations is refuted by decades of trial and failure. The reverse is true: *peace can be negotiated only if the Occupation is first ended.*

Not only human rights, but common humanity and political stability in the Middle East demand an end to the Occupation. There seems no hope of ending it by bilateral negotiation, and a unilateral withdrawal by Israel would leave neither security nor viable government. Difficult as it will be, the only solution I can see requires the international community to take responsibility for the Palestine of the 1967 borders through some occupying mechanism that will be responsible for security and for nurturing the emergence of an independent and viable democratic Palestinian state. Israel's security should be guaranteed within the 1967 boundaries, with any variations negotiated on the more equal playing field that would come with the end of the Occupation. The difficulties would be enormous; perhaps it would prove impossible, but at least it is a conceivable way out of the intolerable present stalemate.

## BACK IN AUSTRALIA
### Australian Jewry and 'The Promise'

My only substantial venture into polemics resulting from my visit to Palestine has been my defence of Peter Kosminsky's TV series *The Promise,* written in response to criticism from the Executive Council of Australian Jewry.[37] Like others who have been tempted, I found it to be a fruitless and unpleasant experience. The Jewish establishment in Australia shows no interest in open discussion that recognises problems and seeks solutions. It is interested only in rejecting every criticism of Israel and discrediting every critic. They firmly close their minds, refuse to recognise a challenge and resist learning any lessons.

Such a common response to independent criticism in Australia – personal denigration, accusations of antisemitism, in my case perhaps senility – of course is not the general Jewish reaction. Many Jews despair at what they believe to be a minority, although very vocal, response by the Israeli lobby, including the section of the commentariat they have so effectively patronised.

There are many who value the great contributions that Jewish people have made to the intellectual, moral and artistic life, and particularly to the pursuit of social justice, in our civilisation. Many Jews are dismayed to see their contributions limited and their moral compasses sometimes distorted by the acceptance of the duty of short-sighted defence of 'Israel right or wrong'. There are many, too, who believe that it would be a tragedy if all the courage and sacrifice and idealism that has gone into the building of Israel should result only in a pariah state because of its denial of justice to Palestinians. If it is to maintain balance among the destabilising forces raging within and without, Israel is in desperate need of trusted but frank and independent critical voices such as the diaspora could provide. Australian Jews could play such a role if they open their eyes and ears and hearts and minds to the messages of the writers, artists, thinkers and people of insight and goodwill in the world, rather than attempt to shoot the messengers. Fortunately, more and more are doing this.[38]

## Law schools and legal education

The main possibility I saw was to do something in the field of legal education, and in this enterprise I found an enthusiastic partner in the Dean of UNSW Law.[39] If Palestine was to emerge as a state it would have to create a new legal system out of the congeries of laws it had inherited from the Ottoman Empire, the British Mandate, Jordan, the military orders of the Occupation, and the organs of the Palestine Authority. It would need a legal profession of high quality and integrity to perform this work. It would need to advise its government and legislature, to staff its courts, advise and represent its citizens, and uphold Palestinian interests, public and private, in the world of international law. It had to produce the kind of judges, law ministers and professional lawyers the new state would require.

In the long run, this profession would have to be produced by Palestine's law schools, the quality and integrity of which would be crucial. During my first trip, I visited all of the West Bank university law schools and formed close ties with some of the deans. I found desperately poor faculties largely dependent on fees from an impoverished student population, whose parents were willing to make great sacrifices so that their children could get a qualification. Senior legal academics had often done their postgraduate study when the only source of scholarships was the Soviet Union. A dean might have a PhD from Azerbaijan, speak fluent Russian, but have no ability to work in English, which is the predominant language used in international trade, international law and research. Few had any experience of life in a democratic country. There was a great need to develop a new generation of law teachers better adapted to producing the graduates with the skills that would be required in a new democratic state. The outside world had been going through the process of building a new order based on the rule of law, human rights and participation in, among other things, modern developments in business law and institutions associated with the digital and electronic revolutions. All this had largely passed the Palestinian law schools by.

This eventually led to a scholarship scheme bringing Palestinian students to conduct doctoral research at UNSW, visits by UNSW legal academics to the West Bank, and a delegation of five deans from West Bank law schools to UNSW. The ground was laid for future collaboration between Australian and Palestinian law schools.

After my experiences and study of the Israel–Palestine struggle, I concluded that peace and justice could only be achieved if the opposing parties gave up recrimination, pushed aside the extremists on both sides, and worked out a way in which both peoples could share the ancient land of Palestine.

# 6
# JUDGES, LAWYERS, EVIDENCE

*Hal Wootten was a judge of the NSW Supreme Court from 1973 to 1983. His judgments included his influential analysis of 'right to silence' issues in McMahon v Gould[1] which 'has not only been a leading case in Australia for many decades, but it has been widely approved throughout the common law world'.[2] Hal found being a judge in the Equity Division intellectually interesting, but he missed having contact with people as he had at UNSW and the Aboriginal Legal Service. From 1976 to 1981, he chaired the NSW Law Reform Commission (LRC). This proved to be a low point in his career. Appointed to lead an inquiry into the legal profession, Hal found himself in a distressing dispute with conservative lawyers, notably Roderick Meagher, then President of the NSW Bar Council. The LRC's suggestion of an independent body to regulate the legal profession was met with (sometimes personal) scorn from some former colleagues at the Bar.[3]*

*Hal's judicial experience is reflected in this chapter, a paper presented at a 2002 symposium on how different disciplines – notably law and anthropology – conceptualised evidence, proof and truth.[4] The context was disputes over the admissibility of evidence from anthropologists about Aboriginal people's relationship with their land. The result was some plain-speaking from Hal about judicial attitudes to expert witnesses, the problems of legalising what are essentially political problems, and the politics of intellectual enquiry.*

## CONFLICTING IMPERATIVES:
## PURSUING TRUTH IN THE COURTS

Recent experiences of expert witnesses in Australian courts have led some to suggest that 'lawyers and scholars are often talking about quite different processes and aims when they speak of evidence, proof and truth – often with serious practical implications in areas such as Indigenous land ownership, heritage, and other contentious social issues'.[5] The aim of this chapter is to explain from a lawyer's perspective the nature of the project in which the law is engaged when it seeks the assistance of expert witnesses – and the extent to which that project is a truth-seeking exercise based on evidence and attempting to anticipate how humanists[6] see their differences with the law, but I have taken the liberty of commenting on some of the issues raised, and of suggesting some factors other than epistemological differences that may underlie the frustration that Australian humanists are feeling about their current involvement in litigation.

### The humanities and the professions

How do the humanities on the one hand differ from the law, or indeed the professions generally, on the other? I speak of the professions in the narrower sense of practical vocations, exemplified in the classical professions of medicine, engineering, architecture, veterinary science and law. Skills based on theoretical knowledge are used to perform some service for the public, the practitioners being trained and certified, and organised into a professional body that monitors standards.[7] As new fields of expertise arise, new vocations aspire to the status of profession. Typically, professions start, not as a field of scholarship, but as the exercise of skills, and study and reflection come as the field grows in complexity. The professions first do it, then think about it. The more virginal humanities think about it, but don't do it. Something of the difference was captured by Justice Oliver Wendell Holmes when he said

'Proof and Truth: The Humanist as Expert', *Australian Academy of the Humanities* (14–15 November 2002).

that law was 'not ... a mystery but a well-known profession'.[8] Mysteries are to be explored and elucidated, professions to be practised.

Professional services bring social responsibilities that humanities don't have. If diseases flourish, dams collapse, or buildings fall down, we point the finger at doctors, engineers or architects. If crime becomes rampant or public liability insurance prohibitive, we ask what the lawyers are up to. But if we have a bad century with lots of wars and genocide, we don't blame the historians; if our leaders talk nonsense, we don't blame the philosophers; if social cohesion decays and families become dysfunctional, we don't hold the anthropologists responsible. We look to them to tell us the truth about what happened, and help us understand why, but we don't expect them to fix it.[9]

At the reflective, researching end of the profession, legal scholars share what I take to be the same broad objective as the humanist: the pursuit of truth in a chosen field of study.[10] They have similar concepts of truth, they pursue it by similar methods, and respond to the same currents of thought sweeping the intellectual world. I stress the obvious to emphasise that humanists acting as expert witnesses are not engaged with law as an intellectual discipline, but with the working of certain social institutions in relation to which lawyers exercise their professional skills, particularly the courts. Just as hospitals are not established for the purposes of medical scholarship, but to deal in a practical way with the problems of patients, courts deal with practical problems in other spheres. It is crucial to consider what the functions of courts are, and how and under what constraints they operate.

## The function of the courts

Humanists sometimes assume, as do other less sophisticated citizens, that courts are established for the purpose of ascertaining truth and tend to be disappointed and injured when they find some other objective getting in the way. The attempt to discover the truth about any complex issue is an extraordinarily difficult, time-consuming and expensive project. Can you imagine any society so ambitious, so flush with resources, so idealistic that it would provide for its citizens machinery to ascertain the truth about every dispute they had?

Many social institutions find a limited amount of truth useful, even desirable, in the pursuit of other ends, but few are funded to seek truth for its own sake – universities and royal commissions spring to mind. In the case of universities, I speak of a passing age; today there is little university funding for the disinterested search for truth. More and more, universities are expected to find their own funding by making themselves useful to commercial interests or vocationally oriented students. Royal commissions are relatively rare, because their search for truth is very expensive, and they not infrequently discover uncomfortable truths. Terms of reference are carefully drawn to limit the issues on which truth may be sought.[11] Royal commissions tend to be so lengthy that by the time they deliver their findings the public has lost interest in the original issue; that indeed is sometimes the reason for setting them up. There is no guarantee that a royal commission will get to the truth, but they illustrate the point that if a government is prepared to spend the time and money to find out the truth, it doesn't leave it to the courts.

What then are courts for? Fundamental is the fact that courts are not standing commissions to search for the truth, but machinery to bring disputes between parties about certain kinds of issues to an end in an acceptable way. While a government can tolerate the circulation of a lot of untruth (indeed, it may welcome much of it and declare it to be the 'truth'), it is usually much more concerned to maintain law and order. A typical government wants to limit violence to that which it controls. It also wants a flourishing economy that it can tax, and this means protecting property, enforcing transactions and, ideally, limiting corruption. These and other objectives varying with the type of government mean that there must be a process for resolving certain classes of disputes. The disputes accorded this treatment – 'justiciable disputes' – are typically matters involving personal freedom and bodily integrity, property, contracts and other commercial relations, and rights-bearing status, but they may include any subject matter the state decides to bring within the arena of legal enforcement. In states that observe the rule of law, disputes involving the state itself, including its claims to punish individuals for breaching the law, are submitted to the same process.[12]

Different styles of society have employed different methods to resolve disputes – sorcery, ordeal, summary execution, banishing disputants to labour camps or psychiatric hospitals, subjecting them to unbearable public denunciation or rejection, to name a few. Sometimes what is described as a court may play a role in endorsing such processes. Today, however, it is increasingly accepted over most of the world that a state's system of dispute resolution should adopt a process of adjudication, in which affected parties have the opportunity to participate by presenting reasoned proofs and argument to an impartial tribunal for decision according to known rules and standards.[13]

In the constitutional and legal tradition to which Australia belongs, courts have a primary role in relation to state-sponsored adjudication. The High Court has described the function of the federal courts as 'the quelling of justiciable controversies, whether between citizens (individual or corporate), between citizens and executive government (in civil and criminal matters), and between the various polities in the federation. This is discharged by ascertainment of facts, application of legal criteria and the exercise, where appropriate, of judicial discretion.'[14]

## Courts and the pursuit of truth

The distinction between the facts and the law, or the 'legal criteria' that are applied to them, is fundamental to the judicial task. Where others might talk of ascertaining the truth, lawyers usually talk of ascertaining 'the facts'. When humanists are called as expert witnesses, it is to assist a court in ascertaining the facts, not the law. It is the ascertainment of the truth about the facts that I discuss in this paper.

It has long been the proud claim of our legal system that justice is administered through courts that are honest, fair, independent, public, available to all, treat everyone equally and uphold the rule of law. Like all human ideals, this ideal is of course not always realised. My point is not to glorify the system but to bring out that the primary claim is not that it gets things right, or discovers the truth, but that it gives parties a 'fair go'. It sees a fair hearing as fundamental. If a decision is arrived at in breach of the rules of 'natural justice', which are procedural rules, it will avail nothing to argue that the decision nevertheless reflects a true finding as to the facts and the law, or, as it is called, rectitude of decision.

Similar ideas have become part of the international conception of human rights. The *Universal Declaration of Human Rights* and the *International Covenant on Civil and Political Rights*, for example, do not prescribe that everyone is entitled to have their rights vindicated on the basis of a correct finding of fact and law but that 'everyone is entitled in full equality to a fair and public hearing by an independent and impartial tribunal'.[15]

Do not misunderstand me. The system seeks truth. That it should do so is implicit in the notion of a 'fair' hearing and in our law's concept of acting judicially, which 'excludes the right to decide arbitrarily, irrationally or unreasonably'.[16] However, truth is often very hard, sometimes impossible, to find, and society cannot indefinitely postpone dispute settlement while the quest proceeds. A number of things may deflect, override or force compromises on a court's search for truth.

## Competing values in the courts

I have already noted how our law privileges procedural justice over the search for truth. Procedure in the common law tends to be adversarial, reflecting the view that the best way to achieve justice is to let parties choose their issues and present their own cases. In contrast to more inquisitorial systems, the court normally has neither the right nor the resources to conduct its own inquiries, and the parties' advocates, not the judge, examine their own witnesses and cross-examine their opponents'.[17] So far as the judge or jury is concerned, the quest for truth remains but is narrowed to what the parties choose to put in issue and the use of the evidence they choose to present. So far as the advocate lawyers are concerned, their primary role in assisting the search is to ensure that the truth-seeker, that is the judge or jury, has the benefit of each party's case being fully and persuasively put.

The search for truth is necessarily curtailed by the requirement to finalise the dispute. As the historian John Lukacs has observed, the 'historian, unlike a judge, is permitted to try a case over and over again, often after finding and employing new evidence'.[18] At law, the parties have their day or days in court, the judge gives a decision and turns to the next case, usually pressured by a daunting list of waiting cases with limited resources for hearing them and the perennial criticism that courts are slow. Scholars, for whom 'truth' is rightly always provisional, find this hard to accept. The anthropologist Patrick Sullivan recently gave a paper about experience as an expert witness with the damning title 'Don't Educate the Judge', which was said to be taken from a lawyer's draft instructions to him as a potential expert witness. The lawyer had actually written that the expert should 'not view the report as an opportunity to re-educate the judge', who had decided the relevant issue in the first part of a hearing deliberately divided into two stages. It is indeed the function of the expert witness to educate the judge on relevant issues (although perhaps not in all the ways favoured by Sullivan), but there will only be one go at doing so.[19]

Another important concern for a dispute settlement system is a high degree of predictability. If every social and commercial transaction gave rise to a dispute, and every dispute went to court, and every case went to hearing, no society could bear either the cost of the system or the effect on the society's functioning. An important reason this does not happen is that courts' decisions are very predictable. The common view that court decisions are unpredictable is based on considering only the tiny minority of matters that go to hearing precisely because they are unpredictable. In the overwhelming mass of transactions, the result of a court hearing is so predictable that a potential dispute doesn't occur or is rapidly settled, and society's business is transacted smoothly. But this is achieved at a price of some rigidity in the process.

## What courts claim to do

If courts merely held out to parties that they could come along and get their disputes decided in accordance with truth and justice, results could rarely be predicted. Instead, courts say: if you apply to the court within a prescribed time, and make claims of a particular kind, and present evidence to a particular effect in accordance with known rules of admissibility, and the court after hearing the other party presenting evidence in accordance with the same rules, and allowing each party to cross-examine the other's witnesses and otherwise test its evidence, is satisfied by that evidence that (in a civil case) on the balance of probabilities what you claim is true, then the court will apply known rules of law to the factual situation so established and make orders of a known kind. It is within that framework that the court conducts its search for truth.

The system does not claim that its finding is a universal truth. It is normally binding only on the parties, and the issue may be relitigated in other cases and different findings made. In the special cases like title to land, where the decision is given *in rem*, or against the whole world, care is taken to give everyone with an adverse interest an opportunity to be a party.

A court's finding is always subject to two caveats about treating it as the truth: it is based only on the evidence that the parties have chosen to place before it; and it is at most a finding of probability, a mere balance of probabilities in civil cases and a higher 'beyond reasonable doubt' standard in criminal cases. If the court can't reach a conclusion, even as to the probabilities, it is still required to give a decision and does so in accordance with known rules about the 'burden of proof'. Broadly speaking, and subject to qualifications, a party alleging something has the burden of proving it. If they leave the judge unable to reach a decision, the case goes against them. So, in the end, a court's finding is not about the real world outside the court. It is only a finding that, in a particular case, a party who has the burden of proving a fact has, or has not, succeeded in persuading the court according to a certain degree of probability.

Humanists normally do not have to make definitive findings. They can, and should, qualify their provisional statement of truth in any way that is appropriate. Courts, however, have to make findings that determine an issue as a basis for subsequent action, and for that purpose a standard of sufficiency of proof has to be adopted. To me, this is one of the most unsatisfactory aspects of the law. The glib statement that civil issues are decided on a balance of probabilities affronts common sense if it is applied with statistical literalism. Do you find a doctor guilty of professional negligence if you think the chances are only 51 to 49 that he or she has been negligent? Is a company that owns 51 of the 100 taxis in a town to be held liable for an accident caused by an unidentified taxi? Some appellate judges have said that the tribunal must be persuaded to a 'belief' or 'satisfaction' in its finding, others that the strength of the evidence necessary to establish a fact on the balance of probabilities may vary according to the nature of what it is sought to prove. The Uniform Evidence Act provides that the court must be 'satisfied that the case has been proved on the balance of probabilities', but that 'in deciding whether it is so satisfied' it is to take into account the 'nature of the cause of action or defence', the 'nature of the subject-matter of the proceeding', and the 'gravity of the matters alleged'.[20] The difficulties are far from resolved, but fortunately in practice a finding rarely depends on treating a party as a mere statistic. More specific evidence is usually available. The higher criminal standard of proof beyond reasonable doubt also has its problems. Those who were once happy to affirm that it was better for 100 guilty men to go free than for one innocent man to be convicted may have second thoughts when the guilty men released into their communities may include terrorists and paedophiles.

## Admitting evidence in the courts

The substantive rules of law prescribe the circumstances that will entitle a party to the benefit of an order of a court or, as lawyers say, a remedy. This creates a potential set of issues on which the court has to be satisfied, but generally speaking these issues may be narrowed by the decision of a party not to contest an issue. The matters that a court has to decide are thus defined by the interaction of rules of law and the pleadings of the parties. The first hurdle for the admission of evidence is that it must be 'relevant', that is, it must have some tendency to prove or disprove a fact in issue.

Since personal involvement in an incident or issue would disqualify a judge or juror, who must have no personal interest in the outcome, the court perforce relies on the testimony of witnesses and the production of documents and other physical evidence. The law of evidence governs the reception of this material. Although it is not a complete description, much of the law of evidence can be understood as a set of exclusionary rules, placing limits on a search for truth ('the facts') that is otherwise conducted in accordance with the ordinary principles of rational inquiry. In an adversarial system the court does not go looking for evidence itself but is limited to what the parties choose to place before it. The exclusionary rules place limits on what evidence will be admitted if another party objects to the evidence.

Some exclusions are in the interests of efficiency and reliability. For example, parties are normally required to produce direct evidence rather than hearsay or opinion, which could be infinite in quantity, dubious in quality and, in the case of hearsay, impossible to test by cross-examination or personal assessment of the witness. Other examples are rules relating to the rejection of evidence with a prejudicial effect outweighing its probative effect, particularly important in criminal cases.

Some exclusions are based on conflicting policy imperatives. Should the quest for truth be pushed to the point of requiring accused persons to incriminate themselves, one spouse to give evidence against another, or a priest or doctor or journalist to reveal confidences, or of allowing police to use evidence they have obtained illegally? These problems arise not because of idiosyncratic concepts of proof and truth but because the search for truth comes into conflict with other important concerns. A much-quoted judgment from a century and a half ago put it like this:

> The discovery and vindication and the establishment of truth
> are main purposes certainly of the existence of Courts of Justice;
> still, for the obtaining of these objects, which, however valuable
> and important, cannot be usefully pursued without moderation,
> cannot be either usefully or creditably pursued unfairly or gained
> by unfair means, not every channel is or ought to be open to
> them. The practical inefficacy of torture is not, I suppose, the
> most weighty objection to that mode of examination. Truth, like
> all other good things, may be loved unwisely – may be pursued
> too keenly – may cost too much.[21]

## Evaluating and interpreting evidence

Evidence, whether in the form of words, behaviour, documents or other physical things, is not 'an open window that gives us direct access to reality', but nor is it, as some sceptics argue, 'a wall, which by definition precludes any access to reality'.[22] The evidence that is admitted has to be evaluated for its credibility and its 'weight', the raw evidence that is accepted has to be interpreted to understand its meaning, and inferences may then have to be drawn to reach conclusions about the issues that have to be decided. Generally speaking, it can be said that the governing principle in these tasks is the search for truth about the matters in issue within the confines of the admitted evidence.

For the process of determining the weight of evidence, there is little in the way of formal rules, and it is done in accordance with commonsense, rational principles that most people would find acceptable. Lawyers know from experience how fallible the whole process is. Documents may be incomplete, erroneous, open to misunderstanding or constructed for other purposes, and may sometimes tell more about those who composed them than their ostensible subject matter. In contrast to some European legal systems, the common law does not accord primacy to documentary evidence and, as a result, has much accumulated experience in evaluating both documents and oral evidence, and the interaction between them.[23]

The evidence of the senses can be wrong for many reasons. Witnesses may be sensorily handicapped or affected by preconceptions or a great variety of biases. Every observation and every interpretation is positioned physically, temporally, culturally and personally, and potentially affected by this positioning. Facts may have to be inferred from very shaky foundations, witnesses may be honestly mistaken, or may be stupid, as may the advocates and the judge. Language is a tricky method of conveying truth, particularly when the communication is between people who inhabit different worlds and speak across boundaries of class, race, culture, gender, generation, locality, nationality or vocational specialisation.

The law recognises that there is a great deal more to oral communication than the words used. Hence, an appellate court that can only read a transcript of a witness's evidence is very reluctant to override a trial judge or juror's assessment of the witness's credibility or meaning, or the conclusions drawn where there is a conflict of testimony. Findings of fact can normally be overturned only if there is no evidence to support a finding of fact or if an inference has been drawn that no reasonable person could draw from the evidence.[24]

Like the witnesses, every fact-finder, whether judge or juror, has particular characteristics, history and social location, and the further a judge or juror is socially, culturally or experientially differentiated from witnesses or parties, the greater will be the risks not only in understanding what they say but in assessing their credibility and understanding their behaviour and motivation. The professional experience of judges, both before and after their appointments, tends to make them reasonably at home with the kinds of litigants and issues that most commonly come to the courts. It is the unfamiliar situation that poses the greatest risk.

In some areas of disputation such problems are mitigated by specialisation, which may take the form of specialised tribunals or courts, or specialised divisions within courts. Persons appointed to these courts or tribunals commonly have prior specialised experience and, in any event, have opportunity to develop it. The specialisation of advocates, with forms of accreditation, is increasingly common. One of the roles of the advocate in all litigation is to help bridge the gulf between client and court.

These various factors help to produce a situation where, in the general run of cases, the courts get by without causing much more than the inevitable dissatisfaction in a situation where usually at least one party must be disappointed. However, even a judge of the English Court of Appeal felt the need to acknowledge in 1923 that 'the habits you are trained in, the people with whom you mix, lead to your having a certain class of ideas of such a nature that, when you have to deal with other ideas, you do not give as sound and accurate judgments as you would wish'.[25] In 1950, Jerome Frank famously criticised the fragility of judicial fact-finding in his *Courts on Trial*.[26] Since then, wave after wave of scholars have busied themselves unmasking many ways in which the human mind may be blinkered, appealing to psychoanalytic, Marxist, feminist, post-colonialist, deconstructionist, cultural and other forms of postmodernist theory that can be applied to judges as readily as to their fellow scholars.

Such studies gradually impact on the general intellectual climate of the community within which the law operates, sometimes with valuable effect. A virtually all-white, male judiciary, for example, obviously had a lot to learn about gender and race, but lawyers sometimes feel like grandmothers being taught to suck eggs. Critics have often said, for example, that neither Frank 'nor any of the other realists can be credited with insights which are not already second nature to any practising lawyer, who does not need to be told how important such elusive personal factors are in the administration of human justice'.[27] However, while the practised trial lawyer and judge may be good at discerning the lack of objectivity in witnesses and in each other, it does not follow that they are equally good at discerning the threats to it in themselves.[28]

Although the constitutional commitment to judicial independence imposes great obstacles to the dismissal of unsatisfactory but honest judges, it is one of many safeguards that the law builds in to increase the level of objectivity of all judges. In most cases, issues are narrowly confined by the relevant rules of law and the pleadings of parties, and judges are required to admit any evidence relevant to those issues tendered by a party in conformity with the rules of evidence so that their scope for selectivity in fact-finding is reduced, although not of course eliminated. They cannot sit in any case in which they have an interest or might reasonably be suspected of bias, they must sit in public and submit to media reporting (usually every word they utter in court is recorded and open to the scrutiny of hindsight), they must listen to advocates putting each party's case to the best advantage, they must give reasons for their decision, they are frequently subject to appeal or review, and final appellate courts consist of three or more members. Both before their appointment and while exercising their office, judges are subject to intense if informal peer review from a fairly tightly knit profession within which reputation is all-important.[29] In recent times there has been a trend to establishing judicial commissions that can entertain complaints about the conduct of judges, and both they and courts themselves conduct conferences and courses to educate [judges] in areas of perceived need or weakness. The training of lawyers has also tended to put more emphasis on a wider education. All this achieves not perfection, but a considerable degree of acceptance and respect in a cynical postmodern world.

## Expert witnesses

For good reason, parties are normally required to call witnesses who can give direct evidence about the relevant facts and be subjected to testing by cross-examination so that the court can draw its own inferences. That is why there are rules against hearsay and against opinion evidence. But this assumes that the issue can be resolved by evidence from witnesses who can give direct evidence of relevant happenings and that inferences can be drawn on the basis of the general knowledge and worldly experience that judges or jurors possess. Judges and jurors will sometimes have to decide issues in areas of knowledge of which they know nothing, or at all events much less than experts in the field. Sometimes relevant facts are reliably known to witnesses only by specialised study or experience, as in the case of historical facts or epidemiological facts, or the breaking strains of materials. Sometimes a layperson is at a loss to know what inference to draw from the facts, or may draw the wrong inference, unless aided by an expert. In such circumstances, the rules against hearsay and opinion are modified to receive evidence from expert witnesses.[30]

Over the eight centuries or so that common law courts have wrestled with this departure from normal rules, five issues came to be identified. First, is the issue one on which expertise is required, or is it within the capacity of the judge or jury to decide, or within their common knowledge? Second, is the area of knowledge recognised as one in which reliable knowledge exists?[31] Third, does the particular witness put forward in fact have knowledge and experience to justify the claim to expertise? Fourth, is the nature and source of information relied on by the expert acceptable? Fifth, is the expert really usurping the function of the judge or jury to decide a 'fact in issue' or even the 'ultimate issue' in the case?

There has been a great deal of uncertainty in the way these issues have been dealt with, some of the distinctions called for being unworkable or difficult to make. The Commonwealth *Evidence Act 1995* expressly abolished the 'common knowledge' and 'fact in issue' and 'ultimate issue' limitations on expert evidence (s 80), and attempted to wrap up the question of expert evidence in the brief statement: 'If a person has specialised knowledge based on the person's training, study or experience, the opinion rule [the general exclusion of opinion evidence, see s 76] does not apply to evidence of an opinion of that person that is wholly or substantially based on that knowledge' (s 79).

With the repeal of the specific exclusionary rules by s 80 and the possible elimination of other older issues by s 79 itself, arguments about the admissibility of expert evidence are likely increasingly to centre round the judge's discretion to exclude evidence if its probative value is substantially outweighed by the danger that the evidence might be unfairly prejudicial to a party; or be misleading or confusing; or cause or result in undue waste of time (s 135).

There is a long-standing tension in courts' relations with expert witnesses. It can be detected as early as 1555 in a defensive comment made when a judge, who needed to call on a grammarian (one of the earliest class of humanist witnesses) because his Latin 'halted a little', self-consciously explained:

> [I]f matters arise in our law which concern other sciences or faculties, we commonly apply for the aid of that science or faculty which it concerns. Which is an honourable and commendable thing in our law. For thereby it appears that we do not despise all other sciences but our own, but we approve of them and encourage them as things worthy of commendation.[32]

While the 'despising' of expert witnesses would vastly overstate the attitudes of most judges, there is no doubt that many judges entertain a basic suspicion of at least some categories of expert witnesses. Surveys have shown that the greatest complaint of Australian judicial officers in relation to expert witnesses is of bias,[33] and this is reflected in rules and guidelines through which courts have increasingly tried to emphasise that an expert's duty when giving evidence is to the court, not the client.[34]

Humanists should not take this suspicion personally, or indeed as a comment on their disciplines. Very few judges have ever encountered a humanist expert. Although humanists in the form of grammarians figure in some very early reported cases,[35] the earliest recorded use of experts by the common law was of surgeons, and medical witnesses have long been the commonest.[36] However, the rise of science and its application in the Industrial Revolution, the growing complexity of business and its greater accountability, and, more recently, the advent of nuclear physics, informatics and genomics are some of the factors that have contributed to a growing range of expert witnesses. However, the overwhelming judicial experience has been, and is of, medical witnesses, followed by other health experts and witnesses from the sciences, technologies, business, and various practical vocations. It is experience from such disciplines that has shaped the attitudes of Australian judicial officers to expert witnesses.

## Humanists and lawyers

Judges have learnt that they must evaluate expert witnesses as much as other witnesses; that expert witnesses also may lie, exaggerate, get carried away by current excitements, contradict each other, allow prejudice or sympathy to colour their evidence, favour the party that calls or pays them, overestimate the certainty of their knowledge, or mistake the latest intellectual fad for the final discovery of truth. If humanists turn out to be immune from the frailties of other experts, that will delight judges, but you cannot expect them to anticipate it.

Meanwhile, humanists called as expert witnesses might well think of themselves as pioneers whose work will have a big influence on future judicial attitudes, among other things, in convincing sceptics that the various humanities can offer knowledge sufficiently 'hard' to be relied on in reaching the kinds of decision courts have to make. They might also bear in mind that the surveys show that another great difficulty judges find with experts is obscurity of language. I would add that if you are trying to tell a judge something that is counter-intuitive, or counter to what passes for common sense, or outside her experience, it will pay to be patient and understanding rather than arrogant. I vividly remember my own experience as a judge 30 years ago when asked to hear a dispute over a computer program. I had never seen a computer and counsel finally gave up trying to explain to me the difference between hardware and software and went off and settled the case.

Courts will acknowledge the expertise of witnesses but will not yield to them authority over an issue that the court has to decide. Historians, for example, should remember that it is not the function of the court to write or declare history. When courts are concerned with the past, it is because the rights of a party to litigation depend on whether a certain event happened or a certain state of affairs existed. If historians can, by application of their scholarship, cast useful light on whether the event happened or the state of affairs existed, courts will usually be grateful for their help.[37] But what they say will not be accepted merely because it comes from an 'authority'; it will have to be shown to have a sound base and will be open to challenge through testing by cross-examination or weighing against contradictory evidence, whether expert or not.

There are no 'authorities' in history in the sense of final arbiters. Everything is contested or contestable; whether it is the evidence for a particular fact, the selection of a particular group of facts as the 'historical' facts, the interpretation placed on them, or the selection, from the myriad of causes that led to an event or state of affairs, of the causes that it is useful to regard as the 'historical' causes. All this is elementary to any historian, spelled out in seminal works like EH Carr's *What is History?*, which in turn has gone the way of all 'authorities' and itself become part of history as other scholars dissect, criticise, revise and agree or disagree with it.[38] It is idle to expect a judge to regard a particular expert witness, however eminent, as embodying the end of historiography.

All this can be acknowledged without leading to the rejection of history as a field of expertise in which courts can find help in making … decisions about past factual situations. It reflects the provisional character of all knowledge and is consistent with the weighing of what the witness says to form a view as to its probability. However, the relativistic view that one version is as good as another would leave courts unable to get help from historians. What, for example, are judges to think when Lyndall Ryan's footnoted authorities for her version of Tasmanian history are criticised in savage detail by Keith Windschuttle and she replies not with reasons for regarding her version as more likely or more accurate, but with the statement that 'we have used the same sources to arrive at different conclusions' and the question 'Two truths are told. Is only one "truth" correct?' Rather than addressing the issue of which version has the stronger claim to approximate the truth, she retreats behind the truism that 'no one can claim a final and complete "truth"'.[39]

However, the last thing I would wish to encourage in humanist witnesses is obsequiousness towards lawyers, either practitioners or judges. There are good social reasons for treating the legal system's normative and adjudicatory authority with respect, but none for endowing it with intellectual authority. Some years ago, I urged on anthropologists that one of their very important functions in native title cases was 'to stand up to lawyers, to detect their ethnocentrism and conservatism, and to resist their tendencies either to mould the law in the interests of powerful clients, or to fall victim to the narcissism of their powerful profession'.[40]

More recently, I was surprised how readily some anthropologists seemed to treat a judge's definition of the legal obligations of an anthropologist in a particular situation as a definition of their professional responsibility. Justice von Doussa took the view that, unless sworn as expert witnesses, it was 'in accordance with community expectations and standards' that anthropologists should act as advocates, and like lawyers pursue the personal advantage of the client.[41] He was not speaking of anthropologists exercising the right of all citizens to advocate things they believe in, but of anthropologists speaking as anthropologists, invoking the authority of their discipline. His analogy with lawyers would blur the crucial distinction between scholarship and advocacy for anthropologists, a distinction which is not blurred for lawyers. Advocacy of particular interests is the professional business of practising barristers and solicitors, but not acceptable in lawyers who accept roles of public service as judges or other independent officers or profess to speak as scholars. Francesca Merlan robustly repudiated the distinction between the 'in court' and 'out of court' standards of anthropologists, asserting that 'if we accept advocacy as at the core of the kind of services that social research can offer, we accept diminishment of the potential of our field, and very likely too, its irrelevance'.[42] Surely, if anthropologists see themselves as scholars dedicated to the pursuit of truth, the important thing for them is not what Justice von Doussa or his hypothesised community expect of them but what they (and their peers) expect of themselves.

## Concepts of truth

Today many scholars would deny the possibility of objectivity in fact-finding. The implicit assumption of the courts is that although one may rarely achieve complete objectivity, this is no reason for abandoning the attempt to get as close to it as one can. Like it or not, that is the task that is given to them in a society based on the rule of law. The law can rule only through its application to facts themselves determined in a manner authorised by law.

What does 'truth' mean to the courts? The courts have no explicit theory of truth or knowledge and, as I have said, are much more likely to talk about 'the facts'. It will be apparent from the earlier description of their processes that courts work with the 'commonsense' assumptions that ordinary litigants bring to their disputes. 'The assumption is that there is a physical world out there and that we are capable of knowledge which corresponds to that physical world.'[43] The primary source of knowledge is our senses, and from the knowledge gained through the senses further knowledge is gained by inference.

Although courts do not enunciate a theory of knowledge, scholars identify what they do as reflecting a correspondence theory of knowledge. Courts operate within the rationalist tradition, with assumptions that a legal scholar has summarised as follows:

epistemology is cognitivist rather than sceptical; a correspondence
theory of truth is generally preferred to a coherence theory
of truth; the mode of decision-making is seen as 'rational', as
contrasted with 'irrational' modes such as battle, compurgation

or ordeal; the characteristic mode of reasoning is induction; the pursuit of truth as a *means* to justice under the law commands a high, but not necessarily an overriding, priority as a social value.[44]

This is not a prescription of how courts should work, but an *ex post facto* description by a scholar who has studied the history of the law of evidence. If there are problems about cognitivist epistemology or the correspondence theory of truth, they are more likely to trouble philosophers than lawyers.

If a humanist challenge is made to the rationalist tradition itself, I will be interested to know what other basis is proposed for a working system of adjudication suitable for a modern democratic state committed to human rights and the rule of law. In particular, epistemological scepticism or relativism would seem to deny the possibility of an effective dispute settlement mechanism based on fact-finding and imply that the holder of such views would not be able to undertake the obligations of expert witness. It has been noted that 'many seemingly sceptical writers about judicial processes invoke standards which are identical or similar to those outlined in the rationalist model of adjudication and that, in law as elsewhere, genuine philosophical sceptics are rare birds'.[45] Moreover, realist legal philosophers who were appointed judges proved 'far less radical in practice than their theoretical views would have led one to predict'.[46]

If the criticism is of specific rules or practices framed within the rational tradition, this will probably tie into debates among lawyers themselves. The rules are under ongoing criticism, review and amendment. If the concern is with the competency or attitudes of particular judges or lawyers, again the issues are matters of common concern, not philosophical difference between disciplines. I have been concerned to discuss the rules, structure and aims of the court system not the quality of its human instruments. The law is no more immune than other disciplines and projects from the difficulty of making anything straight out of the crooked timber of humanity, to use the Kantian metaphor popularised by Isaiah Berlin.[47] The public nature of the legal process, and the obligation of judges to give reasons for their decision, mean that human frailties are exposed and magnified. I have already commented on the weaknesses that are exposed when lawyers are thrown into work in unfamiliar social, cultural and vocational contexts, and it is clear that native title is an area where there is a steep learning curve for lawyers, including learning about the disciplines of anthropology and history with which there have been bruising encounters.[48]

It is also an area that has placed new burdens on historians writing in relevant historical areas, whether or not they are called as expert witnesses. An anthropologist whose discipline has been similarly affected has commented:

> Now that the discipline of history has been overtaken by the
> 'Land Rights Era' it is critically important that practitioners
> realise that what they write today, and equally importantly,
> what they wrote yesterday, whether they themselves are directly
> involved in Native Title proceedings or not, may well find its way
> into processes which affect the real interests of real people, far
> removed from the intellectual debates and comparative comfort
> of academia.[49]

## Reasons for humanists' concerns

The concern of humanists over giving expert evidence is not universal. A distinguished British historian, Richard Evans, has given us a book-length account of a happy experience as an expert witness.[50] In a subsequent review of work on the interaction of memory, history and justice, Evans reflects on the not always happy experiences of historians in litigation arising in various ways out of the Holocaust, and calls for a reassertion of 'history's primary purpose of explaining and understanding the past rather than judging it'.[51] This suggests that the problem for humanists giving expert evidence is not so much with different disciplinary concepts as with the nature and purposes of the particular legal project in which they are asked to assist.

In Australia, significant involvement of scholars from the humanities – anthropologists, linguists, historians, pre-historians – has arisen in recent years principally out of matters arising from attempts to redress the consequences of past treatment of Indigenous peoples, particularly dispossession from land and the removal of children. It does not surprise me that humanists are unhappy about what is happening, for in my view the relegation of these issues to the ordinary courts as issues of private legal rights to be litigated by adversarial processes is totally inappropriate and an abdication of national responsibility. One does not need to suppose defects in legal concepts of truth, proof and evidence to explain why this does not work satisfactorily.

Many of the issues that have to be decided as questions of fact are just the kind of issues that are unsuitable for adversarial judicial determination. Unspecialised judges are called on to decide extraordinarily complex issues about the culture, cultural continuity and history of societies that are quite foreign to what their personal and professional lives have prepared them to do, magnifying the scope for misunderstanding and misinterpretation that, as I have already noted, exists whenever courts have to venture into unfamiliar territory.[52] For the most part the lawyer advocates share their limitations. They all share great linguistic difficulties in communicating with the Indigenous parties, difficulties that are the more dangerous when they are concealed under the illusion that everyone is speaking the same language.[53]

The courts have neither the skills nor the time to settle the issues on the unmediated evidence of Indigenous witnesses, or the potentially available raw data of history, and the parties supply expert witnesses to bridge the gap, particularly anthropologists and historians. But these witnesses, the very nature of whose craft calls for calm, mature, undogmatic and independent consideration, find themselves thrown into a stressful climate of urgent preparation and adversarial expectation to produce clear-cut statements on the basis of which courts can make final findings of fact. While this has to be done when an issue is referred to courts for judicial determination, it is exactly what the modern (or even more the postmodern) scholar rebels against.

More important than procedural difficulties are the substantive issues. What is at stake are great interracial issues of historical responsibility and redress flowing from 200 years of less than enlightened treatment of an Indigenous people by a settler community. In the context of today's standards, Australia – in common with other countries with displaced Indigenous populations – cannot avoid the issue of what responsibility it will accept for the living consequences of the past. Two specific issues that have dramatically surfaced are the consequences of dispossession from land and the consequences of policies that, among other things, concentrated Aboriginals to live under squalid conditions and then removed children because they were living in unsuitable conditions, especially if the mixed race of the children touched nerves of guilt, responsibility or racial pride.

To leave the consequences of these policies to litigation, in private actions based on existing rights in courts designed to settle legal rights by an adversarial system within a relatively homogeneous community, is at once an insult to the Indigenous people and a prostitution of the courts. It is an insult to Indigenous people because what is at stake is not the vindication of rights that they possessed, but redress for what happened to them when they were accorded no rights. In the case of land, even the 1992 *Mabo* doctrine that rejected *terra nullius* and recognised native title left the situation that Indigenous people have no basis for complaining of dispossession by the state prior to 1975, when the *Racial Discrimination Act 1975* made the discriminatory taking of land illegal.[54] By that time, almost all economically viable land had been placed under freehold title that extinguished native title, or leasehold title that either extinguished it altogether or prevailed over it.

In a recent paper to a Native Title Representative Bodies conference,[55] I discussed how this situation developed as a result of a failure of political nerve, which left what should have been a legislative policy issue to resolution in the courts as an issue of existing legal rights. In *Mabo*, the High Court eloquently and bravely confronted the fiction of *terra nullius* and its consequences but could only rule on legal rights, and then only in a way that did not fracture the skeletal structure of the invader's law. Instead of rising to the challenge of creating a new Indigenous policy that could deliver more just outcomes in contemporary conditions, Parliament simply cemented the crippled structure of existing rights into the *Native Title Act 1993*. It left an avenue of escape from the straitjacket in the mediation process. However, instead of accepting the opportunity that mediation offers to go beyond existing rights to seek a mutually beneficial solution, governments refused to negotiate except about whether claimants could establish the existing rights they were forced to claim, and went to the courts to exploit every argument to defeat those rights. The shards of the *Mabo* aspiration lie around us in new case names that threaten to usurp its household status, at least in some Aboriginal communities – *Yorta Yorta, de Rose, Ward, Wilson, Yarmirr.*[56]

In the case of the Stolen Generations, the complaint is not about individual slip-ups by government officers that made their particular actions unlawful (which is the only kind of issue courts can entertain), but about the effects of a legislatively authorised policy under which the powers of government officers superseded the normal rights of parents. The grudging response of the Commonwealth government to the Human Rights Commission's *Bringing them Home* report left the members of the Stolen Generations feeling unrecognised and seeking the only legal redress available – individual actions in the courts, where success depends on the lottery of being able to establish individual illegalities within a system based on legislation. As in the case of land, an issue of national policy was inappropriately relegated to courts because of a failure of political will and imagination.

In the courts, issues of justice are necessarily replaced by strict legalism. Indigenous people who claim native title have to come as individuals or small groups into the courts of the wrongdoers, carrying all the burdens of plaintiffs in adversarial proceedings that pit them against one or more governments and sometimes many property owners.[57] Governments assume the role not of responsible policy makers or negotiators, but adversarial opponents of Indigenous claims, willing to spend on court struggles many millions that are not available for constructive solutions.[58] The victims feel themselves on trial, having to justify themselves in the face of rules of law that were developed in a society from which they were excluded and took no account of their interests.

For a stolen child, a great interracial human tragedy may be reduced to her inability to prove that her long dead illiterate mother did not consent to her removal as a baby. She, of course, has no records and no idea what happened, but in her attempts to gain some recognition of her situation she may find herself the adversary of elderly patrol officers indignant at suggestions that there was anything wrong with the painful jobs they carried out in good faith in their youth, and subject to humiliating cross-examination about her parents' tragic lives, perhaps by a highly paid, aggressive senior counsel anxious to redeem the reputation of his politician father.

Even to access the minimal possibilities that native title holds for most Indigenous people, those seeking native title have to prove that the state has not extinguished their rights by giving their land to someone else, as it was long able to do at the stroke of a pen, and that notwithstanding 200 years of dispossession, the disruption of protection and the regimentation of assimilation, they have maintained a recognisable group identity and a continuity of traditional association with the land. They have to show a relationship with the land that is capable of translation into legal rights in an alien system. Even if they succeed, their rights are subordinate to every other right created in a system that did not even acknowledge the possibility that their rights might exist. All this they will have to do in the face of barristers employed by one or more governments and other interests to destroy their case, and with the object of convincing a judge who, however good his or her intentions, has, like the barristers, grown up, studied and lived in another world, where there are different values, different concepts, different understandings, and different languages.[59] Anthropologists are often caught in the middle, trying to mediate between mutually unintelligible worlds, and painfully aware that the deck is so stacked that telling the truth may well mean the defeat of the claim.[60]

It did not have to be like this. Australia is not bound to mean-spiritedly hold its Indigenous people to the limited legal rights that ingenious lawyers can find surviving two hundred years of trampling on them. We seem to have forgotten that it is open to us to be generous and creative. There are plenty of precedents for creating special laws and special tribunals for issues that are unsuitable for the courts. Less than 30 years ago, both sides of politics joined in a land rights solution for the Northern Territory delivered by a specialised tribunal applying reasonably simple rules of eligibility for the grant of a form of title that were readily understood by everyone.

Across the Tasman, a very similar society has stumbled on a way of considering how to redress the past that is wide-ranging, respectful of Māori and Pakeha culture and interests and much less adversarial, and free to present imaginative solutions to government for its consideration and negotiation with Indigenous people. Problems of colonial mistreatment can be taken up within a holistic framework. The question is not how to ferret out and enforce some legal right that has managed to survive, but how to provide a fair basis for the future. The Waitangi Tribunal regularly sits with a historian member and conducts or coordinates research itself.[61] Nominally the process is hung on the long-ignored Treaty of Waitangi, but its terms are so vague that it imposes little restriction on the creative pursuit of justice and reconciliation. An Australian solution need not await a treaty but, if it is not established earlier, could be embodied in a treaty.

I am not suggesting any of these existing or proposed tribunals as models to be adopted but as evidence that will, imagination and generosity of spirit can devise solutions better than our miserable shunting of issues into courts that cannot deal with them appropriately. Ways can be devised to allow Indigenous voices to be effectively heard, to harness scholars to the task of investigating the past and its consequences in the present, and to bring creative thought to bear on specific recommendations to which the state might respond with political responsibility and a concrete basis for negotiation with Indigenous people if needed.

Australia's native title 'solution' to the land rights issue has often reduced Aboriginal people to fighting over miserable scraps. It would be a pity if it reduced humanists and lawyers to fighting over their relative claims to epistemological purity and sophistication, rather than working as natural allies in the search for an acceptable outcome to our country's relations with its Indigenous people.

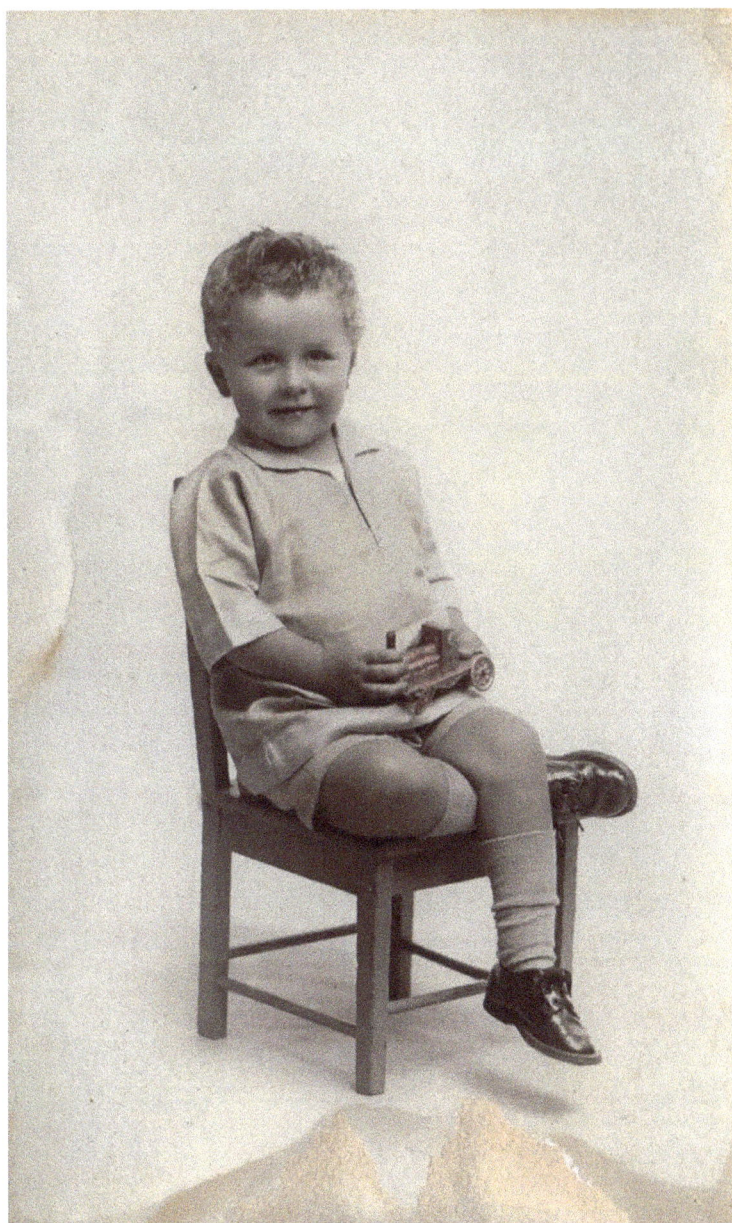

A young Hal Wootten

*Courtesy of Gillian Cowlishaw*

Hal as a student
*Courtesy of Richard Wootten*

Lecturer at the Australian
School of Pacific
Administration,
aged 24
*Courtesy of Gillian Cowlishaw*

Hosting a LAWASIA reception in 1968 with John Kerr for a delegation
from Laos, led by Foreign Secretary Chao Sopsaisana
*Courtesy of UNSW*

UNSW Law's first academics – Garth Nettheim, Tony Blackshield,
Hal and Richard Chisholm
*Courtesy of UNSW*

Dean of Law at UNSW
*Courtesy of UNSW*

Hal greeting visitors for
a LAWASIA function
in the 1970s

*Courtesy of UNSW*

At the Aboriginal tent embassy in Canberra, 1972

*Courtesy of Gillian Cowlishaw*

With Gary Williams and Pancho

*Courtesy of Gillian Cowlishaw*

With Riverbank Frank

*Courtesy of*
*Gillian Cowlishaw*

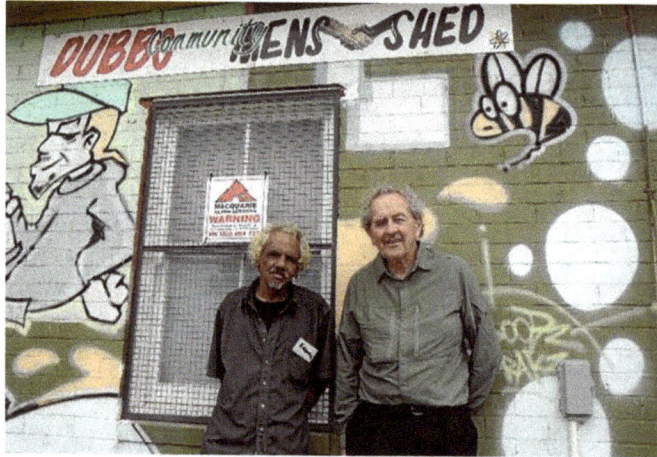

With David Shulman,
and about to be arrested
while on the way to a
demonstration against
illegal settlements in the
South Hebron hills.

*Courtesy of*
*Gillian Cowlishaw*

Birdwatching with Gillian Cowlishaw
*Courtesy of Gillian Cowlishaw*

Hal, aged 90

*Courtesy of Peter Solness*

# 7

# ACCESS TO LAW:
# PAPUA NEW GUINEA
# AND THE ABORIGINAL
# LEGAL SERVICE

*Hal Wootten was consistent in his belief that for the rule of law to have substance, whether in Australia or elsewhere, lawyers had to carry out professional duties of acting for anyone, whatever their status or means, and of contributing to democratic governance. If there were no such lawyers, institutions had to be created to produce them. He addressed this directly in the 1964 article that opens this chapter, concerning the 'pressing problem' of creating a legal profession in Papua New Guinea, and which unsurprisingly includes consideration of the role of legal education towards this goal. He argued that 'the one indispensable requisite (for independence) is an enlightened elite from which can be drawn leaders, at the political and higher administrative levels, capable of making the decisions and carrying out the acts of government which are the substance of independence'.*[1]

*The University of Papua New Guinea opened its School of Law in 1965. Hal's commitment to institution building to enable a profession that would support the rule of law and the protection of all was a theme evident across his career. His early view of the steps needed to establish an independent and Indigenous profession for PNG were followed by his vision for a new kind of law school at UNSW (see chapter 4), his project to support Palestinian law schools (chapter 5), his long association with LAWASIA,*[2] *and, in the body of this chapter, his leadership in creating the Aboriginal Legal Service in the early 1970s.*

## AN INDIGENOUS LEGAL PROFESSION
## FOR NEW GUINEA: A PRESSING PROBLEM

One of the most outstanding of the many marked changes which have
come over the Australian legal profession in recent years has been the
growth of international consciousness.[3] Through conventions, through
increased travel and interchange of visitors, and through the activity of
bodies such as the International Commission of Jurists, lawyers have
become increasingly aware of the common bonds of the profession
which transcend national, racial and political barriers. They have
come to appreciate that the development of an international solidarity
among lawyers can be a significant contribution to the preservation
or development of the rule of law. This is, I believe, one of the
strands from which the interest of the Australian legal profession in
New Guinea has been woven.

Another strand is undoubtedly a general awakening of Australian consciousness of the very difficult responsibility which we
have to discharge in Papua and New Guinea, if we are to bring its
people to independence in the modern world, unscarred by the bitter
tragedies that have preceded and succeeded independence in so many
former colonies.[4] There are, of course, many Australians for whom
what might otherwise be a mere abstract responsibility is quickened by
memories of the part played by many of the people of the Territory
in the last war.

Whatever the reasons, the fact is that the Australian legal profession, through its representative body, the Law Council of Australia,
has for several years been seeking a role it could play in relation to
the Territory. On 28 July 1962, the Executive of the Law Council passed
the following resolution:

The Law Council of Australia is of the view that steps
should be taken to ensure the development among the Indigenous

---

'An Indigenous Legal Profession for New Guinea: A Pressing Problem' (1964) 1(2)
*Australian Bar Gazette* 3–6.

people of the Territories of Papua and New Guinea of a soundly trained and fully qualified legal profession which understands and accepts the rule of law and proper ethical principles of professional practice. The Council offers its full co-operation and support to the Australian Government in the task of helping such a profession to come into existence as rapidly as possible.

## The problem

Implicit in this resolution, and in the subsequent actions of the Law Council, has been a recognition of the fact that, by its very nature, an independent legal profession, such as we know and value, cannot be the creation of a government, and that, if its evolution was to be speeded up, a developed legal profession, such as that of Australia, would have to play a role. The need for speeding up the development of the profession in the Territory could scarcely be more urgent. As it becomes one of the last remaining territories under the supervision of the Trusteeship Council of the United Nations, the external pressures to hasten independence become greater and greater and more and more impatient of the very real difficulties which would ideally call for a cautious pace. And now that the common border with Indonesia has brought the instability and neurotic anti-colonialism of that country to the very doorstep of the Territory, any hope that the development of the Territory might have proceeded in relative isolation from the stresses and strains of the South-East Asia area has disappeared. It is of little use to document the case that, in many new countries, an Indigenous elite has treated its more backward countrymen more harshly than they were ever treated by the former colonial power. There can be no doubt that, within a relatively short space of time, the Territory will be governed by its own Indigenous elite. In that respect we have no choice. The only choice we have is as to the degree of effort we put into seeing that the elite will be a well-educated, sophisticated elite, possessed of the skills necessary for running a modern state.

Quite apart from the ordinary services of the legal profession to the community, independence in the Territory will create an urgent demand for native lawyers as judges, magistrates, administrators,

Cabinet ministers and politicians who have some understanding of the constitution and the working of government under law. Already the first parliament with a native unofficial majority is being elected. From it, there will shortly be selected persons to take embryonic ministerial responsibilities in relation to various departments. In those former colonies where parliamentary government has worked with any degree of success, lawyers have played a significant role and it is surprising how many of the political leaders in such countries are lawyers. To what extent can we expect native lawyers to play a role in the new House of Assembly and to be among those selected for training in the development of ministerial skills for a Cabinet which must someday include law ministers? The very disturbing answer is 'Not at all', because there are *no* native lawyers in the Territory. Nor can there be even one for several years, as the only native law student has just completed his second year at the University of Queensland. After him, there will be a gap of at least a further three years, as next year is the first year in which there is any possibility that other students may join him in legal studies.

## Commission on higher education in the Territory

The opportunity for the Law Council to play a positive role in this situation came last year when it was asked to make recommendations to a Commission on Higher Education in the Territory concerning legal education. The Law Council established a sub-committee[5] to report to it on this matter ... Through the visit to the Territory, the sub-committee had the opportunity to meet and draw on the experience of the Australian lawyers who man the judiciary and the legal profession in the Territory at the present time ... A broad indication can be given of the nature of the problems as seen by the sub-committee and of the solutions which they suggested. The first problem was, of course, the critical urgency of commencing the training of a native legal profession, so that there will be trained personnel with some professional experience by the time their services are in demand for key positions in an independent New Guinea. There is a desperate shortage of natives educated to matriculation standard, and this shortage will continue for a few years, although each year the number available will increase dramatically as the fruits of the Administration's work at lower levels of the education system are progressively reaped. In the meantime, there is strenuous competition from various quarters to persuade the few matriculants available to take up various careers – as teachers, army officers, medical practitioners, agriculture officers and so forth. In this competition, law had been unrepresented. The first task, therefore, was to drive home the point that the provision of an adequate nucleus of lawyers from which Supreme Court judges, law ministers, professional leaders and constitutional experts could be selected was at least as important as the provision of trained personnel in other fields. Indeed, as the sub-committee pointed out:

> Law is so intimately connected with the distribution, exercise and control of political power in every field and with the protection of individual liberty in the clash of political factions that the need for Indigenous lawyers may soon be more keenly felt than the need for Indigenous practitioners of other professions which may be further removed from political conflicts.[6]

A classical illustration of the importance of the first local lawyers in a country is provided in the Sudan, where it was recently the position that, of the first seven Sudanese lawyers trained locally in the law of the Sudan, one was the Chief Justice, three were judges of the High Court, one was Attorney-General, one Minister for Commerce and another Foreign Secretary.

The sub-committee stressed the critical importance of the first group of native lawyers to be trained:

> It is not only that, as the most experienced and mature members of the profession, they will be the obvious candidates for future appointments to ministerial, judicial and academic office. In the meantime, they will be uniquely qualified to contribute to the political life of the Territory in a period of critical constitutional development. Of equal importance is the fact that they will, by the traditions they establish and the example they set, greatly

influence, if not determine, the ultimate ethical and professional standards of the profession. It will depend on them particularly to establish the tradition of a strong, fearless and honourable profession, independent alike of the government and of the bench, which is a prerequisite of justice and of liberty.

## A local Faculty of Law?

There appeared to be very general acceptance of the fact that a university would be set up in the Territory as soon as practicable, and, accordingly, although the sub-committee unreservedly supported this proposal, it did not find it necessary to devote as much attention to this issue, as to whether such a university should contain a local Faculty of Law.[7] The committee found that there were some misgivings about this proposal from the local profession for two quite important reasons. One was a fear that a local faculty might be a sub-standard institution producing an inadequately trained practitioner. The other was that the circumstances of the Territory would not provide the appropriate ethical training and communication of the traditions of the profession which would be possible in an Australian capital. The sub-committee accepted that these two matters were fundamental considerations, and that, unless they could be satisfactorily resolved, a local Faculty of Law should not be established at this stage, however desirable it might be for other reasons.

However, the sub-committee came to the view that there was no reason why training in a local Faculty of Law should not carry with it both proper academic standards and a proper communication of the standards and traditions of the profession. The fears of the development of a lower standard were largely influenced by the fact that, for some years, training of medical practitioners has been provided in the Territory at a lower level than that which is acceptable in Australia. However, as long ago as 31 October 1962, the Law Council had obtained an assurance from the Administration in the following terms: 'It is the unequivocal intention of the Administration that those who are admitted to practice before the courts in this country, whatever their racial origin, will be competently trained by accepted professional standards.'

As there was no policy operating against full professional standards, the problems that had to be faced up to were whether the quality of staff or quality of students would inevitably depress standards. It was recognised that very special efforts would be needed to attract staff of adequate calibre and integrity, and a number of suggestions were made to this end, including a reference to the ways in which this problem had been tackled in Africa. While it is a difficult problem, it is one which can and should be overcome. So far as students were concerned, the sub-committee was very strongly of the view ... that there would be no problem about the inherent ability of students. There would, of course, for some years be difficulties arising from the fact that the language in which students would have to work, namely English, would be essentially a foreign language in their community, and from the general cultural level of the community in which they would study. Again, however, it was considered that these were problems to be tackled and solved and ones which would require a flexible and imaginative approach to the university curriculum in the early years. They were problems which a local Faculty of Law could overcome by appropriate remedial teaching and special courses which could bring students with initial handicaps to a degree standard which they could not hope to reach if left to sink or swim at an Australian university.

So far as the development of proper standards of professional conduct and traditions of independence and fearless advocacy were concerned, the sub-committee suggested that they could be developed consistently with local university training in the following ways:

(a)  by the example of the judges and practitioners of the Territory;
(b)  by the activities as a professional body of the new Law Society of the Territory;
(c)  by active endeavours from student days onwards to bring the potential lawyers into contact with the local profession and to smooth their assimilation into it;
(d)  by the teaching in the Faculty of Law;
(e)  by the fact that some at least of the first practitioners will necessarily be trained in Australia, and, if care is taken to see

that they appreciate the functioning of the Australian profession, they will set the tone of an Indigenous profession as its first members;

(f) by active steps on the part of the Australian profession (including the sponsoring of visits by students and graduates to Australia to work and associate with the Australian profession);

(g) by bringing students and graduates into contact with the legal profession of the world through such bodies as the International Commission of Jurists.

The sub-committee was of the view that once it was accepted that proper academic and professional standards could be maintained consistently with training in the Territory, the case for the early establishment of a Territory Law School was made out on the following grounds:

(a) It will ensure that no educational vacuum will exist in the field of law on independence. On the contrary, a Law School will have been established and grown into a viable institution at a period when it will be most possible to establish high academic and professional standards. It would be tragic if these had to be fought for, for the first time, among the pressures of the possibly turbulent days after independence.

(b) It will provide the Territory with a necessary research institution for the development of the law of the Territory.

(c) It will provide a degree course with content appropriate to the laws and legal problems of the Territory.

(d) In the critical initial period, when matriculated students are in short supply, it will be able to make the most efficient use of the potential student material by adjusting its entry standards and providing compensation in the form of remedial and supplementary teaching.

(e) It will orient the students to the legal needs of the Territory, and will not accustom them to a standard of living which the Territory cannot support or alienate them from the community in which they will serve.

(f)  It will make it possible for the student who is unable to leave the Territory, e.g. because of family commitments, political aspirations, or inability to persuade the powers that be that he should be given a scholarship, to pursue his legal studies. Many eminent lawyers have battled through to qualification against great handicaps, and the people of the Territory should not be denied the opportunity to do this.

(g)  It will provide necessary assistance to other faculties.

(h)  It will provide a centre within the Territory for informed independent and critical discussion of legal issues.

## Development of a local body of law

Underlying the whole of the sub-committee's recommendations was a recognition that the Territory must evolve its own body of law suited to its own conditions, and it could not satisfactorily do this merely by copying the law of an Australian state. Indeed, such an approach would only perpetuate and aggravate the present situation under which the legal system of the Territory caters to a large extent only for the problems of the European community and the small, advanced or entrepreneurial section of the native community. For the great bulk of the population, the only contact with the legal system is through the criminal law, and the cases that come before the courts in this jurisdiction tend to show mainly that legal redress has not been accepted as an adequate substitute for primitive forms of self-help. In moving from village custom to a modern legal system, it is probable that much more could be gained from a study of the legal systems of new African and Asian countries than from that of a developed community such as Australia. All this has implications, not only for the content of the legal system, but for the training of the lawyers who should be oriented towards the real legal problems of their own country rather than towards problems which are important only in a very different type of community ...

## A first step in cooperation

It is of course obvious that, pending the establishment of a local Law School, the only practicable method of training the first and vitally important group of native New Guinea lawyers is by sending them to Australian universities. These students will suffer very great handicaps by comparison with their fellow students who have grown up in Australia and to whom English is their native tongue. Members of the profession in Australia could undoubtedly do a great deal to assist these students, both in their studies and with their personal problems, and it is hoped that a relationship of friendship and assistance will grow up. It would undoubtedly be an enormous contribution to the stability of the Territory if the members of the key profession of law grew up to regard Australian lawyers as their personal friends and colleagues who had been only too willing to help them during the difficult stages of their country's progress towards independence.

———————————

*In his ABC interview with Peter Thompson in 2005, Hal spoke of the three times that he had 'an experience of really belonging warmly to a community'. The first was when he was doing fieldwork in a New Guinea village; the 'second was in the first year or two of the Law School when we managed to really create a community among the law students and the teachers; and the third was when I got involved in starting the Aboriginal Legal Service (ALS), and suddenly felt admitted to the Indigenous community in Sydney ... I felt it was very strange that having those ties with the Indigenous people of New Guinea, I didn't even know the Indigenous people of my own country, and that was something nagging at the back of my mind'.[8]*
*He told the ALS Story Project,*

> *My experience with the ALS was one of the most wonderful and rewarding experiences of my life, for which I feel ... particularly grateful to the Aboriginal community in which I formed such friendships, and which responded with such warmth and generosity*

*to the whole enterprise. It was quite a magical experience for certainly many of the white people and I believe many of the Aboriginal people who took part in it. We were privileged to take part in a unique experience and to do it at a moment in history which had been created by the Aboriginal people of Redfern. There was at that time a great feeling of hope and growing confidence … There was a feeling of community, cooperation and inter-racial warmth.*[9]

*Hal said later that a feeling of being 'privileged to be present at a special moment in history is [one] that many people, black and white, share to this day'.*[10]

*Hal's role in the establishment of the ALS exemplified his approach. He wanted change, not just protest, and so rejected the initial suggestion that he could help by finding 'some lawyers to take a few cases to teach the police a lesson'*[11] *in favour of setting up a lasting institution. He insisted that the ALS would only work if Indigenous people were central in its establishment and operation. He relied on his fellow lawyers' commitment to professional values and commitment to justice as their incentive to be involved. In Redfern, an informal curfew on Indigenous people, backed by police use of street offences (and the 'trifecta' of offensive language, resist arrest, assault police) clearly evidenced legal inequality. Hal was influenced by 'work I had done in organising Australian lawyers to assist the development of an Indigenous legal profession in Papua New Guinea, and to back LAWASIA's efforts to strengthen the legal profession in developing countries'.*[12] *He 'thought on the basis of my experience in doing that … there was a degree of sympathy and idealism in the legal profession that would make it possible to set up a permanent Aboriginal Legal Service'.*[13]

*Hal credited his experience in New Guinea with giving him 'an ability to feel at ease with people who were totally different to myself, different in culture, different in education, and different right through'.*[14] *He was able to span divisions between older campaigners for civil rights*[15] *and younger radical activists*[16] *within the Indigenous community*[17] *and to connect them with the legal profession, describing his role as joining the tributaries together into the river of the ALS. 'We had a committee that couldn't really be dismissed by anybody because it had top figures from the legal establishment, it had strong representation from both the younger and older parts of the Aboriginal community.'*[18]

*His access to and high standing among the profession were vital: when he wrote to barristers and solicitors 'within range of Sydney', 'very large numbers' put their name on the ALS roster and financially supported his venture.*[19] *This included senior members of the profession, including Gordon Samuels, then Vice President of the Bar Council, later Governor of NSW.*[20] *Equally, he attracted high-quality young people who would go on to prestigious careers – lawyers like John McKenzie, Bob Debus, Stephen Norrish, Peter Stapleton, Richard Chisolm and Peter Hidden. His standing meant that he could get action on individual issues, then build further. A clear example was the fall-out from finding that people in an Indigenous reserve at Toomelah had no clean water, although the reserve manager had water trucked in for himself. Hal wrote a letter to the Sydney Morning Herald. On the day of publication, a government minister rang to say a water truckload was on the way to the people of Toomelah. The story attracted publicity for the ALS, leading Bill Wentworth, the Commonwealth Minister for Aboriginal Affairs, to contact Hal offering help – and funding. This led to the establishment in Redfern of an office for the ALS (which had previously used the UNSW Law School as its address), a solicitor, a field officer (Gordon Briscoe), and a secretary. Until then, everything had been done on a voluntary basis – 'it simply never crossed our minds that the government might give us financial support ... [W]hen we did need a bit of money, well we just put our hands in our pockets and that was it. But the whole thing was established on a completely voluntary basis, and nobody, either Aboriginal or white, got a penny for their efforts, they all did it as a matter of dedication.'*[21]

*Hal remained President of the ALS until 1973, when he became a Supreme Court judge: 'My new position required me to terminate what had been one of the richest experiences of my life. I felt I had been able to make a modest contribution to the progress of the movement, but I had been more than amply rewarded by the warmth and generosity of*

*Aboriginals who had admitted me to their friendship, their family circles, and their country missions; who had taken me and my family camping in their special places; who had shared with me their humour, their history, their courage in adversity, the tragedies and joys of their lives.'*[22]

We begin with Hal's commentary on the ALS, explaining the historical origins of conflict between police and Indigenous people. This chapter ends with a shorter reflection from 2005 and Hal's tribute to Bob Bellear, one of his friends and colleagues from Redfern who went on to be the second Indigenous law graduate in Australia and the first appointed as a judge (serving in the District Court of NSW from 1996 to 2005).

# WITH THE ABORIGINAL LEGAL SERVICE, 1970–73

## A neglected field

At the time England first settled Australia, it had no professional police; these came 40 years later with the formation of the London Metropolitan Police in 1829.[23] Australian police thus began with no professional traditions, and they also had a major role that had no counterpart in England, and which in North America had fallen to the military.[24] In Australia, the suppression of Aboriginal resistance to white settlement, insofar as it was a state function, fell largely to the police. Their function was primarily to protect white settlers,[25] and, when they were called in, the expectation was often not that they would identify and arrest suspects, but that they would conduct punitive expeditions and wipe out the troublesome blacks.[26] When Aboriginal resistance was overcome and policy changed from military-style suppression to other forms of control, much of it under the banner of 'protection', police long remained the enforcing instrument of the dominant white society. They were often, for example, associated with the taking of children from their mothers to be brought up in institutions or foster homes. Today, it is still difficult

---

'Aborigines and Police' (1993) 16(1) *University of New South Wales Law Journal* 265–301.

for many Aborigines and police to see each other in non-adversarial roles. For some – on both sides – violence is still anticipated as a likely concomitant of arrest …

## The first Aboriginal Legal Service

The establishment of the first Aboriginal Legal Service (ALS) in 1970 came at the end of a decade of rapidly growing Aboriginal political consciousness and awareness of the possibilities of organised action and protest. It was only in 1963 that Aborigines without a special licence ('the dog collar') had been allowed into hotels in NSW. In the same year, the Yirrkala people petitioned federal parliament to stop mining at Gove, and Victorian Aborigines marched through the streets of Melbourne in defence of Lake Tyers, and three years later the Gurindji went on strike at Wave Hill. The demand for 'land rights', although usually modestly defined, had become a widely unifying demand. The idea of a 'Fourth World' of Indigenous peoples had not emerged, and looking overseas Australian Aborigines were influenced mainly by Black American movements – the 'Freedom Rides' of 1961, the victories of the civil rights movement by both court actions and peaceful protest, and then the more radical advocacy of violence by 'Black Power' movements from 1966 on, the year the Black Panthers[27] were formed.

All this was in the air, but the formation of the ALS was a direct response to a very specific problem: police treatment of Aborigines in Redfern. The concentrated Aboriginal community in Redfern, estimated at well over 12 000, was a relatively recent development, fed by post–World War II Aboriginal migration from rural NSW and interstate as opportunities for employment dried up in rural areas.[28] Redfern became and has remained a staging post for Aborigines migrating to Sydney, a place where supportive company and cheap accommodation can be found until they are channelled by public housing programs into other suburbs. It has also had a substantial nucleus of Aborigines who have made it a permanent home.

Among the migrants there in 1970 was a small number who had completed secondary education. Two of them, who were to play a major role in the establishment and administration of the ALS, were Paul Coe and Gary Williams. They were among a group of young Aborigines who did not see why Aborigines should continue to submit to a degree of police stereotyping and oppression which many older Aborigines had come to accept as part of being Aboriginal. This group thought that they should be able to obtain some protection from the law, and, in their search for some lawyers who might be willing to take some cases on a *pro bono* basis and 'teach the police a lesson', they enlisted the support of some Sydney University law students. The latter, including Eddy Neumann,[29] who was to become the first Secretary of the ALS, approached me and invited me to meet the young Aborigines and their sympathisers. I had recently been appointed Dean of the UNSW Law School, which was to take its first students in 1971, and some of the statements I had made about the aims of the new school led the students to hope for a sympathetic reception. Among the consequences of the meetings which followed were the establishment of Australia's first Aboriginal legal service[30] and the UNSW program of special admission for Aborigines, which led to Paul Coe and Gary Williams enrolling among the first law students in 1971, and many other Aborigines following them.[31]

Having had no experience of Aboriginal–police relations, I was initially bewildered when told of a police-imposed curfew, but was soon convinced when I visited Redfern and saw that any Aborigine on the streets of Redfern after 10.15 pm, even if quietly walking home, was bundled into a patrolling paddy wagon. The standard charge was public drunkenness, but naturally such treatment often led to reaction by an indignant Aborigine which escalated both to additional charges of resisting arrest and assault police, and to physical retaliation by police. In addition, police regularly patrolled hotels frequented by Aborigines, particularly the Empress,[32] and their heavy-handed treatment and oppressive scrutiny of Aborigines often led to violent incidents in and outside the hotel bars. One of the early activities of the ALS was a regular Friday and Saturday night roster of eminent legal and academic observers who spent the evenings with Aborigines in the Redfern hotels.

## Pre-emptive police action

It is doubtful that the police in Redfern had any awareness of the history of the Aboriginal community or the ferment it was going through. The reasoning by which they justified their actions in Redfern was highly logical, albeit in breach of the law and of human rights (a much less well-known concept then, than today). There was a significant number of street thefts from the person, often accompanied by threats or assault, and in Redfern they were often committed by Aborigines who found themselves broke after an evening's drinking. Police reasoned that if all Aborigines could be removed from the streets of Redfern after closing time, there would be a drastic reduction in the incidence of these offences. Hence, a curfew had a certain rationality. Moreover, since an Aborigine was likely to react adversely to arrest, it was only sense to get in first and eliminate the possibility of resistance by firm handling.

The same logic, although now officially disapproved, underlies many police actions which arouse Aboriginal resentment today. The *Cop it Sweet* television documentary showed Redfern police in 1992 stopping an Aborigine driving a newish red Laser, because it was unusual for an Aboriginal to own or have lawful use of such a car.[33] Again, from a police point of view, the action was rational. Few Aborigines are sufficiently affluent to own such a car, so it may well be statistically more likely that such a car driven by an Aborigine is stolen than if it is driven by a white person. From an Aboriginal point of view, the police action was racially motivated harassment; an Aborigine who rises above what police consider his or her normal station in life will immediately be treated as suspect – even more suspect than other Aborigines, who, judging by police arrests, are in any event considered much more likely to commit offences than non-Aborigines.

These practices have compounding effects. Because of their visibility and police stereotyping, Aborigines who do commit offences are more likely to be caught, and those who have not committed them are more likely to be wrongly accused and, in some cases, convicted. Because of their resentment of such police practices, and the lingering imprint of the last 200 years on Aboriginal attitudes to police, Aborigines are more likely to react to police with resentment and hostility, so that the stage is set for offensive language, resist arrest and assault charges. This applies even to routine or well-intentioned police approaches; police who try to establish a friendly relationship with Aboriginal youth on routine beat patrols are likely to be accused of harassing them.

## Myths of equal treatment

When, as ALS President, I initiated contact with the Commissioner of Police,[34] the reaction was that police have to apply the law and cannot distinguish between races: if Aborigines obey the law they will not be in trouble with the police.[35] Officers were taught to treat all citizens the same. This discourse has often been used as a protective screen, to justify a refusal to look at or even acknowledge the existence of Aborigines. Although it has been abandoned at policy and training levels in police services, it is still common at the grassroots level and is being resurrected at a theoretical level by those opposed to special measures for Aborigines.[36]

People do not in fact get treated equally; all sorts of assumptions and stereotypes get built into day-to-day judgments. The policeman who stopped the red Laser would doubtless say that he stopped any driver who aroused his suspicions, irrespective of race. Those who exercise power are often influenced by prejudices or erroneous beliefs in ways of which they are unaware. You do not have equal treatment if Aboriginal populations are policed more intensely than other groups, so that more of their peccadillos will be observed, and the pressure of more intense scrutiny will spark more frequent reaction. It is essential to get behind slogans and see what is happening in particular cases.

Moreover, to treat in a similar manner people who are different or unequal does not necessarily produce equality.[37] When the vagrancy law made it an offence to be without visible means of support, it did not operate equally on rich and poor. Not only are Aborigines typically the poorest of the poor, they are culturally different, and the application of a policy which does not recognise cultural difference will be unfair, particularly if the policy incorporates norms from one culture. Many Aborigines, for example, speak in a way very different to what is regarded as decorous by white Australians, and have different attitudes to drinking in public, sleeping in parks, and otherwise using public space. They are used to a less hierarchical society and may treat people in authority differently. Many think it rude to look other people in the eye, while many whites regard avoidance of eye contact as shiftiness, and suspicious. All these things affect the operation of street offences legislation, which is often applied to the detriment of Aborigines.

## Peace-keeping or law enforcement

To the not inconsiderable extent that police have, as the equal treatment discourse claims, rejected discretion in policing Aborigines and proceeded automatically to arrest for breaches of the law, they have acted both in a discriminatory manner, because other groups are not similarly policed,[38] and in breach of good police practice. In his book *Police, Force or Service?*[39] John Avery, who was later to become NSW Commissioner of Police, discusses a distinction between the 'law enforcer' and the 'peace-keeper', the contacts made with the public by the former being 'more of a punitive and inquisitive nature, while the latter is more concerned with assisting citizens … [P]eacekeeping also involves the attempt to control a situation, to achieve the police objective of quiet and good order and the absence of trouble, by means other than the formal processes of arresting or reporting for the purposes of having summonses issued'.[40] He also refers to the distinction between 'humanitarian' and 'authoritarian' officers, the former believing that 'words are generally more effective than physical force in conflict situations', whereas the latter, 'the traditionalists believing in the efficacy of force, are quick to pass judgments and are often formal and inflexible during their conflict interventions'.[41] Avery treats it as obvious that the approach of humanitarian peace-keeping is desirable, although of course not always appropriate,[42] and that it involves 'the use of a considerable amount of discretion … Police cannot enforce all the laws all the time, even if they tried, nor does anyone expect them to do so.'[43] The typical arrest figures for many Aboriginal areas make it clear that police usually operate there primarily as authoritarian law enforcers rather than humane peace-keepers.

## Police cooperation

The officially expressed attitude of the ALS was that:

> ... while it will defend Aborigines strongly against any
> interference with their rights, whether by Police or anyone
> else, it considers that the long-term interests of both Police
> and Aboriginals, and of the community, are best served by the
> growth of mutual understanding and respect between the two
> groups. While the Service has provided legal representation
> for Aborigines in conflict with Police, it has also looked for
> opportunities to promote cooperation and has pursued these
> in preference to public criticism of Police activities which might
> prejudice such cooperation.[44]

The Police Commissioner reacted in a proper, if not enthusiastic, manner to the establishment of the ALS. He circularised police informing them about the ALS and agreed to the display in all police stations of a notice giving information about contacting the ALS, and some officers actively referred Aborigines to the ALS.[45] The Commissioner nominated a liaison officer, and he was helpful on occasions. Soon after the ALS started, the situation in the Redfern hotels seemed explosive, and we asked that a conference be held between five Aborigines and five police officers and myself to discuss the conflict. It proved a useful meeting and, for a time at least, there was a lowering of tension.

Although the insistence on the equal treatment hypothesis and a defensive attitude to complaints limited discussion with the top levels of the Police Force, there were some officers who were more interested in realities. Inspector Fred Longbottom, the head of the Special Squad, which was concerned with political and potentially subversive issues, was a remarkable man to find in such a position at that time, having a genuine belief in the right of peaceful protest and respect for those who were willing to protest against injustice. For example, he was keen to cooperate with the ALS to ensure that Aboriginal marches and demonstrations could be held and carried off effectively and peacefully. Had he not been there, the actions of other officers with a more heavy-handed approach might well have triggered violent reactions. Certainly, there were some, both Aboriginal and nonAboriginal, who were ready for such a response, and were concerned that the ALS was a device to turn Aborigines away from more radical and extra-legal activities.

When the ALS learnt that Redfern was to come under a new inspector, Bob Beath, who had been responsible for handling demonstrations against the Springbok tour, which had erupted into violence between police and Aborigines on several occasions,[46] there was considerable foreboding. However, he turned out to be, as he claimed, a professional policeman, and a very realistic one, without other axes to grind. From the beginning, his attitude to the ALS was: 'You want peace and good relations in Redfern, so do I. Let us work together to achieve it.' Today such willingness to unbend and negotiate would be widely acknowledged as good police practice. In 1970 it was rare. The ALS was able to negotiate with him ways of avoiding incidents between police and Aborigines, and he continued to be helpful when he was transferred to Dubbo.

One of Inspector Beath's professional precepts was that he was responsible for the police under him and did not want them to get hurt. This made him keen to avoid trouble, not exacerbate it. I found the same precept operative with the Commissioner of the Federal Police when, at the request of Paul Coe, I went to Canberra on the weekend of 29–30 July 1972, when there was to be a large Aboriginal gathering at the Tent Embassy, and fears were held that there would be a repetition of a violent struggle that had occurred between police and Aborigines the previous weekend. On that occasion there had been no less than a pitched battle. The Commissioner assured me that he did not want his men to get hurt, and I was able to assure him that those organising the Aboriginal demonstration did not want their people to get hurt, particularly because so many women and children were there. I believe that this common interest, and the negotiation that grew out of it, had a lot to do with the day going off peacefully. Had this peaceful outcome not eventuated, there might well have been a serious long-term deterioration in Aboriginal–police relations.

## Aboriginal organisations

The Aboriginal Legal Service introduced me to the empowering potential of organisations for Aborigines. It enabled Aborigines to do what they could never have done acting as individuals – provide a general legal service for Aborigines, including legal advice, representation in court, and the making of representations to and negotiation with police forces and other arms of government. Originally, professional legal work was done by lawyers who agreed to be on a panel to do fee work, but the possibilities on this basis, though valuable at the time, were limited. Many Aborigines lived in areas where there were many Aborigines and few lawyers, insufficient (even if they had been willing) to provide the needed service on a voluntary basis. Moreover, lawyers acting ad hoc in individual cases could only rarely establish the rapport with, and build up the knowledge and expertise to communicate with, understand and effectively represent, their very different clients. Nor could they provide the basis of experience and accumulated knowledge to identify common Aboriginal problems and seek solutions to them.

But, more fundamentally, submitting oneself as an object of charity to a lawyer, who acted simply as an expert in using the dominant legal system of which his client was often ignorant, but to which the client had to submit, was a completely disempowering experience ... By contrast, the ALS model provided an empowering experience for many. From the beginning, a major part of the controlling Council was Aboriginal, and this rapidly became a majority, and before long the Council was totally Aboriginal, although dependent for legal advice on non-Aboriginal lawyers. The employment of salaried lawyers, and Aboriginal support staff, became possible with government funding, initially on a modest basis through the support of a Liberal Minister for Aboriginal Affairs, Bill Wentworth, in 1970, and then on a fully funded basis promised by Gough Whitlam in the 1972 election.

The ALS provided an important and empowering experience for Aborigines in controlling part of their affairs. The Council and a Management Committee were elected, and any Aborigine could join the ALS without fee and stand for office. Those elected obtained experience in management, budgeting and decision-making, hitherto rare experiences for Aborigines. They determined the priorities and the practices and attitudes for the organisation. So far as possible, Aboriginal staff were employed, and where Aborigines were not available, as in professional areas, those employed were responsible to the elected Aboriginal Council. Aboriginal clients came not for white charity, but on a basis of entitlement to a community-based Aboriginal organisation.

So attractive was this early experience in self-determination that the model was followed in the establishment not only of other legal services across Australia, but in other fields. An immediate reaction of Aborigines who had been involved in the ALS was to establish the first Aboriginal Medical Service, which still operates successfully in Redfern, and has become a model for many other health services. In view of some recent theoretical criticism of the funding of Aboriginal organisations,[47] it should be noted that the alternative to the Aboriginal-controlled organisations was not some imaginary independent, individual provision of services, but 'mainstreaming'; that is, the delivery of services by bureaucracies over which Aborigines had no control, either as individuals or as communities.

Naturally the road has not been easy or smooth for these exercises in self-determination, modest as they were, among a people whose initiative had so often been crushed or denied in the past. The organisation is a concept with no counterpart in small-scale face-to-face Aboriginal society, where the slow pace of technological, demographic and natural change, and the limited contact with outsiders, meant that few challenges were posed to the notion of a timeless law regulating human affairs, and few opportunities were presented for social engineering. Decisions within a stable framework could be made by consensus or influenced by persons of traditional authority. There were no funds to account for. In using the Western concept of an accountable, democratic organisation, there have been failures as well as successes, and ups and downs within the organisations that have survived, but I believe that the establishment of the ALS began one of the great steps forward for Aborigines.

The establishment of the ALS fundamentally altered relations with police, who could no longer assume that Aborigines would plead guilty to whatever they were charged with, or that complaints about police conduct would never be made or pressed. Initially most police seemed to resent the change, but today it is usually accepted as part of the natural order of things.

One thing that has largely disappeared is the old paternalistic activity of the local policeman, who exercised a personal discipline, particularly over young Aborigines who would be given 'a boot up the backside' and taken home to their parents. Some older, conservative Aborigines mourn the change, saying that when they were young, they would never have been allowed to get away with what young people do today. In some Aboriginal communities there are warm memories of police who were paternalistic but put much effort into genuinely beneficial welfare activities.[48]

## Changing police policies

I resigned the presidency of the ALS in 1973 when I became a Supreme Court judge, mainly in civil jurisdictions where I saw little either of Aborigines or police.[49] In the years 1970 to 1973, the ALS had been primarily concerned with getting into operation a system to provide legal advice and representation for Aborigines in conflict with the criminal law, and with building support and participation in the Aboriginal community. These were big tasks carried out with limited resources, and little time or energy was available for proactive measures to influence police policies and attitudes. Nor was the time ripe on the police side. The NSW Force remained locked in its 'equal treatment' discourse, which effectively refused to acknowledge Aboriginality. It was not until 1980, when it established an Aboriginal Liaison Unit, that the Force moved away from that position. Other police forces had also abandoned the notion that they could ignore Aboriginality and attempted to develop relations with Aboriginal communities and organisations.

The changing police policies towards Aborigines in the 1980s were in some degree a response to major changes in federal and state policies to Aborigines across the board, to great changes in Aboriginal communities themselves, and to the growing sense of a national Aboriginal identity that had been dramatically expressed in the 1971 Tent Embassy, and in the Aboriginal response to Australia Day 1988 and other Bicentennial celebrations.

## Community policing

But even more important were changes internal to police forces themselves, nowhere more strikingly expressed than in John Avery's appointment as Police Commissioner in NSW in 1984. In 1981, when an Inspector, he had published *Police, Force or Service?* He saw a critical situation in which … attempting to achieve social peace 'by increasing legislation and coercive forces' was an expensive mistake.[50] His solution was 'to bring the people into the functions of social control'. Notwithstanding their sometimes more dramatic functions, 'by far the largest area of police functions lies in routine peace-keeping activities'. He argued that 'it is the police function to assist the public with social control'. He commended the view that 'what the police chief must do is to focus the entire institutional effort around one job, that of the police officer closest to the community', and advocated a change of name from Force to Service.[51]

Today[52] 'community policing' is a well-accepted philosophy of police services in Australia. I have encountered police who see this as a reason for denying recognition to specifically Aboriginal issues – the police deal with 'the community', not with particular groups who are expected to submerge their viewpoint under a general community umbrella. Fortunately, this is not the dominant view, and was certainly not the view of Avery, who wrote with considerable perceptiveness of the Aboriginal situation:

> The police image with Aboriginals is lamentably poor for a number of reasons, particularly the differing perspectives on life or what has been described as 'the great cultural gap'. It has been suggested that police are the grinding edge of the white society on the black. Police, in common with other members of non-Aboriginal racial groups in Australia, must come to recognise the significance of Aboriginality. With indifferent arrogance, the white people have carelessly endeavoured to force

this people to become like unto our own flawed racial image. The relations between police and Aboriginals will improve when other residents on this continent allow them to rediscover the dignity and pride which were once theirs, and assist them to preserve their heritage.[53]

By 1988, 'community policing' had been widely embraced by Australian Police 'Forces', which were engaged in changing into Police 'Services'.[54]

## THE INFLUENCE OF THE ALS

From the outset the Service was resolutely non-political. We did not exist to tell Aboriginals what they should seek, but only to provide them with the legal services they needed. We did, however, hope that its effect would go beyond the righting of individual injustices, important as that was, and would contribute to a growth of pride, dignity and self-respect in the Aboriginal community. In this we were not disappointed. As soon as the Legal Service started to take shape, Aboriginals saw the possibilities of the model for health, and in no time at all there was an Aboriginal Medical Service, with our Field Officer, Gordon Briscoe[55] as President, and our Councillor Mum Shirl as Field Officer. Gary Foley went to Adelaide to help set up a legal service, which was known as the Aboriginal Legal Rights Movement. After the advent of the Whitlam Government, community-controlled service organisations of various kinds mushroomed across Australia. The two Aboriginal students in the first year of the UNSW Law School were followed by a steady stream. The next year there was Pat O'Shane, the first Aboriginal magistrate, in 1978 Bob Bellear, the first Aboriginal judge. Police grumbled that Aboriginals were no longer prepared to 'cop it sweet'.

'The Aboriginal Legal Service' (unpublished speech, 2005).

## TRIBUTE TO BOB BELLEAR, 1944–2005

*Hal met his friend Bob Bellear in Redfern when the community of which he was part took a stand against police racism. It made Bellear decide to become a lawyer which, as Hal explains here, he did with great and original distinction.*

With the passing of Bob Bellear, the UNSW Law School lost a uniquely distinguished graduate, of whom it is justly proud. Bob was the first Indigenous judge in Australia, having been appointed to the NSW District Court in 1996.

Bob's ancestry combined two severely disadvantaged groups: Australian Aboriginals and the Pacific Islanders brought to Australia in the course of the infamous Kanaka trade.[56] He overcame tremendous handicaps to enter the Law School in 1974, graduate in 1978 and gain admission to the Bar in 1979.

In happier circumstances, Bob may well have chosen a career other than law. He was moved to embrace it not for its material rewards, nor for love of the subtleties of legal reasoning, nor for the charms of adversarial litigation. These things were not calculated to attract a person who was unpretentious and generous by nature, direct and spontaneous in thought and action, and compassionate and conciliatory by disposition. Famously, he decided to do law as a result of observing the unjust treatment of Aboriginal people by police, seeing law as an avenue for redressing the balance. True to this intent, his subsequent career progressed from counsel for Indigenous and other disadvantaged defendants, to counsel assisting the Royal Commission into Aboriginal Deaths in Custody, to Public Defender and finally to judge in the court that dealt with the great bulk of criminal work above the level of magistrate.

Having chosen law as a career, he pursued it with integrity, commitment, dignity, courtesy and humanity. Injustice, dishonesty, cruelty or hypocrisy could move him to anger, but not make him bitter, vengeful or unfair. His path-breaking career and his imposing presence meant that he was constantly held up as an example to inspire young Aboriginals, a difficult role that he accepted with grace and no hint of pomposity.

# 8

# THE ROYAL COMMISSION
# INTO ABORIGINAL DEATHS
# IN CUSTODY

*The Royal Commission into Aboriginal Deaths in Custody was established in 1987 in response to media reports instigated by several Indigenous families who believed police were responsible for their son's or cousin's death in custody. The number of recognised deaths soon mounted to 99 and the number of Royal Commissioners from one to six. What began as an investigation into the immediate causes of these deaths turned into an inquiry into fundamental issues concerning the treatment of Aboriginal people in Australian society. As one of the Royal Commissioners, Hal Wootten was centrally involved in the Commission's work, investigating and reporting on 18 deaths in NSW, Victoria and Tasmania.[1] He provided the Regional Report for these states[2] and contributed to the final reports of the RCIADIC published in 1991. This involved a huge output of writing,[3] which relied on intensive investigation and research.[4]*

*This chapter begins with extracts from Hal's reports on the deaths of Lloyd Boney, Malcolm Smith, David Gundy, Clarrie Nean, Mark Quayle and Harrison Day. They exemplify Hal's ability to connect human agency and social structures – the actions of detainees and police and prison officers and the historical and social determinants of those actions. They also express his simmering anger at injustice. These extracts on individual cases are followed by material drawn from Hal's Regional Report. Hal's reflections on the RCIADIC, and its critics, conclude the chapter.*

# SIX INDIGENOUS DEATHS IN CUSTODY
## Lloyd Boney: 'A typical death in custody'

A number of features of Lloyd's life were typical of many Aboriginal men of his age, and his death was typical of many of those who have died in custody. He reached working age at a time when the main opportunities for Aboriginal employment in the pastoral industry, which was the only real industry in the area in which he lived, had largely disappeared. Consequently, like many other young Aboriginals, he grew up with little direct contact with rural life and without the opportunity to acquire or to use rural skills. Instead, he lived in a town where all the power, all the businesses and all the resources were in the hands of white people who in most ways belonged to a separate, dominant community. He grew up in a home and among peers to whom formal education meant little; went to a school which he found alien and alienating; and acquired the habit of spending his time, in the absence of other ways of using it, in sociality heavily laced with alcohol. His death too was typical of the way in which many of the deaths in custody have occurred among Aboriginal men of a similar or younger age group. He was heavily intoxicated when arrested, was locked in a cell which was known to be unsafe with no company and no supervision, was left with the means to hang himself from a point in the cells by his own clothes and was found hanged within a short period after coming into custody.

It was to be expected that police would not have a high opinion of Lloyd. They repeatedly saw him as a result of his violence towards women and sometimes suffered the effects of his violent rage themselves. The negative side of his life, particularly his violence, is well documented as this was the main concern of those in the dominant white community who kept most of the records where he lived. They defined him as a problem.

Yet clearly, they were seeing only one side of a multi-faceted person. Just as his death appeared different to the Aboriginal community, so did

---

The full text of the reports can be found at <austlii.edu.au/au/other/IndigLRes/rciadic>.

his life. He was, like all members of that community, closely involved in the kinship networks. He had a real and undisguised love for his young son. He had close friends, some of them respected and active members of the community, who were very concerned about his death. The very strength of the reaction to his death in the Aboriginal community says something about the respect and affection in which he was held, as well as about the state of Aboriginal relationships with the dominant white community and the police in particular.

Lloyd Boney's death was the death which finally precipitated the establishment of the Royal Commission a few days after he died. The reaction that it produced in the local community was and remains profound.

## Malcolm Smith:
### An Aboriginal death (and life) in custody

The story of Malcolm Charles Smith is the story of a life destroyed, not by the misconduct of police and prison officers, but in large measure by the regular operation of the system of self-righteous, heartless and racist destruction of Aboriginal families that went on under the name of protection or welfare well into the second half of this century. At 1.25 pm on 29 December 1982 Malcolm Charles Smith, an Aboriginal prisoner at Long Bay, Sydney, went into a toilet cubicle and locked the door behind him. About half a minute afterwards, a piercing scream came from the cubicle. Prison officers rushed to the door and, when there was no response to their inquiries, knocked it off its hinges and found that the handle of an artist's paint brush had been driven through Malcolm Smith's left eye, so that only the metal sheath and hairs were protruding. He was quickly attended to by nursing staff and a doctor and transferred to Prince Henry Hospital, as an emergency case. Despite all possible care, he died at 11.41 am on 5 January 1983.

So much for *how* Malcolm died. Why did he die? Why was he in prison, seeking to pluck out his eye? The answer begins (depending on how long a perspective one takes), somewhere between 26 January 1788 and 5 May 1965. On the former day there commenced the European settlement that, in Rowley's phrase, was to mean 'the progress of the

Aboriginal from tribesman to inmate'.[5] It was to spread across the continent, overwhelming people like the Paakantji, who occupied the rich hunter-gatherer habitat on the banks of the Darling, and the Ngiyampaa, their neighbours to the north-east. By the operation of massacre, individual killing, introduced diseases, destruction of food supplies, sexual exploitation, introduction of alcohol and dispossession from the land with which their whole life was entwined, these peoples were reduced to small remnants and many of them herded without regard to tribal affiliations into what were in effect concentration camps, although known as stations or 'missions', where they were denied civil rights in the name of protection and forced into a state of dependency in which many are still enmeshed. Whoever made the policies they enforced, it was usually the police that Aboriginals saw as the immediate agents of oppression.

Some bold spirits managed to maintain a precarious independence. Malcolm's parents, Gladys, of Paakantji descent, who lost an arm in a shooting accident at 16, and her husband, Joseph, of Ngiyampaa descent, lived a roving fugitive life along the Darling between Ivanhoe, Menindee and Wentworth, travelling in horse-drawn vehicles and sleeping under tarpaulins, and supporting themselves by casual work on stations and fruit blocks, and by hunting and fishing, as their family grew to 13 children. Always on the move, their constant concern was to escape the attentions of 'the welfare', and its agents the police, lest they suffer the fate of so many Aboriginal families and be forced to live on a reserve or have their children snatched away, often never to be seen again.

Gradually they came to settle with related families at Dareton, near Wentworth, where irrigation farmers valued the easily accessible pool of casual labour. They lived in humpies built from discarded materials, where Gladys cared for her large family while Joe built a reputation as a reliable worker. Here disaster struck. Gladys died and despite the efforts of Joe and his elder daughters, 'the welfare' caught up with the younger children.

Immediately prior to 5 May 1965, the other date from which Malcolm's story may be commenced, he was a happy, healthy and free 11-year-old, albeit grubby, living in a humpy, and truant from a school made unattractive by racial prejudice and irrelevance to his life. He was taken away from his family by police, cut off from his family, whom he did not see again until he was 19, and sent to Kempsey, over 1500 kilometres away on the coast, beyond the boundaries of their accessible world. When he finally rediscovered them at the age of 19, it was too late for him to start a normal life. The intervening eight years, mainly in despotic institutions of various kinds, had left him illiterate and innumerate, unskilled, and without experience of normal society. He had been taught a model of human life based not on mutual respect, cooperation, responsibility, initiative, self-expression and love, but on dominance and subservience, rigid discipline and conformity, repression and dependence, humiliation and fear, with escape or defiance as the only room for initiative. He had experienced the law as a system which gave him no rights, no representation and no consideration, ignored the existence of his family, and treated him as having no place outside an institution.

Instead of being socialised into the family and kin network so important to Aboriginals, he had been 'socialised' to survive in institutional communities. He was to spend nine years of the remaining nine years [and] eight months of his life in gaols, where he found greater opportunities for freedom and privacy than he had known for the previous eight years in juvenile homes. In gaol he was respected by staff and prisoners alike for his strong character, leadership, sporting prowess and artistic talent, and there he built his friendships and social relations. His five intervals of liberty, totalling only eight months, offered an environment with which he was ill-equipped to cope and little opportunity for employment or constructive activity. The first two occasions lasted two or three months, the rest only a few weeks. All but the last ended as a result of petty theft or illegal use of a motor car. The society which had deprived him of the opportunity to grow up in a family and learn to live in a free community offered him no assistance whatsoever in adjustment or rehabilitation but visited his every lapse with penal sentences. In many cases the sentences were extremely harsh.

Yet the bonds to his family formed in early childhood remained strong, and it was in a misguided attempt to assume the role of its protector that he committed his one serious crime, killing a man whom he believed to be ill-treating his sister. In gaol he had assumed the role of protector of weaker prisoners, but in his inexperience of life outside gaol, he so misjudged the situation that his distraught sister disowned him as a brother and other members of his family gave evidence against him. Returned to gaol, he was seen by his prisoner friends as a changed man, obsessed with religion he little understood and carrying a Bible he could not read. Burdened by guilt, he became psychotic and embarked on a series of self-mutilatory acts, culminating in his fatal third attempt to put out his eye in obedience to the Biblical text: 'If thy eye offend thee, pluck it out.'

His death is part of the abiding legacy of the appalling treatment of Aboriginals that went on well into the second half of this century in the name of protection or welfare. It is history, but history of critical importance today. It is history that few Australians know, and which our historians are only now piecing together.

Without a knowledge of it, we cannot hope to understand Aboriginal–White relations today, for they are deeply moulded by that history. We will not understand the ill-suppressed hatred which many Aboriginals feel towards police and their deep distrust of officialdom generally. We will fail to appreciate how many Aboriginal men and women there are now in the community carrying deep scars from that history, scars that prejudice not only their own lives but those of their children. We will run the risk that, as has happened so often, we will repeat the mistakes of the past.

The attempt to 'solve the Aboriginal problem' by the deliberate destruction of families and communities, which was the policy of the Aborigines Protection Board, and to some extent its successor, the Aborigines Welfare Board, not only wrecked individual lives but is seen by many Aboriginals as falling squarely within the modern definition of genocide. Few would openly advocate such policies today but, unless continuing positive steps are taken to understand and counteract them, there is a risk that long-standing racist attitudes will continue to influence the formulation and implementation even of more enlightened policies. In particular, it is essential to stop treating Aboriginals as dependent people, whose welfare is looked after by others who know better than they and give them back the opportunities for self-reliance, independence and self-respect that were so cruelly taken away and denied them for most of the last 200 years.

So long as Aboriginals are being detained and imprisoned at 10 to 20 times the rate of non-Aboriginals, many will die in custody. So long as Aboriginals live in depressed communities without equal opportunities and hope for the future, so long as they remain an alienated, dispossessed people embittered by wrongs that have not been recognised or redressed, they will continue to come in conflict with the law and be taken into custody. So long as Aboriginals outside custody are dying 20 years and more earlier than non-Aboriginals, as the result of a high incidence of lifestyle diseases, and of the alcoholism and violence which the stresses and frustrations of their lives produce, many will inevitably die in custody as well.

General community attitudes underpin government policies and the work of police, courts and prisons. They are often expressed in hurtful actions by insensitive and uninformed people. There is need for increasing public awareness of the history of Aboriginal affairs and the factors presently operating, including the insidious effect of often unconscious racism. It is my hope that this report and other reports of the Commission will contribute to that result.

## David Gundy: Lawless policing

*The investigation and report into David Gundy's death was one of Hal's most difficult. This was not a standard death in custody. David Gundy died when a shotgun, held by Sergeant Terry Dawson who burst into Mr Gundy's bedroom early one morning, discharged when he grabbed it and the officer pulled back. Police were looking for John Porter, who had shot at two police officers, killing one. Mr Gundy had only a tangential, non-criminal connection with Porter. The warrant to search his house was obtained unlawfully.*

*Hal's report again distinguished between human agency and social structures. No blame was attached to Terry Dawson, whose bravery was acknowledged. But that was not enough: the officer should never have been there. There was no legal authority for the raid. Hal's criticism was directed at the senior officers who treated the need to have legal authority for their actions as a tiresome constraint to be slipped. In this respect, there is a strong connection between Hal's critique and the Wood Commission's disclosure of the process corruption besetting the NSW Police.[6] Several officers involved in Mr Gundy's death would later attract the critical attention of the Wood Commission. The survival of undesirable elements of police culture beyond the Wood Commission because of the NSW Government's limited adoption of its reform agenda indicates the continuing relevance of Hal's warnings about police and law.*

David John Gundy, a 29-year-old Aboriginal man, died as a result of receiving a wound prior to 6 am on 27 April 1989 when a police shotgun discharged in his bedroom during an unlawful police raid on his home. Police had no legal right to be in his home at all, much less to point a loaded and cocked shotgun at him. Sergeant Dawson, who held the shotgun, had no intention of injuring David Gundy and was no more to blame than other police involved in planning and carrying out the unlawful raid. He was a senior member of a small elite of permanent SWOS (Special Weapons and Operations Section), police who were dedicated to courageously carrying out dangerous assignments but lacked the humility to consider the lawfulness of their methods. Even now they continue to see the incident as a one-off, unforeseeable event for which David Gundy, if anyone, was responsible. They allowed their enthusiasm for their task to lead them to make serious misjudgments and to treat SWOS guidelines, the Police Instructions, and the law and its processes disdainfully. Regrettably, to this day, police have refused to recognise the shortcomings in the training and methods of SWOS, the unlawfulness of the raid or the patent untruth on which it was based. Instead, they have sought to denigrate and blame David Gundy for what happened, although he was in truth a law-abiding, hard-working family man. It is in the nature of things that a unit such as SWOS will develop a very high degree of self-esteem, confidence and certainty about its own proficiency and rectitude. But the downside of this necessary confidence is the risk of self-satisfaction, self-righteousness, arrogance and lack of concern for the law. One detects an assumption that the law will look after police acting to catch a serious criminal, and inconvenient legal rules can be safely ignored. Police felt entitled to make their own law. [Officers in units such as SWOS] must have complete commitment to what they are doing and complete faith in the superiority of their cause over that of those against whom they pit themselves. While this produces qualities of bravery, loyalty and dedication to duty which are admirable within their context, it also produces a high degree of self-righteousness which easily progresses to arrogance and a tunnel vison which leaves little room for respect for dissent or conflict of opinion, or for political, legal or moral restraints which stand in the way of what is seen to be the task in hand.

## Clarrie Nean: Alcohol and dispossession

Clarence Alec Nean junior ('Clarrie') a 33-year-old Aboriginal man, died at Dubbo Base Hospital at 9.30 pm on 15 August 1982. He had collapsed earlier that day in Walgett Police Station, where he was spending four days on a warrant for non-payment of a fine of $80, imposed for taking a tin of sardines and sauce valued at $1.07 from a local supermarket while he was intoxicated.

No blame can be attached to the police in whose care he was, nor to the ambulance officers, hospital staff and doctors who treated him after he collapsed. He died of a brain haemorrhage. His death was the culmination of a life that had been tragically shaped by the circumstances in which he and his parents and Aboriginals generally lived, and ended with years reduced to futility by his addiction to alcohol. The offence for which he was placed in custody was committed under the influence of alcohol, and the fall that led to his death was probably the result of alcohol withdrawal.

The most useful question that can be asked is what is there in the background of this man that casts light on why he was a chronic alcoholic at the age 33? From a study of the large number of official files in which his life is documented, and the evidence of living witnesses, two major stresses on the development of his self-esteem and the integration of his personality emerge. One is his highly disturbed childhood, in which he spent nine of his first 15 years in a series of foster homes and institutions. The other, itself linked to the first, is the stress of growing up as an Aboriginal in a society in which Aboriginals were marginalised, denigrated and denied dignity and control of their lives by a racist bureaucracy. The Aboriginals of north-western NSW were brutally dispossessed of their land in the early 1840s and their resistance mercilessly crushed by the end of that decade. Left with no land on which to find food and live, they became dependent on white settlers who used their labour for a minimum return and exploited the women. Later, the Aborigines Protection Board established stations on which they could live under the control of its managers and small reserves where they could live under the supervision of the police. They were left with no rights to control their own lives or those of their children, and it was difficult to escape dependence on the official and private white community and frequent humiliation at its hands. One of the few temporary escapes available was the consumption of alcohol, the illegality of which served to cement the power of police over them.

## Mark Quayle: 'A most peculiar custody'

*Mark Quayle was taken to hospital in Wilcannia, suffering from alcohol withdrawal. Medical staff called police, who took him away from the hospital and locked him in a dark cell where he hanged himself. Hal later referred to this case as a definitive example of an Aboriginal person being treated as less than human.[7]*

While no other person intended or took part in his death, it resulted from shocking and callous disregard for his welfare on the part of a hospital sister, a doctor of the Royal Flying Doctor Service and two police officers. I find it impossible to believe that so many experienced people could have been so reckless in the care of a seriously ill person dependent on them, were it not for the dehumanised stereotype of Aboriginals so common in Australia and in the small towns of western NSW in particular. In that stereotype a police cell is a natural and proper place for an Aboriginal.

There is not the slightest reason to believe that any other person was directly involved in his death. Indirectly, however, the responsibility for his death lies on Sister Heathcote, Dr Ryan and Constables Coombs and Morris, all of whom acted in breach of their legal, professional and moral duties towards a person who was in their care and dependent on their proper attention. But while their conduct has to be examined and assessed, it would be wrong to smugly scapegoat them as monstrous individuals. Underlying their uncaring conduct, which treated Mark as less than an equal human being, are attitudes to Aboriginals which are widespread, not only among police and in hospitals, but in the wider community. His death is a challenge to the conscience of all Australians.

## Harrison Day: The past and the future

Harrison Day, an Aboriginal in his early 40s, died on 23 June 1982 in Echuca District Hospital, where he was taken from Echuca Police Station in the throes of an epileptic fit. It is clear that there was no violence or foul play associated with his death, and none was alleged. The concern of his Aboriginal friends and relatives is of a different kind. They believe that the police must have known that Harrison, whom they frequently locked up, was an epileptic. Was he, they ask, treated with due regard to his condition, which called for regular medication and for close observation so that he would receive immediate assistance if he fitted? ...

A descendant of proud Yoti Yoti ancestors who courageously resisted the taking of their lands a century and a half ago, and a skilled bushman and a kind and gentle man, Harrison Day stands in a 200-year tradition going back to Bennelong, of upstanding, well-adjusted Aboriginals from whom the white invasion took land, livelihood and independence and gave instead alcohol and disease. That after 200 years we had no better answer for his situation than the revolving doors of courts, police cells, hotels and hospitals is a great indictment of our imagination and of our humanity. It illustrates how systemic oppression of Aboriginals can remain entrenched in institutions, even in the guise of impersonal application of laws applying equally to all.

# THE REGIONAL REPORT
## The enduring effect of the past on the present

A number of people of goodwill have asked me what I have to tell them after my two-and-a-half years' experience as a Royal Commissioner inquiring into Aboriginal deaths in custody. I answer their question in this way. While it is important to divert Aboriginals from custody, to make their custody safer, and to ensure that any deaths are properly investigated, the great challenge to this country is to eliminate the grossly disproportionate rate of incarceration of Aboriginal people. How is this to be done? It does not take much close contact with Aboriginal people to convince one that the explanation for their disproportionate conflict with the criminal justice system does not lie in greater viciousness and criminality of character in comparison with the rest of society. One encounters as much gentleness, kindness, integrity and desire for a peaceful life among them as among the rest of the population.

What does become clear is that most Aboriginals have a continuing identity as Aboriginals which sets them apart culturally and historically as a separate community of people, encapsulated within a larger community. Relations between those two communities are built on inequality arising from a long-standing, unresolved injustice and tensions which result from it affect the lives of individuals and communities in all kinds of ways. The dominant white community has over two centuries mostly tried to deal with the issue by destroying the Aboriginal identity – either by physical extermination or by genetic or cultural absorption. Even today many of those who accept that a major effort must be made to overcome Aboriginal disadvantage in matters such as health, education, employment and so on accept this only on the basis that there must be only one people recognised in Australia, and that any assistance to Aboriginals is not to enable their separate flowering as a people within the country but to help them 'catch up' and 'be like us'.

Royal Commission into Aboriginal Deaths in Custody (Regional Report of
    Inquiry in New South Wales, Victoria and Tasmania, 1991) 8, 17–18.

Early in my inquiries, I formed a strong conviction that a concentration solely on the immediate circumstances of individual deaths would not be very rewarding in terms of the understanding it would give of why Aboriginals were in custody and dying in custody. It soon became clear that the greatest reason why so many Aboriginals died in custody was that there were so many Aboriginals in custody. They were being locked up at quite staggering rates. Once one excluded the hypothesis that Aboriginal deaths in custody were the result of systematic murder or ill-treatment by police officers and prison officers, all that could be learnt from the immediate circumstances of particular deaths were points of safe and humane custodial procedures and cell design. While these matters are important, they are for the most part not matters of peculiar application to Aboriginals. They involve matters which were just as important in relation to non-Aboriginal prisoners – matters such as the elimination from cells of potential hanging points, the regular inspection of prisoners, the seeking of medical attention for unconscious or non-rousable prisoners, alertness for the existence of other conditions masked by alcohol or other drugs, a humane reaction to disturbed, depressed or angry prisoners and so on. All of these require attention, but in large measure they can be readily discerned once one starts to examine deaths in custody ... Many of them have received attention by custodial authorities around the country, although there is still much room for improvement.

Putting to one side these procedural and architectural issues, what could be learnt from the study of the deaths that might increase understanding of why Aboriginals are coming into custody and as a result are dying in custody in such large numbers? ... I concluded that the most fruitful way of studying the individual deaths was to see each death not as an isolated event but in the context of, and indeed as the culmination of, a life. Because of the extraordinary level of institutionalisation, supervision and incarceration that has been imposed on the Aboriginal population, it was possible to learn a great deal about the life story of each individual who had died from files that were readily accessible. Of course one has to be wary of taking these materials, compiled almost entirely by white public servants, at their face value … Often official records and reports tell more about the person who wrote them, and that person's attitude to the Aboriginal subject, than they do about the Aboriginal. However, the files often contain enough clues to give a glimpse of what was going on and one can soon learn to 'read between the lines'. Usually, somewhere in the files, there are some observations from some perceptive officer whose comments reveal the limited viewpoints of others. In addition, in most cases, it has been possible to supplement the material on the files with statements or evidence from other people who knew the Aboriginal concerned, and particularly from his friends or relatives.

My hope was that a careful use of available material would yield some insight into the way in which the circumstances of Aboriginal life in Australia, the cultural patterns of the Aboriginals themselves, and the policies and institutions of the dominant society which had dispossessed them, interacted to produce the situation where that individual had ended up in custody and died in custody instead of achieving some happier outcome to his life. The knowledge so gained … does enable their lives to be looked at as a whole, their communities to be looked at as a whole and the critical events of their lives to be seen in the context of a range of factors. The relations of Aboriginals and Aboriginal communities with the dominant white society then emerged as the most important of the factors for explaining what was happening.

My first, and I believe my most successful attempt to place a death in the context of a life, was in the Report of the Inquiry into the Death of Malcolm Charles Smith. This report generated an extraordinary reaction in the media, and the story of Malcolm Smith has continued to touch the hearts and imagination of many people. It brought out … the shattering effect on Aboriginal lives of the well-intentioned but self-righteous and culturally arrogant policies of taking Aboriginal children away from their families and seeking to shape them by institutionalisation to conform to the standards and expectations of white society. The institutions of the dominant society did succeed in severing Malcolm's ties over the critical years of adolescence and youth with the deprived Aboriginal family that had let him often run free, unwashed and undisciplined instead of attending school, but had given him love, warmth, self-esteem and a chance to be a member of a social group. But society achieved this severance only at the cost of making Malcolm a person who was adjusted solely to life in institutions and remained locked up for almost his entire life.

The attempt to understand the life of Malcolm Smith was particularly successful partly because of the dramatic nature of his story, the wealth of material available, and the impact he had made on people who remembered him, but also because of the amount of time I was able to give to studying and writing his story. As the number of reports to be written built up and deadlines approached, I was not able to give the same attention to all. However, in a further 16 reports I was able in a greater or lesser degree to put the death in the context of a life story.

In my 18th report, that on the death of David John Gundy, I did not place such emphasis on the life of the man who died. The hearing and the writing of the report took place under very severe time pressures, and the amount of material relating to his death, as a result of previous investigations, was overwhelming. But in any event, I did not consider his life as relevant to his death as was the case with the others on whose deaths I reported. His death was not the consequence of the working out of factors in his own life. The temporary custody in which he met his death was not something to which his life and his past conduct had led him. It was accidental that he was the victim of an arrogant and unlawful police raid by officers who neither knew nor cared who might be in the house they were raiding. Consequently, it seemed to me more important in the little time available to me to write the report, to seek to understand the culture of the police which led them to make a fruitless and unjustified raid on his home, rather than the cultural background that had led to David Gundy being in that particular house at that particular moment …

Anyone who attempts to write about Aboriginals in modern Australia must be conscious of the limitations of what can be achieved, the risks of misinterpreting, of ending up in gross simplification or suffocating detail, and the inevitability of hostile reactions from those on one side or another, or on both sides, whose sensitivities are affronted.

However distasteful it be to admit, there is a cultural or racial divide in Australia, on one side of which there is the Aboriginal community (itself an aggregation of many smaller communities) and on the other side the non-Aboriginal communities, with all the complexities and subcultures of which it is composed. Almost anyone who seeks to write will be on one side of that divide or the other and will be conditioned by personal and cultural experience to see certain things and interpret them in certain ways.

There is a view popular in some quarters, both Aboriginal and non-Aboriginal, that non-Aboriginals have no right or capacity to write about Aboriginals. While it is proper to be conscious of how any individual writer's account and interpretation is shaped and constricted by his or her life experience, the denial of anyone's right to discuss a matter must be rejected. What [is] desperately needed are people on both sides of the divide trying to understand each other. Indeed, what is most needed is that people on both sides of the divide should try to understand and write about the divide itself, what put it there, what keeps it there, what its consequences are, and how it can be bridged.

Few white Australians understand how racism continues to affect Aboriginals and what an all-pervasive part of their experience it is. If there is to be a real change in the position of Aboriginals in Australian society, the non-Aboriginal community has to develop an understanding of the widespread, insidious, dehumanising and debilitating effects of racism and work to reduce its influence. The many Aboriginals working constructively for the advancement of their people in their own organisations and communities and government departments, or eloquently pleading their people's cause in the media or through books and plays, or winning the world's esteem for their art, have shattered the stereotype of the unsophisticated Aboriginal who was for so long the butt of the cartoonists' cheap racism. For all but the most prejudiced, they have also shattered the stereotype of the noisy, drunken, importunate and untidy Aboriginal in the parks or streets who, although usually a small minority in any community, was often the only Aboriginals noticed by most whites. However, it is by no means clear that the old stereotypes are being replaced by realistic knowledge.

Most Aboriginals remain conscious of their identity as a people – the original people of Australia – and continue to seek recognition of that identity. The dominant European community has stumbled from one approach to another in relation to Aboriginals – extermination, exploitation, segregation pending extinction, forced assimilation, 'expected' assimilation, assimilation 'chosen' but without alternatives, and 'integration', the last an unclear concept often hard to distinguish in practice from assimilation. In more recent times there has been adoption of policies such as self-management and self-determination but limited success in giving them real content. Not the least part of the problem is that Aboriginals have for so long been cut off from power, from control of their own lives and communities, and from the exercise of authority and management of resources and institutions that it is not easy for them to suddenly meet the often unrealistic and inappropriate expectations and requirements of white officialdom. Until very recently there has been virtually no willingness to recognise Aboriginals as a dispossessed people with whom a just reconciliation should be sought ...

White Australians have shied away from confronting these issues, sometimes in complete ignorance of the past treatment of Aboriginals in this country, sometimes fearful of a challenge to the legitimacy of the white occupation of Australia, sometimes for the protection of vested interests which they see as possibly threatened by the recognition of Aboriginal rights, sometimes for racist reasons, sometimes in an arrogant ethno-centric rejection of cultural pluralism, and sometimes in an unjust and unrealistic invocation of ideas of equality. But the issue will not go away. It will only grow as an issue of conscience, justice, civil harmony and international reputation.

The great lesson that stands out is that non-Aboriginals, who currently hold virtually all the power in dealing with Aboriginals, have to give up the usually well-intentioned efforts to do things for or to Aboriginals, to give up the assumption that they know what is best for Aboriginals, and to stop treating Aboriginals as aberrant or backward individuals who have to be led, educated, manipulated and re-shaped into the image of the dominant community. Instead, Aboriginals must be recognised for what they are, a people in their own right with their own culture, history, values and right to take part on an equal footing in finding their place in Australia.

They are a people who through the processes of colonisation were stripped of resources and, in south-eastern Australia at least, had their culture changed almost beyond recognition. Nevertheless, they have retained and value, and are entitled to respect for, their distinct Aboriginal identity. They have maintained their identity and their culture in the face of deliberate attempts to destroy it, and in the face of having to live in a situation where economic, political and social power, control of resources, control of the media, control of education, control of employment and indeed most forms of power have been vested in the competing dominant culture.

What is needed is a redress of that balance so that there is genuine respect and genuine room for Aboriginal culture and identity. This must be accompanied by a real transfer of resources to the people who were so cruelly deprived of them, and it must be a real transfer to their control, not the use of resources to manipulate their responses in a way congenial to the dominant culture.

## REFLECTIONS ON THE ROYAL COMMISSION

Reflecting on the Royal Commission more than 20 years after it finished, I realise that many of my readers will have come to political consciousness and lived in a world in which Aboriginals are always in the news, always a source of national anxiety and a challenge to Australia's international credentials. They may assume that the Royal Commission was established as part of this ongoing concern, to find answers to the deepening Aboriginal malaise that still defies solution today. Let me give some perspective.

For nearly 50 years I lived in the Great Australian Silence,[8] and its corollary, the Great Aboriginal Invisibility. Different events brought them to an end for different people. For me they vanished in 1970 when

I met a brilliant group of charismatic young Aboriginals and found a niche working with them to establish the first Aboriginal Legal Service.

For many other Australians, the Silence and the Invisibility were shattered in 1972 by the magisterial voice of Gough Whitlam, whose government ushered in what was conceived as a period of self-determination, exemplified in the thousands of government-funded but Aboriginal-controlled organisations that appeared in following years, and the Woodward Report as a first step in the realisation of land rights.

Before long, it became apparent that the Great Australian Silence and the Great Aboriginal Invisibility had been only episodes in a more enduring and frequently recurring phenomenon, which I will call the Great Australian Complacency. Once it became clear that the Fraser Government did not intend to dismantle the Whitlam legacy, Aboriginal issues fell out of focus for many people, including myself. Solutions, it seemed, were in hand, and one could focus on other issues – the environment, multiculturalism, the Murdoch takeover, Indonesia or whatever.

What should have been worrying signs, among them the growing campaign stemming from John Pat's death in custody at Roebourne in 1983,[9] went largely unnoticed. In 1987, a confident nation looked forward to celebrating its bicentenary the following year with head held high.

The Complacency was interrupted by Moral Panic as deaths in custody unexpectedly became news. In the first half of the year, 11 Aboriginal deaths in custody, five by hanging, set the stage for a horrifying denouement. In just six weeks between 24 June and 6 August 1987 there were five Aboriginal deaths in custody, all by hanging, and four in police cells. As death after inexplicable death hit the headlines, anxiety and bewilderment grew. Was it credible that so many, mostly young, Aboriginal men would hang themselves, and how could they do so unaided with the meagre resources of a prison cell?

Unwilling to accept a growing Aboriginal belief that police were resuming an old policy of killing Aboriginals, but having no explanation of their own, governments sought to clear the air with the knee-jerk appointment of a Royal Commission to inquire into every Aboriginal death in custody since the 1 January 1980 and into the way they had been investigated at the time.

More than 100 families became convinced that they had lost a member in a death covered by the terms of reference and their expectations of an exhaustive inquiry into those deaths became a governing factor in subsequent events. It was not possible for governments to call off inquiries when it became clear that it was not difficult for an unaided prisoner to hang himself and that Aboriginal prisoners were not hanging themselves, or otherwise taking their lives, at a greater rate than non-Aboriginal prisoners.

What cried out for investigation was not the likelihood of foul play but why so many Aboriginals were falling foul of the justice system and spending time in custody. This was not the purpose for which the Commission had been established and governments were naturally cautious in expanding what was already proving to be a mammoth task: in effect around 100 Royal Commissions into separate deaths, each occurring in its own peculiar circumstances. Eventually it was accepted that the newly identified central issue could not be ignored, and a grudging amendment to the National Commissioner's terms of reference made clear by implication that it was part of his task to report on 'underlying issues associated with the deaths'.[10] It read more like an afterthought – as indeed it was – than a change in the Commission's focus, but it was the hook on which Commissioner Johnston hung most of his massive five-volume report ...

It was only the National Commissioner's terms of reference that received this modest amendment, and he was provided with a research unit to assist him. The rest of us (apart from Patrick Dodson, a non-lawyer who was later appointed with the specific task of investigating underlying issues in Western Australia) remained focused on meticulous inquiry into individual deaths and their subsequent investigation. When in the course of our inquiries we encountered material that might assist Commissioner Johnston in his additional task, as we inevitably did, we recorded it in our reports to him.

Each Commissioner was free to adopt his own style of reporting. My view was that I could best contribute to a national understanding of what was happening if I presented the death I had investigated as the culmination of a life lived in shaping circumstances, rather than an isolated event. By serendipity, my first report, about Malcolm Smith, was released on a day when news was slack and was read by *The Age*'s Canberra reporter. As a result, it attracted considerable media attention and commentary, and even became the subject of a popular song and a documentary film.[11] Later reports, released in Spartan format at strategically selected times by governments with no desire to encourage the airing of critical comment, often disappeared with little trace.

Nevertheless, enough filtered out in the Commission's many individual death reports to create some receptivity for the culmination of its work in Commissioner Johnston's monumental National Report. Like everyone who worked close to this gentle, kindly man, with his dry wit and passionate dedication to justice, I developed not only affection, but also a deep respect for his courage and dedication. The conception and writing of the National Report required both.

Some elements of the National Report were given. Drawing on the individual death reports, it had to describe the immediate circumstances and causes of the deaths, and the adequacy of their investigation. While in a small number of cases the cause of death has remained controversial for some people, the findings of the Commission and the recommendations flowing from them have been generally accepted. The great issue confronted by Commissioner Johnston and his latter-day critics was how far and in what directions it was appropriate for the National Report to go in discussing issues 'underlying' the deaths.

Cultural determinists like Gary Johns argue that the Report should have recognised that the Aboriginal condition was due to adherence to an outmoded culture and have been concerned to recommend and facilitate the shedding of that culture in favour of 'the' modern culture.[12] His criticisms naively treat cultures as if they were items of clothing to be donned and doffed at will and would make assimilation the overriding aim of policy.

The criminologist Don Weatherburn argues that the issue should have been treated as a criminological one within the relatively narrow bounds of practical criminology and criticises the National Report for being more ambitious.[13] Along with Noel Pearson, he has wrongly assumed that the National Report failed to highlight alcohol and other issues playing major causal roles in relation to Aboriginal imprisonment.[14]

Noel Pearson, who has been by far the most powerful intellectual contributor to the Aboriginal policy debate in recent years, has varied in his policy emphases but places priority on the issues of alcohol, welfare dependence, education and economic development. Despite his predilection for disparaging the National Report, his priorities do not conflict with its priorities.

I have argued elsewhere that Noel Pearson's real complaint is that instead of headlining his issues of priority, the National Report headlined the historic destruction of Aboriginal society by European intrusion and the continuing disempowerment of Aboriginal people that followed.[15] While he would agree on the importance of this history, Pearson is able to take its recognition for granted in a way the Commission could not. It was in part the work of the Commission itself, along with the High Court's *Mabo* decision the following year,[16] and the ongoing messages of the 'new historians' and the reconciliation movement, that there is a general recognition that Aboriginal disadvantage is not the result of Aboriginal inferiority and shortcoming, but of a history of dispossession, institutionalisation, and continuing disempowerment. This has cleared the way for a more open and rational discussion of what may be done to change the Aboriginal condition.

Elliott Johnston's strategy was to use the recognition of historical disadvantage as the launching pad for a national call on all Australians, black and white, to join together for a massive and holistic attack on all aspects of Aboriginal disadvantage. He relied neither on guilt nor denigration, but on the sense of justice and fair play he believed to be present in mainstream Australian society, and on the desire and willingness to take control over their own lives that he believed to be present but stifled in Aboriginal communities.

It was not an empty rhetorical call that the National Report made. It was backed by a detailed program to tackle every major aspect of the overall disadvantage found in the Aboriginal society that was producing the candidates for deaths in custody. Whether the problem was related to alcohol and drug abuse, unemployment, education, children and youth, health, housing, community infrastructure, policing, the effect of imprisonment, service delivery, community reconciliation, or the fulfilment of international obligations, the National Report sought to provide what was in effect a manual of best practice, based on the advice of recognised experts in the various fields, and the lessons of the Commission's own vast inquiry into particular lives and deaths in custody.

The 339 recommendations of the National Report were not an unprioritised wish list. They were framed by a five-volume discussion examining each issue, its importance and its relevance to other issues. Two issues come to stand out as one reads the Report as a whole. One is the destructive and undermining effect of alcohol abuse, the subject to which two chapters are devoted and which pervades many other chapters.[17] The Report does not treat Aboriginals as mere victims of alcohol but as people who must take responsibility for their use of it, and major recommendations relate to giving Aboriginal communities effective control over its availability.[18]

The issue that received the greatest emphasis of all was the importance of delivering the assistance that Aboriginal communities need in ways that did not perpetuate or reinforce the dependence and disempowerment that had characterised government policies in the past. Commissioner Johnston saw an ingrained pattern of white domination in policymaking, service delivery and community relations that had survived the years of so-called self-determination. He targeted this disempowerment, advocating an end of domination and the return of control of their lives and communities to Aboriginal hands.[19] This is reflected in recommendation after recommendation.

Twenty years later, people ask what has been the effect of the Royal Commission? There [is] no doubt that in relation to its original and central focus, the Commission has resulted, despite the odd egregious exception,[20] in much better care of all at-risk prisoners, black and white, and much more thorough and transparent investigation of the deaths that do occur.

In relation to the many specific areas of disadvantage on which the Report made recommendations, I have no qualification to speak in detail.

However, over the years I have heard little informed criticism of the specialised recommendations and have often had Aboriginals volunteer how useful the recommendations have been to them in seeking support for particular programs.

It is common for Aboriginal and other critics to make a broad-brush complaint that the recommendations of the Commission have not been implemented. Establishing how far this is true would require a detailed study of many areas of policy, and so far as I know, this has not been done. If the task were to be undertaken, it would require judgments about what was effective implementation, which would likely be exceedingly controversial.

One early study of Commonwealth implementation that I made for the Aboriginal and Torres Strait Islander Social Justice Commissioner highlighted that what was claimed to be implementation was often expensive bureaucratic activity that produced little or no impact on the ground.[21] It is pleasing to find 14 years later that, while the anarchic, unproductive and self-justifying character of bureaucratic activity on which I stumbled in 1994 still marks Aboriginal policy, it is now the subject of serious academic study.[22] It is clearly problematic to argue from the limited success of its bureaucratic implementation that the National Report was itself defective.

Certainly, some key messages of the National Report have been decisively rejected in practice. Its guiding principle, that Aboriginals should at every point be given as much control as possible over their own lives, has been spectacularly abandoned in the Northern Territory Intervention.[23] The idea that imprisonment should be a punishment of last resort has been negated as Aboriginals have been caught up in wave after wave of vengeful and self-defeating law and order policies that have filled prisons with inmates of all kinds. This has been one, although by no means the sole, reason that figures for Aboriginal imprisonment have gone through the roof.

High rates of imprisonment remain today, as the Commission found 20 years ago, not as an isolated feature of Aboriginal society, but as an integral part of communities characterised by many interacting features that are judged distressingly disadvantageous and dysfunctional by mainstream society. A brief return of the Great Australian Complacency after the Royal Commission and the *Mabo* decision was strongly challenged, particularly by Noel Pearson.[24] It again ended in Moral Panic, notably expressed in the way in which the Northern Territory Intervention has been conceived and implemented.

There are many strongly expressed opinions about the depth of the malaise in Aboriginal society and what is required to remedy it, but apart from a few areas where statistics speak louder than words, remarkably little research-based evidence exists to found these opinions. Like other commentators, I am left to speculate. I find myself coming back to the conclusion that Commissioner Johnston reached about what he regarded as the most important prerequisite for the success of his program.

He nominated three essential prerequisites for success.[25] The second was assistance from the broader society and the third was the delivery of that assistance in a manner that did not create welfare dependence. However, the first and the most crucial was the desire and capacity of Aboriginal people to put an end to their disadvantaged situation and to take control of their own lives. He affirmed a passionate conviction that they would do so, based on the number of initiatives they had taken and were taking at the time. He gave many examples.[26] In other words he proceeded on the assumption that Aboriginals wanted to make, and given the chance would make, substantial efforts to achieve what the mainstream community regards as desirable change or 'progress', that they wanted to embrace modernity, 'to be like us'.

Many of course do and have gone on to join what we could call a very successful Aboriginal middle class. They are not part of what is conceived as the problem: those who have been left behind in many bounded Aboriginal communities, and in some city and rural town populations.[27] The assumption that these people are willing, indeed anxious, to be 'like us' was not peculiar to Commissioner Johnston but is shared by his critics and supporters alike. He differed from the rest of us only in feeling the need to give reasons for his assumption; most of us treat the superiority and compelling attractiveness of our way of life as requiring no argument.

However, it is undeniable that, even when opportunities are available, many Aboriginals show little inclination to seek or persist with paid employment, to make the changes to their lifestyles recommended in the interests of achieving a longer and healthy life, to follow medical regimes, to renounce the established rites of passage through conflict with police and imprisonment, to live in nuclear families in unshared houses on unshared incomes, to insist that reluctant children go to school every day, or to forego the pleasures of alcoholic socialising.

Why this is so has been much debated by Australian anthropologists in recent years with no conclusive outcome,[28] and I am not qualified to offer one. I wonder, however, whether we underestimate and fail to understand how difficult and complex is the transition from an egalitarian hunter-gatherer society, in which one's only capital is social capital in the form of interpersonal relationships, to a modern capitalist society based on individual accumulation. As one observes the continued indifference of many Aboriginal people to what are generally considered benefits of modernity, as well as to its authority, one is reminded of Clastres' view of hunter-gatherer society as a site of resistance to state-formation.[29]

Looking down from the heights of modernity, it is easy to fail to realise the warmth and joys and satisfactions of lives that we see only as distressed and dysfunctional, and that surrendering them may be a price that people may not be willing to pay for the problematic advantages of modernity. Perhaps it is not surprising that many Aboriginals do not respond to the stifling solicitude or ill-concealed contempt of smug advisers and administrators who patently regard their communities, their way of life, their social bonds, their mutual caring and sharing, their emphasis on personal autonomy, their deep ties to country and much that makes them what they are, as at best valueless or unfortunate handicaps, at worst the stigma of inferiority and depravity. The resistance to progress that mainstream society pathologises may to them be a defence of what they experience as 'havens in a heartless world'.[30]

White Australia has always had difficulty in finding either an ear with which to listen to Aboriginal Australia or a voice in which to speak to it. One remembers Stanner as a rare example of a person who had an ear to listen and the rarer ability to distil what he heard to a wider white world.[31] It is not easy to listen to Aboriginals, for they have no spokesperson and speak with many voices and have learnt to be distrustful. It takes time and patience and rapport, things that are hard to muster in bureaucracies, so the listening and interpreting has usually to be done outside government. It is not a fly-in fly-out task on the relatively useless consultation model.

Two of the most successful occasions on which white Australia found a voice to speak to Aboriginal Australia were Paul Keating's Redfern speech and Kevin Rudd's Apology. But it is not enough to apologise for past failures. If we want Aboriginals to listen, we must be able to talk about a future, not just an inevitable future on our model, but a future that recognises the value of Aboriginal society for those who live in it, and their view of an acceptable future.

Can Australia offer a future that does not just provide a path for individual Aboriginals to leave their communities and be integrated into mainstream society, but a future for Aboriginal communities in today's world? Jon Altman and his colleagues in the Centre for Aboriginal Economic Policy Research have argued for the viability of a hybrid economy, part subsistence and part market-based, to underwrite a future for remote communities.[32] Noel Pearson has sought to build in Cape York the institutional basis for an Aboriginal society that can control alcohol, promote individual responsibility, achieve high educational outcomes and develop an economic base which allows its members to live in both worlds.[33]

Commissioner Johnston would have been happy with either outcome, as long as it was the result of Aboriginal choices. Perhaps both are doomed to failure, as the cultural determinists and neo-conservative economists would argue. If that is so, it is hard to see a future other than continuing painful disintegration for many Aboriginal communities. If Commissioner Johnston proves to have been wrong when he rejected any 'doubt that Aboriginal people are capable of, determined to and will in fact exercise self-determination',[34] the National Report will in retrospect come to be seen as the great swansong of the self-determination era.

# ONE LAST MATTER

I get somewhat impatient with those who sanctimoniously point out that Indigenous incarceration rates have risen not fallen since the Royal Commission, as though it is the Commission's fault, and they are absolved of responsibility.[35] They speak as if the Commission had given them ointment to rub on a wound and it hadn't healed. There are no magic ointments or silver bullets for complex social problems, and the Commission never claimed to have one. It examined the deaths and the lives of 99 people who had died in custody. It told the stories of these 99 people and the history from which they and their communities had emerged so that it could be seen that these were not worthless people but fellow human beings who had been disadvantaged and suffered. It said that if people continued to live in deprived, disadvantaged and dysfunctional communities, imprisonment rates would continue to be high. It identified problems in these communities as seen by experts who had studied them, by the people who lived in them and by Commissioners who had spent three or four years of intense stress and effort listening to them. It identified what experts and the people themselves saw as the best way to tackle the problems. It said the most serious problem was alcohol and the most fruitful way of tackling it was by reducing its availability. Finally, it said you will never get anywhere unless you respect Aboriginal people, recognise their difference, and let them take control of their lives.

Our commissions expired, we went home and left it to you, those who hold power in Australian society. You, not the Commissioners, have been responsible for the last 20 years. What have you done in those 20 years? Have you done anything to reduce the availability of alcohol, or have you turned your head while profiteers go on exploiting Indigenous misery? Have you seriously tried to find constructive alternatives to the revolving gate of prison, or have you acquiesced in the expensive and inefficient punitive policies that always bear most harshly on the

'Reflections on the 20th Anniversary of the Royal Commission into Aboriginal Deaths in Custody' (2011) 7(27) *Indigenous Law Bulletin* 3–8.

disadvantaged? Have you kept abreast of changing problems in the communities and new expertise in tackling them? Have you engaged with Noel [Pearson]'s vision?

The National Report was not a revelation from on high, not a font of perennial wisdom, not the end of history, but a passing moment in it. It was a response to the problems of the time, by people of the time, using the tools of the time. Take what you can from it and move on. It is now your thinking, your imagination, your dedication and your professional commitment that is needed.

# 9

# *MABO*, NATIVE TITLE AND SQUANDERED OPPORTUNITIES

*In the iconic case of* Mabo,[1] *the High Court of Australia rejected the fiction of terra nullius and ruled that the continuance of native title was consistent with the common law's 'skeleton of principle'[2] and, consequently, with the Crown's radical property title. In his speech on being awarded an Honorary LLD by UNSW in 1994, Hal Wootten spoke bluntly about the significance of the* Mabo *case:*

> Mabo *compelled the non-Aboriginal Australian community to confront an issue that it had previously been able to ignore or misrepresent, namely that our nation has been built on the dispossession, often violently, brutally and cruelly, of the previous owners of Australia, the Aboriginal people, who still live among us as the most disadvantaged group in the community.[3]*

Mabo *launched Hal into 'one of the most hectic and demanding periods' of his life.[4] Outraged by the often ignorant and offensive criticism of judges who, by convention, could not answer back,[5] Hal engaged in a torrent of writing and public speaking. This ranged from scathing polemic to legal analysis to academic argument. His opponents should not be underestimated: people suggesting that the decision was the result of a communist plot may now sound absurd, but such claims were made by powerful members of the Australian establishment. Hal explicated the decision and its consequences to judges.[6] He explained to anthropologists the jurisprudence of the common law and judicial decision-making,[7] and also gave them some frank advice: 'the characteristic of anthropologists I wish to emphasise here is their frequent tendency to treat lawyers with undue deference and respect. If I could adapt the advice of two of our eminent politicians, don't let the bastards run over you, it is your job to keep them honest.'*[8] *He corrected the ahistorical claims of Professor Geoffrey Blainey.*[9] *Hal also commented on why these matters were being faced in the courts rather than in parliament, and the reasons for and limitations of doing so.*[10]

*Of the impacts of* Mabo *on Hal, two stand out. The first is that it led to the establishment of the National Native Title Tribunal to which Hal was appointed as Deputy President. The second is that, once again, Hal found himself in close contact with Aboriginal people for whom he had such respect and affection.*

*The material gathered in this chapter shows Hal's high regard for the High Court of Australia, his disappointment at the way in which the opportunities that its decision had opened were squandered, and his sense of a country changing, however grindingly slowly – and how lawyers' nudges contributed to that change.*

## THE LAWYERS' PROBLEM

The *Mabo* decision recognised that there are two systems of land law in Australia, and that there have been two ever since the British introduced the second in 1788. But the recognition did not offer equality; it is to the courts of the introduced system that Aboriginal people must turn for the recognition, registration and protection of their native title. In this process Aboriginal people, who have the most authoritative knowledge of native custom, will be dependent on the lawyers, who have the least ...

Lawyers coming from a common law background expect to find rights defined with a high degree of precision and certainty. They are used to ascertaining rights by reference to deliberately formulated rules to be found by recourse to authoritative written statements in legislation, case law or legal textbooks. The discipline of writing the rules down

Extracts from 'The End of Dispossession? Anthropologists and Lawyers in the Native Title Process' in J Finlayson and D Smith (eds), *Native Title* (Centre for Aboriginal Economic Policy Research, 1995), 106, 107, 112.

in a permanent form, and the constant exposure to interpretation in the courts, mean that they can usually be stated with a considerable degree of certainty as to their terms, even if they contain concepts the application of which leaves room for judgment and discretion.

Where rights in land are concerned, several centuries of capitalism and industrialism have worked to bring title to an individualised, alienable and recorded form so that it can be dealt with in a certain fashion as a security and a commodity. This entails certainty as to the exact scope of the rights of a clearly identifiable set of individuals at any given point, and certainty as to how that allocation of rights may be changed, including a clear definition of who may change them and how, and what will happen to those rights on the demise of one or more or all of the individuals. Those are the kinds of things that lawyers recognise as rights, and the sort of things that many lawyers will be expecting anthropologists to find.

In a non-literate, non-capitalist, non-industrial, relatively small, face-to-face subsistence society, the situation is very different.[11] The identity of the holders of rights in land, the nature of those rights, and the circumstances in which they may be acquired, lost, modified, transferred or succeeded to can only be determined by reference to oral tradition. Such a society does not have the same pressures for certainty. The face-to-face, rather than impersonal, nature of the society, and the relative unimportance of property other than land, which in any event is not a commodity, tends, especially in a hunter-gatherer society, to make personal relations much more important than property rights, sharing more socially valued than personal appropriation, and constant negotiation of relationships a normal feature of life. Precision as to boundaries, for example, may be critically important to agriculturists, industrialists or bankers, but not necessarily so for hunters and gatherers. On the other hand, the powerful forces associated with sacred sites may give the transgression of certain areas a significance rarely matched in a Western society ...

It is the natural tendency of lawyers to assimilate native title rights to the common law rights with which they are familiar. Communal title is foreign to them and can easily be overlooked or treated as of no importance. As already noted, the common law is individualistic and craves clear and certain definition of rights and operates in a society where land is a commodity with a value quantifiable in money terms. The Aboriginal relationship to land is communal, complex, often contingent and negotiable, and part of a spiritual as well as an economic order.

When an individual Aboriginal says, 'this is my land', all these things are taken for granted. The Aboriginal is not saying 'I have an indefeasible, alienable fee simple for which I am accountable to no one'. Rather he or she is asserting an important position in a complex web of relationships and responsibilities, in which people may have, as well as very definite rights, potential or contingent secondary rights which may or may not be asserted, and rights to ask or to negotiate which may or may not be exercised.

## A CHEER FOR THE *MABO* NUDGERS

What were the long-standing precedents which the High Court overruled? Cases in which the whites who had driven Aborigines off their land were squabbling among themselves about their titles! Never was the possibility of subsisting Aboriginal rights even considered; never was an Aboriginal represented. Some precedents!

Far from being an invention of the High Court, native land title has been recognised by European scholars since the 15th century and was given effect to in many countries. But unlike the United States, Canada and New Zealand, Australia proceeded on the assumption that its Indigenous people did not have a system of rights to land, with the most horrendous consequences when Aborigines tried to defend those rights against the settlers. An error born in ignorance and racial arrogance, the assumption became a lie when its falsity was exposed. In 1841, the head of the Colonial Office noted 'the important and unexpected fact that these tribes had proprietary rights to the Soil'.

'A Cheer for the Mabo Nudgers' (1993) 3(62) *Aboriginal Law Bulletin* 2.

In 1888, Sir Henry Parkes declined to invite Aborigines to the Centenary celebrations with the words: 'And remind them that we have robbed them?'. In 1992, there were pitifully few who had not been dispossessed, but a common law which prided itself on respect for property could hardly have denied them what by every honest reason was theirs.

We hear a lot about guilt these days, but only from people who are denying their guilt. Some say that they should not be called upon to do justice to Aborigines because they are not personally responsible for what happened to them. They work themselves into positive paroxysms of guiltlessness. In what other sphere of public affairs do we regard guilt as the only reason for action? ...

Many people gave the world little nudges in the direction of the *Mabo* decision. Aborigines and Islanders who had the courage and persistence to fight for their rights, lawyers who supported them in a hard slog over 12 years, citizens who encouraged them, are now being painted as the contemporary tools of a communist conspiracy. What a sinister bunch of little nudgers! Every bit as bad as that other six on the High Court! I salute them all.

As for the mining industry, it needs defending against some of the spokesmen who give it such a bad name. To listen to them ranting against conservationists and denigrating Aborigines you might think the industry was incurably destructive and racist. Don't be misled. Many parts of it are making great efforts to be environmentally sensitive, and some are learning to do business constructively with Aborigines.

# SHOULD THE HIGH COURT HAVE LEFT THE ISSUE TO PARLIAMENT?

## The limits of case law

Unlike legislatures, our courts do not have a free hand to craft solutions to the injustices that history has left in its trail. They cannot make fresh starts. Normally they apply the law or develop it in response to new problems or changing circumstances. One can sympathise with Justice Dawson, the only dissenter in *Mabo*, who concluded: 'If traditional land rights … are to be afforded …, the responsibility *both legal and moral*, lies with the legislature and not with the courts.'[12] However, as Justice Brennan drily observed five months later, 'Legislatures have disappointed the theorists' who maintain that it is the exclusive function of the legislature to reform the law and have left the courts with 'a substantial part of the responsibility for keeping the law in a serviceable state'.[13]

## The Court's responsibility

Did the Court transgress the limits of acceptable judicial action in shaping the law?[14] I would give an emphatic 'no'. The so-called precedents in my view barely qualified for this title and lacked cogency by normal tests. Nevertheless, the Court treated them with great seriousness because of their age and their relevance to property. However, overruling them did not fracture the essential skeleton of the law; indeed, in the absence of statute, the Court's doctrine of native title would have neither upset any existing title nor limited the Crown's freedom to dispose of land in the future. On the other hand, to endorse the existing understanding of the law would have meant endorsing a chapter of injustice in Australian history that was deeply troubling to the nation's conscience and damaging to its international reputation. It would have left the law in a state where unjust dispossession could continue in the future.

---

'Response to Lecture Delivered by Sir Gerard Brennan' (Speech, Hal Wootten Lecture, UNSW, 23 August 2012) <www.unsw.edu.au/law-justice/news-events/events/annual-hal-wootten-lecture>.

A different view of the law did not have to be invented. It was there in common law materials, to be found in Privy Council decisions relating to other parts of the British Empire, and the development of the common law in other jurisdictions, particularly the United States, New Zealand and Canada. The case for changing the law was overwhelming, and the means were at hand to do so by ordinary common law processes. Should the Court have left the task to the legislature?

The problem was one which had been created not by the legislature but by the courts themselves, and by inadvertence not deliberation. The issue of whether the law would protect the land rights of Aboriginals had only once been raised in the courts, in the 'Gove case',[15] and then before a single judge who did not have the High Court's authority to review the law. Otherwise, in so far as the courts had decided the question adversely to Aboriginals, they had done so without hearing them and considering their position, and hence in breach of natural justice.

The problem was therefore very much a judicial responsibility, and capable of being dealt with by ordinary judicial processes, without significant disruptive effects. The argument for leaving it to the legislature was essentially that the situation had existed for a long time. It was, however, not a problem that had readily lent itself to legislative solution. It was very much a national problem, in the sense that it was a nation-wide problem, but it was one which the national parliament had no power at all to tackle until 1967, and thereafter had found considerable difficulty in tackling without the agreement of all states. The Aboriginal people of Gove had gone to court only after parliament had failed to respond to their bark petition of 1963. It would not have lain well in the mouth of the judiciary to say that a problem created by judicial decision should be left to the legislature, when it was known as a matter of political reality that the chances of the legislature coming to grips with it in the foreseeable future were very slight.

Moreover, the Court would have been leaving the legislature to deal with the issue on a basis it considered wrong. By setting the law right in *Mabo*, the High Court did not take away the power of parliament to deal with the issue, which remained totally under the control of the Commonwealth and, subject to inconsistent federal laws, of state parliaments. The real complaint of the *Mabo* critics was not that the legislature was prevented from dealing with the issue, but that it was forced to confront it.

## *MABO* AT TWENTY

As *Mabo* recedes into history, memory becomes precious. My first memory of *Mabo,* 20 years later, is surprise, then admiration. Another 20 years before, Justice Blackburn's decision rejecting the possibility of common law native title did not surprise.[16] It simply confirmed what I had been taught at law school, and had never had reason to doubt, that the only source of title to land in Australia was the Crown. In the intervening years the *Aboriginal Land Rights (Northern Territory) Act 1976* and the NSW *Aboriginal Land Rights Act 1983* had served to confirm my assumption that the path to Aboriginal land rights lay in the political not the legal field.

So *Mabo* was humbling for me, and surprise was accompanied by admiration and respect both for the imagination, skill and devotion of the lawyers, led by Ron Castan QC, and for the judges who had had the courage, imagination and legal craftsmanship to find a way after two centuries to insist that the law recognise the obvious but long-ignored basic fact that Europeans had settled in a land occupied and owned by Aboriginal people.

I shared the view common among those who welcomed the decision that in itself *Mabo* would 'give rights to only a very small percentage of the indigenous population'.[17] However, it opened the way to new ways of imagining the nation, not only for 'whites', but also for Aboriginal people, who for the first time could stand on some firm moral high ground that did not depend on sympathy for disadvantage or victimhood.

---

Extracts from 'Mabo at Twenty: A Personal Retrospective' in Toni Bauman and Lydia Glick (eds), *The Limits of Change: Mabo and Native Title Twenty Years On* (Aboriginal Studies Press for AIATSIS, 2012) ch 34.

At 70, I had long ceased active practice as a lawyer, but an occasion to examine the judgments in detail soon came. Earlier, the Australian Conservation Foundation had initiated a study of the interaction of Aboriginal people and national parks, and I was asked to consider the impact of the *Mabo* decision. This led me to a detailed study of the decision, and its relation to the national parks legislation of each state and territory.[18] Much of the work I did was reduced to historical interest by subsequent legislation. However, my study of *Mabo* led me to make a general submission discussing the appropriate Commonwealth response, which I forwarded to the Prime Minister, members of federal Cabinet, and interested organisations in October 1992.[19]

I followed up on two concerns. One was that the process of recognition and registration of native title should not open the door to the fragmentation and privatisation of the traditional communal native title, as had happened with deleterious consequences in some overseas jurisdictions … This problem has been avoided in Australia. Under Part 3 of the *Native Title Act 1993* (Cth) (the Act), proceedings are focused on 'the native title claim group', embracing 'all the persons … who, according to their traditional laws and customs, hold the common or group rights and interests comprising the particular native title claimed' (s 61).

Another concern was with the conceptualisation of native title as a 'bundle of rights', rather than the robust undivided right of 'possession, occupation, use and enjoyment as against the whole world', which the High Court had declared in *Mabo*. Early in discussions of *Mabo*, commentators associated with the mining industry advocated the 'bundle of rights' concept, and some went on to opine that these rights consisted only of those that Aboriginal people had traditionally exercised: hunting and gathering yes, but mining and forestry no.[20] This view would freeze Aboriginal titles into museum pieces, I argued. Surely it is reasonable, where there is no express limitation or concurrent title shown, to assume that prima facie the occupiers of an area have a right to do anything lawful on it, whether the occasion or the capacity to do it has hitherto arisen or not.

It was suggested that the 'bundle of rights' was favourable to native title because it allowed the survival of a residual title in the case of a competing title that was partially inconsistent. However, I could see no reason why this required postulation of a bundle of rights; the law is familiar with the idea of a law or right being overridden 'to the extent of the inconsistency', without any need to reduce the subordinate law or right to a bundle of specific rights.

My concern that this conceptualisation of native title might be written into the draft legislation led me to make representations through the Minister for Aboriginal Affairs and Special Adviser Phillip Toyne.[21] Whether or not these affected the outcome, the final Act does not express or assume a 'bundle of rights'. Section 223 defines native title only by a general reference to 'the communal, group or individual rights and interests of Aboriginal peoples or Torres Strait Islanders in relation to land or waters'. Section 225, which defines the term 'determination of native title', requires that a determination that native title exists shall include a determination, 'whether the native title rights and interests confer possession, occupation, use and enjoyment of that land or waters on the native title holders to the exclusion of all others' (s 225(e)). By requiring consideration of the possibility of a comprehensive *Mabo* title in every case, the Act negates the assumption that native title will, typically, consist only of a bundle of discrete rights to perform particular activities.

However, the notion of a bundle of rights remains alive and has been used by the High Court in *Fejo* and *Ward*.[22] The direct consequences so far have been to justify partial as against complete extinguishment in the presence of competing titles, but there is concern that it may harbour a tendency to conceptualise native title in a demeaning way.[23]

## The battle for public opinion

It is easy to forget today that Australia might well have ended up with the abolition or purely token recognition of native title, accompanied no doubt by some minor genuflections to Aboriginal interests. Abolition was what some state premiers, notably Richard Court of Western Australia,[24] wanted, and the federal Opposition, with much support from industry, wanted to leave it to the states. In the 18 months between *Mabo* and the passing of the Native Title Act in December

1993, two struggles went on: one over the drafting and passing of the legislation, the other for the 'hearts and minds' of the public to whose attitudes the legislators were sensitive.

The relatively successful outcome of the first struggle was due to a surprising conjunction. The dispersed and autonomous nature of Aboriginal society has always made it hard for more than local leadership to emerge and act with authority. However, *Mabo* proved a catalyst. An impressive and effective Aboriginal leadership emerged on to the national stage.

By a stroke of good fortune, they found themselves matched with a maverick Prime Minister who had the imagination and humanity, and the courage and integrity, to engage with them. Paul Keating[25] was an unknown quantity in Indigenous affairs; how would he respond? I was heartened to hear on the grapevine that, with a fitting metaphor, the 'boy from Bankstown' had said to his staff: 'We Australians have to wake up to the fact that we are prowling around in someone else's backyard.' In December 1992, he delivered his famous Redfern Park speech, identifying *Mabo* as one of the 'practical building blocks of change' that Australia needed:

> By doing away with the bizarre conceit that this continent had
> no owners prior to the settlement of Europeans, *Mabo* establishes
> a fundamental truth and lays the basis for justice. It will be much
> easier to work from that basis than has ever been the case in
> the past. For that reason alone, we should ignore the isolated
> outbreaks of hysteria and hostility of the past few months.[26]

The 'isolated outbreaks of hysteria and hostility' intensified and became relentless. Remarkably, Keating held to his principled stand for nearly 18 months during a ruthless campaign to turn public opinion against *Mabo* and the recognition of native title. It was not a populist campaign led by shock jocks, tabloids, ideological columnists and letter writers, although they were there. Not only leading miners (who might have been regarded as the usual suspects) but eminent businessmen from various fields, politicians, historians, knights of the realm, senior lawyers and retired judges presented themselves as guardians of the nation and competed in viciousness of attack on those who had betrayed it.

There is no better place to observe the elect at work on their mission than in the proceedings of the Samuel Griffith Society,[27] which held its annual conference in July 1993 ... Bill Hassall, a lawyer and President of the Liberal Party in Western Australia, said:

> If we are to come to grips with *Mabo,* we must see it as part
> of a wider agenda ... Put very simply, the wider agenda is to
> create an Aboriginal, separate, sovereign state geographically
> within Australia, but not part of, or tenuously only a part of, the
> Australian nation. Once more the Aboriginal people are being
> used – used by people whose aim is to weaken and destroy the
> nation we know, for reasons which can only be assumed to be
> as inverted, perverse and obscure as those which have driven
> Marxists and other totalitarian thinkers in all ages.[28]

The 'wider agenda' had been exposed in a speech by Hugh Morgan, a miner of enormous standing who was later President of the Business Council of Australia and on the Board of the Reserve Bank. Four months after the *Mabo* judgment, in what was no throwaway line but part of the annual Joe and Enid Lyons Memorial Lecture at the Australian National University, he had revealed that the decision of the 'gang of six' in the High Court was the culmination of a communist plot hatched in the 1930s.[29]

The Samuel Griffith Society was also the site for some of the vehement criticism of the High Court from senior lawyers and former judges who spoke like voices from the past, oblivious to the jurisprudence of the 20th century. No less an authority than the Hon. Peter Connolly CBE QC, former President of the Australian Bar Association, President of the Law Council of Australia, and Queensland Supreme Court judge, accused the Court of 'a disregard for the legal system carefully built up by its predecessors and for the established rights of the Australian community', and described *Mabo* as 'a naked assumption of power by a body quite unfitted to make the political and social decisions which are involved'. His address, along with another by SEK Hulme AM QC, who described the doctrine of native title as 'a sheer invention of the High Court', was reprinted by the Association of Mining and Exploration Companies for a distribution that included barristers and schools.[30]

Not only were the decision and the judges misrepresented and attacked in the most extravagant and contemptuous language, but there was licence to speak of Aboriginal people in the most derogatory terms that would normally have been shunned as racist. We were told that Aboriginal claims had been rightly ignored because they were a worthless people. Hugh Morgan recalled that 'Aboriginal culture was [so] much less powerful than the culture of the Europeans that there was never any possibility of its survival'.[31] For Henry Bosch, a leading businessman, they were 'a backward Stone Age people' who had 'been getting away with murder for 200 years'.[32] According to the then Chief Minister of the Northern Territory, Marshall Perron, they were 'centuries behind us in their cultural attitudes'.[33]

The eminent historian Geoffrey Blainey condemned the Court for 'such an unusual view of Australian history', produced by judges 'noteworthy in their ignorance',[34] yet their conclusions can be supported from his own works. Along with others, he played into fears that Aboriginal people would acquire large areas of land at the expense of non-Aboriginals, a result at once unfair and a threat to security.[35]

There was a pressing need for some counter to these heavyweights of the establishment who had been mobilised to save the nation in its time of mortal danger. So, although I had no role in the production of the *Mabo* decision, I did find a role in defending it. I have always felt status and respectability more of an encumbrance and embarrassment than advantage in my personal life, but they can be accumulated as a form of capital to be expended in good causes. In the previous decade I had been able to draw on capital accumulated as a barrister, QC, law dean, university chancellor and Supreme Court judge for the benefit of the environment when I became President of the Australian Conservation Foundation. Since then, I had added to this capital through service as a Royal Commissioner into Aboriginal Deaths in Custody and appointment as a Companion of the Order of Australia, which I had thought might come in handy some day. What better cause than the defence of the legitimacy, indeed primacy, of the Aboriginal presence in Australia!

Recalling my own role this period, I am reminded of the title of Spike Milligan's wartime memoir, *Adolf Hitler: My Part in his Downfall*. I was one foot-soldier on one small front in the *Mabo* wars, where the aim was to hold the fort while the main battle was fought at the political and legislative levels. Yet 1993 proved to be one of the most hectic and demanding periods of my life. I found myself appearing on both national and commercial television, on radio, responding by letters to the editor or interview to the press, writing articles for newspapers, addressing a range of community clubs, labour groups, speaking at university seminars and conferences, seizing any opportunity to spread the message.

It was important to keep that message clear and uncomplicated. Looking back ..., I see that I hammered three points: that only a small number of Aboriginal people would benefit, that every title that anyone else held would take priority, and that far from their being given anything or specially treated, they were merely belatedly getting the right that all others enjoyed – the right to inherit land from their forebears. These were arguments designed to reassure non-Aboriginal people that their backyards and other property were not threatened and nothing unfair to them was happening. Unfortunately, some extravagant and unfounded claims made by a number of maverick Aboriginal groups had given some credibility to their fears ... [It] was much easier to defend the justice of the decision to non-Aboriginal than to Aboriginal people. However, the urgent task was to hold on to what the High Court had recognised, to hold the fort in public opinion while those at the centre of things converted the status of native title from mere common law at the mercy of any state into a right protected by Commonwealth law and the *Racial Discrimination Act 1975* (Cth).

At the University of Technology, Sydney, I gave an occasional address which became an op-ed in the *Sydney Morning Herald* ... A breakfast address to the Evatt Foundation resulted in another op-ed in the *Sydney Morning Herald*, and to a radio interview on 2GB ... I gave a detailed reply to the legal and historical criticisms of *Mabo* in a paper to a conference at Sydney University, explaining how the legal system has been developed over centuries, and defending the judges' use of historical knowledge. Later, I revisited all the jurisprudential criticisms of the decision in my address to a judicial conference. My position in the conservation movement provided a platform to address environmentalists concerned that national parks and other reserves were threatened ... To appeal to another interest, I drafted and secured support for an ecumenical statement on *Mabo*'s 'message' which appeared in the press ... signed by senior representatives of the Australian Council of Churches, the Syrian Orthodox Church, the Armenian Apostolic Church, the Roman Catholic Church, the Executive Council of Australian Jewry, the Australian Federation of Islamic Councils, the Lutheran Church, the Greek Orthodox Church, the Churches of Christ, and the Uniting Church, and, by way of secular endorsement, the five non-Aboriginal people who had served as Royal Commissioners into Aboriginal Deaths in Custody. It declared:

> The message [of *Mabo*] is simple. This continent once belonged to many Aboriginal peoples. Over two centuries, most of it was taken from them piece by piece without compensation. Where this has happened, it cannot now be undone; a new nation has been built and is here to stay. But some groups of Aboriginal people, mostly in remote areas, still have their traditional land. Simple justice requires that we respect their rights, no less than we respect the rights of other Australians who have inherited land. Indeed, because land often has sacred significance to Aboriginal people, we should avoid their displacement wherever possible, even for money compensation. If we wish to use their land, we should seek to negotiate terms acceptable to them as has often been successfully done in the past.

It went on to say that:

> Its challenge is to accept the fact that the building of modern
> Australia has involved Aboriginal dispossession, and to accept
> responsibility for dealing justly with the consequences, and to call
> on all Australians to speak out for the principles of recognition of
> surviving Aboriginal rights to and, negotiation wherever possible,
> support for the Racial Discrimination Act, and patient progress
> towards reconciliation.

In summary, I was one of many people who in a spontaneous and
completely uncoordinated fashion responded individually in the various
ways open to us to a powerful campaign which was seeking to swing
public opinion against *Mabo*. What effect our efforts had must remain
moot, but at least we know that our opponents' campaign did not prevent
an outcome acceptable to the Aboriginal negotiators.

## The National Native Title Tribunal

Native title had been saved from infanticide, but it was a stunted child,
bearing the marks of its difficult birth in the judicial process. In the
Native Title Act no attempt had been made to rethink and reshape
the concept with the policy-making freedom of the legislative process.
Perhaps that would have been impossible or dangerous to attempt at
the time.

But I saw a ray of hope in the fact that claims were initially to go
to mediation, where anything was possible. All that was needed was
an imaginative and generous spirit in the governments that would be
the principal respondents. The nation was committed to reconciliation.
If a claim could be seen not as a legal threat to a state's assets, but as
an opportunity for doing justice to a particular dispossessed group by
any reasonable means available, the Act might become a real path to
reconciliation.

The appointment as President of the National Native Title Tribunal
of Robert French, a respected judge who was capable, enlightened and

humane, was a promising start.[36] So I readily accepted when, in the middle of 1994, I was invited to become a part-time Deputy President for three years. It was exhilarating to work in such a novel institution with a congenial leader and colleagues. It was rewarding and heartwarming to visit Indigenous communities enlivened and enthused by the spirit of *Mabo*, and to learn of their usually very reasonable aspirations ...

Initially my hopes were high. Frustrating lack of progress could, for a while, be put down to the novelty of the problems. However, gradually a pattern emerged. Again and again, government representatives adopted a purely defensive role. They invariably wanted yet more information from the claimants. The inference from their behaviour was that if Indigenous claimants could demonstrate beyond a shadow of a doubt that they would win some degree of native title if they went to court, then it was possible that that degree of native title might be agreed to. Beyond that, nothing. I found myself rebuked by government representatives for suggesting that they might consider a more imaginative approach. Despite its admirable President, the Tribunal had achieved very little by the time my term expired in 1997. Looking back six years later and reflecting on two areas of Indigenous policy that politicians had left to the courts – the compensation of removed children and the historic dispossession from the land – I wrote:

> To leave the consequences of these policies to litigation in private
> actions based on existing rights, in courts designed to settle legal
> rights by an adversary system within a relatively homogeneous
> community, is at once an insult to the Indigenous people and
> a prostitution of the courts. It is an insult to Indigenous people
> because what is at stake is not the vindication of rights that they
> possessed, but redress for what happened to them when they
> were accorded no rights. [Litigation such as *Mabo* and *Wik*]
> developed as a result of a failure of political nerve, which left
> what should have been a legislative policy issue to resolution in
> the courts as an issue of existing rights. In *Mabo*, the High Court
> eloquently and bravely confronted the fiction of *terra nullius*

and its consequences, but could only rule on legal rights, and then only in a way that did not fracture the skeletal structure of the invader's law. Instead of rising to the challenge of creating a new Indigenous policy that could deliver more just outcomes in contemporary conditions, Parliament simply cemented the crippled structure of existing rights into the *Native Title Act 1993*. It left an avenue of escape from the straitjacket in the mediation process. However, instead of accepting the opportunity that mediation offers to go beyond existing rights to seek a mutually beneficial solution, governments refused to negotiate except about whether claimants could establish the existing rights they were forced to claim, and went to the courts to exploit every argument to defeat those rights. The shards of the *Mabo* aspiration lie around us in new case names that threaten to usurp its household status, at least in some Aboriginal communities – *Yorta Yorta*,[37] *de Rose*,[38] *Ward*,[39] *Wilson*,[40] *Yarmirr*.[41]

A lot of *Mabo* water has flowed under the bridge since I left the scene, including legislative amendments, judicial decisions, mediation agreements and decisions on policy and practice. Others are better qualified than I to draw up a balance sheet, but I permit myself a final thought. Sometimes I reflect that if all the money that has been spent on litigating native title had been spent acquiring land interests for Indigenous people, either from public resources or on the market, much more would have been achieved. But then I remind myself that this was never an alternative. Without *Mabo* and the Native Title Act it is unlikely that much at all would have happened. Some justice is better than none. But what an opportunity was squandered!

# NATIVE TITLE IN A LONG PERSPECTIVE

Looking at native title from any point in the last ten years [to 2002], it towers over you and makes it hard to see anything beyond. In my perspective of 30 years ago, native title no longer towers, but is one mountain to be climbed on a journey to a destination beyond. One can ask, how did we come to take the track up this mountain? Would it have been better to take another route? Is it leading us where we want to go?

Everyone has their own idea about where they want to go. I know what mine was 30 years ago, because I recently stumbled across a submission I made to a Senate Committee at the time, a time when there were officially 140 000 Aboriginals. At the end of a long submission covering many issues, I said:

> We need to tackle the problem with the dedication,
> concentration of resources, and determination to succeed that
> we would bring to a war. If 140 000 of our countrymen were
> prisoners of war in a foreign country, we would not rest until
> they were released. Yet within this land a large part of 140 000
> of our countrymen are prisoners of an historical injustice and its
> consequences – ignorance, malnutrition, poverty, discrimination,
> disease, lack of opportunity, destruction of their individual
> personality and their social fabric. Many live in conditions
> that would be considered appalling in a prisoner of war camp,
> and are subjected from birth to a brainwashing about their
> inferiority that no military power has yet attempted on its
> captives. To liberate these our countrymen, we have only one
> enemy to overcome – ourselves – our apathy and indifference,
> our selfishness, our turning of the head.

I didn't have a prescription for how Aboriginals should live their lives. The goal was simply to release them from all the imprisoning factors

---

Paper presented at the Native Title Representative Bodies Conference (Geraldton, 3 September 2002).

that prevented them from being free and equal citizens – genuinely not merely formally equal – who could make their own decisions about their lives and find their own future.

Today, I still aspire to the same ultimate destination for the road that winds through the foothills of land rights (which I passionately advocated in the submission), native title, apology, recognition, rights, treaty, all the various intermediate goals. They are all steps to an end, and we all need to know where we are heading, and not get bogged down at some point on the way.

Things have changed a lot in the last 30 years. They were changing even as I spoke to the Senate Committee. A few months later, Gough Whitlam said:

> If there is one ambition my Government places above all
> others, if there is one achievement for which I hope we shall be
> remembered, if there is one cause for which future historians will
> salute us, it is this: that the Government I lead removed a stain
> from our national honour and brought back justice and equality
> to the Aboriginal people.[42]

It was majestic rhetoric, but it was a lot more. Government vastly increased the resources to tackle disadvantage, and formally abandoned assimilation in favour of restoring to Aboriginals 'the power to make their own decisions about their way of life'. It developed a proposal for land rights that was to deliver half the Northern Territory into Aboriginal ownership, with access to mining royalties that sustained two powerful land councils to defend Aboriginal interests and help them manage their land. The Fraser Government did not seek to undo the Whitlam revolution, which was the basis of bipartisan policy for two decades. Labor returned to power in 1983 with a promise of national land rights, but in the face of a contemptible campaign by the West Australian mining industry, Prime Minister Hawke caved in.

My close involvement in Aboriginal issues resumed in 1988, with three stressful years as a Royal Commissioner into Aboriginal Deaths in Custody. Among the things I learnt again, and emphasised in what

I wrote, was how racism continued to confine Aboriginal achievement, and how Aboriginal people hungered for recognition as a distinct people with a legitimate presence in Australia.

The great achievement of *Mabo* was to tackle these two things head on. It roundly rejected the racism of *terra nullius* that lay at the heart of Australian law and recognised Aboriginal people as the original owners of the land, from whom it had been filched piece by piece over the years. Nothing that has happened since can take that away. These statements by the highest court in the land had an enduring effect on the way Indigenous and non-Indigenous people see each other and see themselves. As a declaration of national recognition, and as a redemptive confession and atonement on behalf of the nation, *Mabo* was magnificent.

But native title cannot be judged only by these criteria. Implemented through the Native Title Act, it has become the national land rights process. While some outcomes can be praised, overall the process has been a failure by almost every criterion. It has been inordinately expensive, extremely slow, only fortuitously related to sensible land use, stressful and divisive for Aboriginal participants, unresponsive to Aboriginal needs and wishes, and arbitrary, haphazard and minimal in its delivery of benefit to Aboriginal people.

This is not a criticism of the *Mabo* judges. The problem with any judicial solution is that it can only proceed by declaring existing rights. Unlike a legislature, a court is not free to engage in social engineering, to make and implement policies by creating or redistributing rights in society. The court could recognise but not create rights, as the legislature could and had done in the Northern Territory, creating inalienable freehold, with special rights in relation to mining. The High Court had to find the rights existing somewhere, and that could only be in native custom, which had originated in small scale, local, hunter-gatherer societies and had neither been devised to meet the problems of life in 21st century capitalist society, nor had a chance to adapt to those problems.

The attempt to fit into the requirements of native title often pressures people to reinvent themselves in artificial ways and opens up divisions within communities that had been painfully forged, not out of undisturbed kin groups on their ancestral land, but out of people thrown together by dispossession, family disruption and bureaucratic convenience. If custom can be found, it is translated into rights stated in the language of a totally different system, on which it has to rely for its protection. The very act of writing down the authoritative custom of a preliterate society, which depended not on the exegesis of a text by experts, but on the nurturing and negotiation of its custodians, inevitably gives it an alien rigidity and inflexibility and cripples its development.

But worse still is the arbitrariness of trying to slip native title at a chance point of time into another system of law, where it is subject to the effect of all kinds of decisions taken at many different times for many different reasons, none of which included concern for native title. Native title always contained the fundamental anomaly that the longer and the more intensely a community had suffered, the less chance there was of native title surviving.

Now we see the detailed arbitrariness that provoked the anguished outburst of Justice McHugh in *Ward*.[43] A solemn court of eminent judges sounded like children playing 'he loves me, he loves me not' with the petals of a flower: 'This reservation extinguishes, this reservation doesn't, this pastoral lease extinguishes, this one doesn't'. Sometimes it was more like: 'this little piggy goes to market' – 'this little title goes back to the Federal Court to see how far it's been extinguished'. I shouldn't make fun of judges doing their best. Everything is done with respectable legal logic; the trouble is that it has no relation to justice, workability or commonsense outcomes. And as Justice McHugh said, the 'decks are always stacked against the native title holders'.[44]

He also rightly said that the problem of Aboriginal dispossession cannot be satisfactorily dealt with through 'a system that simply seeks to declare and enforce the legal rights of the parties, irrespective of their merits'.[45] We have such a system because legislators squibbed the issue of national land rights in the 1980s. Conceivably the situation might have been retrieved after *Mabo*, if the community had been able to accept the message of the justice of Aboriginal claims and the need to address them, but also to recognise the need for a process more flexible and imaginative than the judicial process can be. However, the Aboriginal leadership was flat out preventing the modest gains from *Mabo* being legislated away, and people like myself were preoccupied reassuring the public that the heavens hadn't fallen in, as the miners and some eminent lawyers, historians and politicians claimed.

There was another opportunity when mediation of claims began under the Native Title Act. I used to hope that a government would come along and say, 'Well this claim signals to us that the Aboriginal people in this area have a grievance. Before we get into the technicalities of native title, let us look at the broad picture in the area. Tell us what you would like to happen and we will look at what is possible.' Instead, governments invariably sent their lawyers along, hugging their cards to their chests, in effect saying to the claimants 'If you can convince us that it is 100 per cent certain that we will lose if we go to court, we will be prepared to settle.' If, as mediator, I tried to suggest a more flexible approach, I was quickly given to understand that I was exceeding my proper function.

Every now and then, hopes are raised of a better approach, but usually they are dashed. Claimants find that a government is more likely to become flexible if they have it over a barrel than if they appeal to its sense of justice and its imagination. It would still be possible for governments to approach native title claims in the way I have suggested, and to revisit determinations already made, either within or outside the framework of native title. In fact, the 1998 amendments relating to ILUAs (Indigenous Land Use Agreements) have provided a very useful tool for making agreements with strong legal effect.

Unlikely as such a change in government attitudes may seem at the moment, it is more likely than government adoption of Justice McHugh's bold and difficulty-ridden suggestion of 'an arbitral system that declares what the rights of the parties *ought to be* according to the justice and circumstances of the individual case'.[46] A change such as I have suggested could produce results much more quickly than a treaty process, and indeed could provide stepping-stones to a treaty. Cautious governments could experiment incrementally with new ideas. If they were interested in having issues arbitrated, they could experiment on a case-by-case basis in the course of negotiating ILUAs. Perhaps over time something like the spirit of New Zealand's Waitangi process could grow in the Australian scene.

We have climbed so far up the native title mountain that simply going back is not an option. Any genuinely fair proposals to speed the process would be welcome, although Aboriginal interests have reason to be cautious. Like certainty, speed and efficiency have a way of becoming code words for sacrificing Aboriginal interests. Unless governments are prepared to rethink their attitudes, the native title process may drag on for a long time, as Aboriginal people try to salvage what they can.

That's how native title looks in my long perspective, but what lies beyond it? In 1970, it struck me that the young activists, who had grown up in the bush where pastoralists dominated society, thought that owning land was the key to power and independence. Even then that was no longer true, but it still affects the thinking of many Aboriginals today. Land is important for spiritual or historical attachment, but except for the few who are fortunately located, land can easily be a burden or a trap.

For most people, black and white, independence and access to opportunity depends, and will increasingly depend, on education. Lack of education remains one of the great imprisoning factors, keeping Aboriginals on the margins of affluent modern society. Parents owe it to their children to see that they do get an education, and, with their non-Aboriginal friends, parents should treat the flaws in the education system as problems to be tackled, not allow them to disqualify another generation from the opportunities for full participation in the world that is their right.

Some people worry that education means cultural change. Culture is not some fixed thing that human beings carry with them through changing circumstances. It is something they make anew every day as they respond to new circumstances. They keep what is valuable and move on from the rest. The right to choose what to keep and where to move on is self-determination. Education enlarges both capacity to choose and the range of choices available. Whatever happens to native title, education will be central to the journey onward.

Like it or not, we will all live in the 21st century. There will be nowhere to hide. It will follow you to Tibet or Shangri-la or the remotest outstation in Australia, and it is to the circumstances of the 21st century that culture will have to respond. It is proving a difficult time for all of us. Many white Australians feel ashamed of responses our governments are making, at home and abroad, and of our own inability to respond adequately to social problems that exist under our noses. Aboriginal communities are particularly under the spotlight, mainly because people in them are finding the courage and the voice to stand up and say 'enough is enough'. Noel Pearson is surely right in identifying as major factors still imprisoning Aboriginal people: alcohol and drugs, isolation from a real economy, and government help that, however well meant, disables instead of empowers. These problems exist irrespective of whether people have been dispossessed or enjoy land rights or native title. They have to be confronted whatever happens to native title.

As Pearson and many others have said, in the end the solutions must come through people themselves taking responsibility. A great Aboriginal writer, Kevin Gilbert, said it powerfully over 25 years ago through the voice of Grandfather Koori:

> You can't find value in yourself until you build it by respecting
> yourself through living right. If you tolerate crumminess,
> gutlessness, meanness, wife bashing, kid bashing and neglect then
> you'll never get the strength to climb out of hell ... If our people
> cannot change how it is amongst themselves, then the Aboriginal
> people will never climb back out of hell. Each Aboriginal has to
> be another Aboriginal's keeper; each Aboriginal has to uphold the
> rules of right living because if we don't do these things then our
> Aboriginality will die out till there's nothing left ... like the coals
> of a long dead campfire.[47]

We all need a vision. As a prophet of another dispossessed people said thousands of years ago, 'where there is no vision, the people perish'.[48] Kevin Gilbert saw Aboriginals perishing unless they upheld the rules of right living, and only they can do that. My whitefella vision for

Aboriginals is for them to be free and empowered to make their own choices among the opportunities the world offers.

But we need a joint vision of how we fit together. Michael Mansell asked whether Aboriginals were going to be Australian Aboriginals or Aboriginal Australians. I would suggest another possibility. We all have many identities, not one. My hope would be that Aboriginals will feel able to be both Aboriginal and Australian. But for that to work, people like myself will have to give up thinking that we have just one identity, that we are *the* Australians. We must learn to accept that we too have multiple identities, that we are whites or Anglos or whatever as well as Australians. That would be another blow to racism and *terra nullius*, and a step closer to the goal I saw in 1970 – a time when my imprisoned countrymen will be free of their fetters, and there will be truly free and equal relations between black and white.

That is the main game, and we should keep our eye on the prize, whatever happens to native title. Within this room there are hundreds of people, black and white, who have worked together for reasons much deeper than native title. Australian politics seems to be infested with people who lack the vision, the generosity of spirit, or the courage to realise the bright hope of *Mabo*. They may further emasculate native title, as much for lack of imagination as deliberate ill will. We must not let them, or the disappointments they bring, undermine our commitment to walk together as the long journey goes on.

## THE MEANING OF LAND IN INDIGENOUS CULTURE

*In* Wik *in 1996, the High Court of Australia decided that native title and pastoral leases could co-exist,*[49] *attracting the same shrill, inaccurate opposition as had Mabo. In a paper at the Wik Summit in 1997, Hal found himself once more defending the High Court of*

'Paper' in Noel Pearson and Karin Calley (eds), *The Wik Summit Papers* (Cape York Land Council, 21–24 January 1997) 118–22.

*Australia against ignorant and malicious critics. By this time, he had experience working on the National Native Title Tribunal, with direct experience of the issues.*

[One] can't avoid the conclusion that there is more interest in generating fear and justifying draconian solutions than in defining and solving problems. Over the last few years, I have had the privilege in the course of working with Wik and other Aboriginal peoples to get an inkling of what the recognition of their native title interests means to them, even when they will only be able to enjoy access to their land for limited traditional purposes. It is clearly bound up with their sense of identity and self-respect and more than once I've listened to Aboriginal people say, with deep emotion, 'if we do not have our land, we will not know who we are', or 'if we do not have our land, our children will not know who they are'. And the people who are saying this are expressing no wish to interfere with pastoralists using their land under the white man's law, and do not see the presence of pastoralists as an obstacle, so long as they are recognised as traditional owners and allowed appropriate access. They have said, as Aboriginal people have said here, 'You respect our law, and we will respect yours.'

## THE CHALLENGE OF *MABO*

All over the world, Indigenous people are asserting their claims to a better deal from the states in which they have been involuntarily encapsulated. In almost every case their attention has been focused on the loss of the land which was so central to their identity and way of life. Increasingly they have come to assert rights, both domestically recognised legal rights and internationally recognised human rights, rather than simply argue for political responses.

The only thing that is strange about Australia's position is how long we took to face the issues. When the High Court was confronted by the

'Mabo: Issues and Challenges' (1994) 1(4) *The Judicial Review* 364–65.

*Mabo* claim, it did no more than justice and honesty demanded. In so doing it propelled the law and lawyers into a key position in carrying forward the important task of building a just and durable relationship between Australia and its Indigenous people. Judges in various courts and tribunals will now face a challenge different from anything they faced before in this country – the challenge of recognising, seeking to understand and respecting cultural difference within the very substance of the law.

But the challenge will be a special version of the challenge faced by Australians in many walks of life. Can we deal with our Indigenous people on a basis of equality, abandoning the assumption that we already know, or that we know what is best, and instead learn to listen to new ways of seeing the world, rather than trying to force Aboriginal concepts into our existing moulds of thought?

# 10

# SACRED SITES, THE STOLEN GENERATIONS AND LOOKING FORWARD

*Hal Wootten's knowledge of both law and anthropology meant that he was drawn to disputes about white developers' plans to disrupt or destroy places of special significance to Indigenous people – inaccurately but unavoidably labelled 'sacred sites'. This became the fourth major area of Indigenous law and policy in which Hal became officially involved.*

*The* Aboriginal and Torres Strait Islander Heritage Protection Act 1984 *empowers the Commonwealth Minister for Aboriginal Affairs to commission reports on areas of significance to Indigenous people that are under threat from developers or from other interference. Such reports must address both the significance of the site and the impact of any proposed development. The Minister must consider a report before deciding on the future of the site. Disputes about sacred sites raised difficult issues, including conflicts between Indigenous and non-Indigenous concepts of knowledge; the power of mining companies; and the limits of respect for Indigenous cultures.*

*Hal was appointed a rapporteur by the Minister, Robert Tickner, on four disputes about the development of sacred sites: the Alice Springs dam; mining at Iron Knob; Boobera Lagoon; and the Century Mine in Carpentaria. In the first piece reproduced here, he looks back on the significance of these cases. In the second, he comments on another area of investigation, report and controversy – the Stolen Generations inquiry. In the third, he provides more general reflections on the future.*

## SACRED SITES

### Resolving disputes over sacred sites

My contribution to this symposium arises out of some practical experiences of the way the Australian state has negotiated claims for the protection of Indigenous 'sacred' places that were threatened by private or public claims to exploit or remake the landscape in pursuit of wealth or public safety or amenity. For many readers, this topic will bring to mind the unhappy experience of the Hindmarsh Bridge affair, where such a conflict dragged out through inquiries and litigation over some seven years and left behind bitter recrimination about the genuineness of Indigenous claims, the appropriateness of processes for evaluating them, and the proper role of experts such as anthropologists in those processes.[1] It is unfortunate that this particular dispute is so dominant in public perceptions of such conflicts, and continues to frustrate the development of more appropriate procedures for their resolution, because it is not typical of the outcomes of Australian Government intervention, as my experiences will show.

In April 1992, I was asked by the then federal Minister for Aboriginal and Torres Strait Islander Affairs, Mr Tickner, to prepare a report for him in relation to an application by some Alice Springs Aboriginals seeking the protection, under the *Aboriginal and Torres Strait Islander Heritage Protection Act 1984*, of some sites that would be destroyed by the construction of a dam, which the Northern Territory Government was planning in the Todd River above the town.[2] For me it was to be the start of nearly a decade's involvement in 'the negotiation of the sacred' in a quite literal sense: the endeavour to find terms and conditions for resolving conflicts between Aboriginal claims for respect of the special significance that certain areas of land had for them, and claims to exploit those areas for private gain or public utility.

---

'Resolving Disputes over Sacred Sites: Some Experiences in the 1990s' in Elizabeth Burns Coleman and Kevin White (eds), *Negotiating the Sacred: Blasphemy and Sacrilege in a Multicultural Society* (ANU Press, 2008) 191–203.

The first application referred to me arose out of a dispute between some Alice Springs Aboriginals, represented by the Central Land Council, and the Northern Territory Government, which was proposing to build a major dam for flood mitigation purposes on land that had particular significance for the Aboriginals, or, as was said in common parlance, contained sacred sites. The Territory Government claimed that a major benefit of the dam would be to save the lives of Aboriginals who might otherwise drown in the Todd River when a flood reached town. Undoubtedly some of the Alice Springs townspeople saw the dam as a potential site for water-based recreation, but the Territory Government strongly resisted the suggestion that it would be so used.

My report was to be the principal basis of the Minister's decision whether or not to protect the site, and under the legislation he could not act until he had received and considered my report. Because a lot of time had been used up in fruitless attempts to get an agreed settlement, the last interim declaration the Minister could make would expire in a little over a month, and the Territory Government's bulldozers were ready to commence work immediately it expired. So I, a secular non-Aboriginal lawyer, had about a month to come to an understanding of the Act; the nature of the significance Aboriginals attached to land and, in particular, that Aboriginal women in Alice Springs attached to parts of the upper Todd River; the reasons why the Territory Government had decided to build a flood mitigation dam at this particular place; and everything relevant to the Minister's weighing the desirability of the dam against the desirability of protecting the sites. There was no standing machinery for the implementation of the Act, and I made inquiries and wrote the report unassisted by any staff.

As it turned out, this was to be the first of four appointments as a rapporteur to the Minister. Later, I dealt with challenges to BHP's mining of a site at Iron Knob in South Australia, to the recreational and pastoral use of Boobera Lagoon in northern NSW, and to some of the mining proposed in the Century Mine project in the Queensland Gulf. In each case my first task was to see if there was a possibility of an agreed solution that would relieve the Minister of the need to make an invidious decision, and then, if no settlement was possible, to collate the materials and considerations relevant to a wise decision. Mercifully, in the other three cases I did not face such an acute time constraint as I did at Alice Springs.

That such conflicts involved the 'sacred' on one side at least is acknowledged in the common designation of such areas as 'sacred sites', although a community that seems willing enough to acknowledge the sacredness of sites at an abstract level may become sceptical of their genuineness when particular claims are advanced, or reluctant to concede that their protection should override the pursuit of wealth or projects conceived in the public interest. Recognition of the need to provide legal protection for Indigenous heritage came late to Australia, and initially was often conceived as underpinned by the requirements of archaeological and anthropological scholarship rather than by respect for Indigenous values, beliefs and feelings. In other words, it was directed to the concerns of non-Aboriginal, rather than Aboriginal people, about the preservation of sites and relics.[3]

The *Aboriginal and Torres Strait Islander Heritage Protection Act 1984* was framed as a last resort measure, enabling Aboriginals to seek Commonwealth protection only if state or territory law did not provide effective protection for a significant Aboriginal area, that is, 'an area of particular significance to Aboriginals in accordance with Aboriginal tradition'. This is the terminology of the Act, which does not use the word 'sacred'.

## Sacredness and significance

The category of the 'sacred', and the items assigned to the category, are constructs of the culture that uses the term. One could not expect that it would translate with ready equivalence between cultures as different as the modern, capitalist, predominantly secular culture of mainstream Australia (which itself would contain many differences of interpretation), and the cultures of Aboriginal groups or individuals.[4] Had the Aboriginal heritage legislation followed popular terminology and required decisions as to whether sites were 'sacred', it would have been very difficult to apply. However, the problem has always been avoided. Although the early legislation did use the term 'sacred site', it defined it to mean 'a site that is sacred to Aboriginals *or is otherwise of significance according to Aboriginal tradition.*'[5] The *Aboriginal and Torres Strait Islander Heritage Protection Act 1984* drops the word 'sacred' entirely, but retains the requirement that the particular significance arise out of 'Aboriginal tradition', which is defined to mean 'the body of traditions, observances, customs and beliefs of Aboriginals[6] generally or of a particular community or group of Aboriginals, and includes any such traditions, observances, customs or beliefs relating to particular persons, areas, objects or relationships'.

As a result, there has been no need to debate whether sites are 'sacred', and the phrase 'particular significance', while susceptible to a number of different interpretations, has not, so far as I am aware, given rise to any difficulties. In my Boobera Lagoon report,[7] for example, I noted that the phrase had been discussed by some members of the High Court in the Tasmanian Dam case,[8] and went on to say that:

> the remarks of the judges support the view that 'particular' is directed only to the existence of a distinguishing characteristic, not to a particular level of significance.

> In seeking a distinguishing characteristic, two possibilities have been pointed out. The area might have particular significance for Aboriginal people in contrast to its significance to other people, or it might have particular significance in contrast to the significance which all land or waters have for Aboriginals. On either view, it is clear that Boobera Lagoon has particular significance at least to the Aboriginal people associated with the Toomelah Boggabilla area.[9]

## Comparing the incommensurable

Underlying my task in each case was the question: 'How does one measure the value of protecting an Aboriginal site against the value of some proposed activity that threatens it?'. Or to put it crudely, 'How much is one prepared to pay to protect an Aboriginal site?'. That in essence is what the Minister has to determine at the end of the inquiry, unless an agreement can be brokered. There is invariably a price tag to protection, and the currency in which the price has to be paid varies – it may be money, perhaps in the form of lost GNP or revenue or export earnings; it may be in jobs or other opportunities foregone; it may be in the loss of the chance of water-based recreation for people living in a hot, dry climate, as in the Boobera Lagoon case, or it may be, as the Territory Government was suggesting in my first assignment, in terms of lives that would be lost.

Of course, it will not be the Minister, or the rapporteur who advises him, who will pay the direct price – they will not lose the profits or get drowned. The burden may fall on a private company, a government, individuals or some form of community interest. But the responsibility is the Minister's and there will usually be a political price to pay, and for both the Minister and rapporteur there may be other forms of unpleasantness. After the Alice Springs dam was stopped, I had to suffer the misrepresenting of my report and the traducing of my character under parliamentary privilege by the Territory Ministers of the day, with the Minister for Transport and Works saying,

> I tell Mr Tickner, Mr Wootten and the Leader of the Opposition that they will be hounded. Despite the fact that they will be long gone from the public arena, I will hound them next time there is a flood that causes damage or loss of life. Wherever they might be, whether it is in one year's time or 10 years' time, I will ensure that they are reminded of this little charade, this shameful exercise, perpetrated on the people of the Northern Territory.

So far, 12 years have passed uneventfully, and I sometimes wonder if I have the powers of the sacred sites to thank, but I still keep an eye on the Alice Springs weather reports.

I have not heard anyone advocate that all Aboriginal sites should be preserved intact, whatever the consequences, although I have encountered the view that sites should never be given special protection against lawful activities, because, it is argued, this would amount to racial discrimination. Once you put these extreme views aside, you become involved in a balancing of interests, a negotiation. Consistent with this, the Act requires the report to deal on the one hand with the particular significance of the area to Aboriginals and the nature and extent of the threat to it, and on the other hand with the effect of protection on the proprietary or pecuniary interests of other persons.

How do you balance one against the other? A philosopher might say that the conflicting interests are of such radically different kinds that one cannot weigh one against the other; they are simply incommensurable. However, lawyers, and others responsible for bringing disputes to an end, learn to be pragmatic. In a recent paper to the Academy of the Humanities,[10] I compared the pursuit of truth by historians and by courts. Historians have the luxury of dealing in provisional truth. They never have to make a final decision, they can decline to make a decision at all. Courts necessarily have a quite different approach, which is not to pursue truth for its own sake, but to respect it as one factor among a number in their task of putting an end to disputes as justly as possible. In essence a court does not and cannot say to parties 'These findings are the truth about your dispute'. It can only say,

This is the closest we can get to the truth following a just and practicable procedure and with the time and resources available. We hope we got it right, but whether it's right or wrong, it is the basis on which you have to conduct your affairs for the future. Stop arguing and get on with life.

It is the same with the protection of a site. The competing interests may be incommensurable, but a decision has to be made or the bulldozers will roll. A failure to make a decision amounts to a decision that the site will not be protected.

How then does one go about weighing the contesting claims? The conflicting interests may be logically incommensurable, but reasonable people make choices between incommensurable things every day. Popular wisdom says that apples and oranges are not commensurable, but few people would have difficulty in choosing between ten apples and one orange, or between a good apple and a bad orange, or an apple worth a dollar and an orange worth a cent, and a dietician may give you other information that facilitates a choice.

This example illustrates two points. One is that finding out more about the objects of comparison may make choice easier, although it won't necessarily do so. The other is that you may be able to find criteria by which very different things can be compared. In our capitalist society, money is often invoked to play this role. Market economists, for example, tend to think that everything can be given a monetary value. I once heard an economist making a case for nuclear power add in so many hundred thousand dollars for each life that would be lost, assuring his audience that he had an actuarial basis for what he was doing. And I believe the Australian Bureau of Agriculture and Resource Economics has calculated that it would be cheaper to move the inhabitants of low-lying Pacific islands to Australia than cut the consumption of greenhouse gas-producing fossil fuels. I have not seen an attempt to put a money value on a sacred site, although questions sometimes arise as to whether Aboriginals will accept monetary compensation for interference with a site, and opposing interests are quick to argue that willingness to accept financial compensation would show that the claim of significance is not bona fide.

## The role of rapporteur

So what does a rapporteur do? I preface my answer with the observation that in exercising any legal power or function under Australian law, one is constrained by some basic features of our legal system. We are a community that accepts the rule of law. Any exercise of power must find its authority in the law and be carried out within the limits of the conferred power and in accordance with any conditions or requirements attached to it. A power or function is conferred for a particular purpose, which is either expressly stated in the law or inferred from the nature of the law, and it can't be used for any other purpose. In exercising the power, all relevant factors, and no irrelevant factors, must be taken into account. Again, what factors are relevant may be expressly stated in the law or inferred from its purpose.

A power to make a decision that may adversely affect someone's interests must also be exercised in accordance with the principles of natural justice, unless legislation otherwise provides. This means particularly that the person exercising the power should not be biased, or reasonably open to the suspicion of bias, and should give a fair hearing to anyone whose rights may be affected.

The role of the rapporteur is thus a quasi-judicial one; he or she must be independent and give a fair hearing to all interests affected and report fairly to the Minister, not omitting anything that is relevant to be taken into account or giving weight to anything that is not relevant. The functions of the Minister and the rapporteur are thus confined within a procedural mould and cannot be exercised arbitrarily.

As a rapporteur I had to subject both sides of the balance to scrutiny and evaluation. Scrutinising and evaluating Aboriginal beliefs is an invidious task, particularly for a non-Aboriginal person. It is not surprising that people – any people – would resent having what are essentially religious beliefs scrutinised, particularly by someone who does not share those beliefs, or even the cultural framework within which they exist. It is not surprising that women may be reluctant to have their beliefs, especially gender-restricted beliefs, evaluated by a man. And it is certainly to be expected that many Aboriginals may resent having their beliefs evaluated by members of the dominant community that dispossessed them. These conflicts were among issues considered by Elizabeth Evatt when she was appointed to review the Act in 1995, and she made recommendations designed to mitigate or eliminate them, which the present government has not adopted.[11]

For my part, I simply had to live with these problems and do what I could to minimise their effects. Over and above the resentment of intrusion on their privacy and the inner sanctum of belief that might be felt by anyone whose beliefs are subjected to scrutiny, I have observed three specific things causing hurt or anger to Aboriginal people in these applications. One is scepticism of their veracity or bona fides, another is the ridiculing of their beliefs (a deplorable feature of the Coronation Hill dispute), and a third is the presumption of arguing that a belief is in some sense 'disproved' by showing that people have flouted it without incurring adverse consequences. It must be particularly galling to Aboriginals that these hurts are so frequently offered by the most ignorant and bigoted of white Australians, who are secure in a sense of their own intellectual superiority that is not obvious to anyone but themselves.

In coming to grips with the Aboriginal claim, a rapporteur will usually have the benefit of at least one anthropological report as well as direct input from Aboriginal people themselves. Sometimes a report may be obtained by one or more interested parties and then offered adversarially to the rapporteur. In less contentious cases there may be agreement on retaining a particular anthropologist to report. Sometimes there is complaint that anthropologists should not be used, but competent anthropologists are of enormous value. Their professional knowledge enables them to provide a context for the claim, and to cast light on its plausibility and its significance. In addition, their linguistic and fieldwork skills enable them to collate evidence from Aboriginals that would take an inordinate time for the rapporteur to collect, if indeed it were possible. Sometimes, the anthropologist may have worked in the relevant community for a long time.

## The Alice Springs dam case

In the Alice Springs dam case, I found that there was undisputed and long authenticated evidence of the beliefs in question. The sites derived their significance from two Dreaming tracks that converged in the area. One was the path of Two Women whose mythical journey started far to the south-west in Pitjantjatjara country, the other the path of a group of Uncircumcised Boys who travelled from the area of Port Augusta to the north coast of Australia. Women from distant lands and tribal groups who shared the Two Sisters story had on several occasions travelled to Alice Springs to support the claim of the Arrernte women, who put their views forcibly to me in a large meeting from which all other men were excluded. They confided to me, for transmission to the Minister, 'secret women's business' that would normally never be disclosed to men.

With the cooperation of the Northern Territory Solicitor-General, who represented the Territory Government, and acted throughout with the utmost professionalism and good sense, arrangements were worked out for handling the 'secret women's business'. It was agreed that it could be revealed to the [Commonwealth] Minister and myself, as the women had volunteered, and supplied to the Northern Territory Government on the basis that the details would be confidential to a female anthropologist employed by the government. Fortunately, in the Territory the parties were accustomed to devising ways of dealing with confidential material in land claims, and one of the problems on which the Hindmarsh Bridge application later foundered was thus avoided.

Investigating the claim was a novel and moving experience for me. I recorded some of the problems I wrestled with in the following section of the report, which was frequently quoted from during the subsequent Hindmarsh Bridge disputation:

7.1.9 To reveal these beliefs to anyone not entitled to know them under Aboriginal tradition (including other Aboriginals and even people of the opposite sex in the same community) is itself a kind of desecration, and it has been done reluctantly and painfully on the basis that it is necessary to prevent the destruction of important sites. I feel a personal obligation to respect the confidentiality of the information given to me. Moreover, I would not wish my report to be the vehicle for the public trivialisation and ridicule of Aboriginal beliefs in the media by uncomprehending people, a situation which was such a shocking feature of the debate over Coronation Hill.

7.1.10 It is difficult for those of us who have grown up in Western European culture to appreciate the nature of the attachment to and concerns about such areas on the part of Aboriginals. Our perceptions of values which we categorise as spiritual, religious, sacred, traditional, and political are shaped by our own culture and do not necessarily fit with categories or with concerns in Aboriginal culture. This is exemplified by the absence from the English language of any word corresponding to what we unhappily translate as 'the Dreaming'. The anthropologist's report in this case stresses, for example, that our division between sacred and secular realms does not correspond to traditional Aboriginal ideas. The Western notion of knowledge as objective and scientifically based does not square with the Aboriginal notion of knowledge, which in the fields with which we are concerned, derives from authoritative statement by a person who, in terms of traditional authority, was qualified to define the knowledge.

7.1.11 Western civilisations have long been accustomed to the notion of traditions as being recorded and authenticated in written texts, and more recently to their being interpreted and their correctness tested in a rationalist manner in the light of the results of historical and scientific inquiry. It is not easy for those who have grown up and been formally and informally educated in this culture to understand and empathise with traditions communicated by oral narrative, song, art and dance, and having an authority quite independent of historical, scientific and rationalist scrutiny.

7.1.12 One way in which Aboriginals stress the importance of sites in the area is by voicing the belief that destruction of the sites would lead to devastating social consequences and particularly consequences to all women, including non-Aboriginal women, and to relations between the sexes. While I refer to this as an indication of the degree of importance attached by Aboriginals to the sites, I warn against the tendency of Europeans to trivialise Aboriginal beliefs by treating such fear of consequences as their essence.

7.1.13 I can assure the curious that the confidentiality is not because the information would be found titillating, shocking or even particularly interesting by Western standards. It simply lacks significance in Western culture, and I could not claim to appreciate its significance to Aboriginals. The issue should not be whether, judged by the norms and values of our secular culture or our religions, the sites are important, but whether they are important to Aboriginals in terms of the norms and values of their traditional culture and beliefs. In other words, the issue is not whether we can understand and share the Aboriginal beliefs, but whether, knowing they are genuinely held, we can therefore respect them.[12]

It became clear to me that there were strongly and widely held beliefs that would be severely affronted by interference with the sites, that a significant number of women would suffer great anxiety because they believed that apocalyptic consequences would follow, and that many Aboriginals saw the matter as a test case of white Australia's respect. But should this prevail against the building of a dam that would not only protect the town from flood damage, but save lives of people who might otherwise be drowned in floods, as a number of Aboriginals had been in the past?

I found the issue easier to resolve than I had feared. It is not possible to go into the matter fully here, but a detailed examination of the dam proposal showed that by normal engineering standards the dam was uneconomic, returning over its life less than 33 cents in material terms for every dollar spent, and that there were other ways of reducing flood damage to the town. The case for the dam therefore rested heavily on its potential for saving lives. However, investigation showed that there had been seven drownings in 20 years, and most of these, probably all, could have been prevented by relatively simple steps that could be implemented in the future. I asked rhetorically whether anyone who had $20 million to spend on saving Aboriginal lives would use it on building this dam.

On receipt of my report the federal Minister prohibited the building of the dam.

## Mining at Iron Knob

The next matter referred to me involved a claim to protect an area from mining at BHP's mine at Iron Knob in South Australia, a step that would sterilise millions of dollars' worth of iron ore. The Aboriginal people in the area had lived an urbanised life for some time, and when the elderly Aboriginal woman who had instigated the claim died, there was no local person who could speak authoritatively to it. With financial assistance from BHP, which acted throughout in a very sympathetic and cooperative fashion, senior traditional Aboriginal men and women from other tribes far to the north were brought to Iron Knob. Although they had never visited the area before, they knew of the country in detail through songs and dances that recorded the stories attached to a Dreaming track that passed through Iron Knob on the way to their own country. They were immediately able to recognise and explain the mythical significance of the various features of the landscape.

For reasons that are too complex to go into here, this case would have presented me with a difficult balance to draw up, but the matter took a surprising twist. The BHP manager became committed to the importance of preserving Aboriginal culture, offering money for books, films, dancing companies, and visits by local to more traditional peoples. The Aboriginal people were grateful and impressed, but still unable to agree to the destruction of the site. The impasse was broken when the manager offered to dig up the sacred site and install it on land the company would provide for a cultural centre at Whyalla. I expected this proposal to get no support, as the actual location of the site seemed critical to its significance, but to my surprise the proposal was immediately embraced by the leading Aboriginal spokeswoman, and a deal was done. Some of the men, however, seemed uneasy, and I was not unduly surprised to learn a few years later that the Aboriginals had regretted their decision and persuaded the company to leave the site undisturbed.

## Boobera Lagoon

In May 1995, I was appointed rapporteur in relation to Boobera Lagoon, an old path of the MacIntyre River in NSW near the Queensland border. According to the mythology of the local Aboriginal people, the Lagoon was made by and is now the resting place of a local version of the Rainbow Serpent, a being that appears in Aboriginal mythology in many places. There was no doubt about the genuineness of the claim, which had long been documented by anthropologists and consistently pursued by local Aboriginals whenever an opportunity had arisen over the years. The most acute among many issues was that the Lagoon had become a major waterskiing site, providing the only water-based recreation for the inhabitants of the hot, dry, dusty Goondiwindi area, but one that the Aboriginals found offensive and disrespectful to what they treasured as a sacred place. Also at issue was the effect of cattle depastured around the Lagoon, most acutely where a Travelling Stock Route bordered the Lagoon. Apart from spiritual desecration, the Aboriginals were concerned that both the waterskiing and the cattle were causing serious environmental damage to the Lagoon.

The matter proved difficult. The Aboriginals had been fighting for the protection of the Lagoon for many years, and although they were quite happy to share its enjoyment with non-Aboriginals who treated it respectfully, they would not condone waterskiing or continued environmental damage. The non-Aboriginal side was no less intransigent. The local authority managing the Travelling Stock Route would not even agree to watering cattle with water pumped into troughs from the Lagoon, a procedure that would have allowed its bank to be fenced off. One could not but feel sympathy for the water-skiers who had been using the Lagoon for many years and had come to regard it as a major feature of family and community recreation for which no substitute was available. There are many aspects canvassed in my report in the course of weighing up the competing claims, but in the end I recommended that waterskiing be banned and arrangements made to keep travelling stock off the Lagoon bank.

The recommendation was to have a chequered history. My report had been commissioned by the Labor Minister, Robert Tickner, but by the time I presented it in August 1995 the government had changed and Senator Herron, a Queensland Liberal, was the Minister.[13] Although I believed that my report made a persuasive case for banning the waterskiing and taking other steps to protect the Lagoon, I held out little hope of a positive outcome, particularly given that the move was opposed by the Deputy Prime Minister, who held the adjoining federal seat.

Several years passed with no decision announced ... Then, under ministerial rearrangements, the Aboriginal Heritage Section was transferred on 17 December 1998 to the Department of the Environment, and Senator Herron, I am told, breathed a sigh of relief. However, the Prime Minister decreed that he must deal with the matter before handing it over. To everyone's surprise, he banned the waterskiing, softening the blow with a grant of $5 million to construct a new waterskiing site near Goondiwindi. There were a number of postponements, but ultimately the new site was constructed and quiet descended on the Lagoon. It is a declared Aboriginal place under NSW law and is now managed by a committee with a majority of Aboriginal members. They are gradually negotiating increased protection from cattle damage around the Lagoon, and on recent inquiry I was told that the only blight on their satisfaction was that the $5 million to build the new waterskiing site was taken out of Aboriginal Heritage Protection Funds.

## Mining in 'blackfella country'

About the Century Mine negotiations, there is little to say. The Carpentaria Land Council made an application under the Act for the protection of some sites within the proposed mining lease, but there was never a real problem. The company was determined that sites would not become an issue and was willing to make whatever concessions were necessary on that score, as well as anxious to lay the foundations for the future operation of the mine in a way that would bring real benefits to the local communities. The parent company was Applera Corp–Celera Genomics Group, and one sensed that the disastrous experience of Bougainville Copper was never far from the minds of its executives. Many matters were negotiated, but I believe the real underlying issue was that many Aboriginals, including Murrandoo Yanner, the influential Director of the Carpentaria Land Council, still saw and treasured the Gulf as essentially 'blackfella country', and did not want its character changed by the intrusion of a major mine. The issue was summed up for me by an incident at a Darwin seminar when Tracker Tilmouth, the very able and entrepreneurial Director of the Central Land Council, was waxing lyrical about the successful enterprises of the Council and the opportunities available in business partnerships. When he finished, Murrandoo stood up and asked, 'Well Tracker, they are all fine things, but when do you get time to be a blackfella?'

That seems to me the dilemma that every Aboriginal faces. How do you remain a blackfella while engaging with what the modern world has to offer? What are you prepared to forego to hang on to the things that you find essential to your identity? To the extent that I am a bleeding heart, my heart bleeds for the individual Aboriginals who every day have to make painful decisions and compromises in the course of finding a satisfying and dignified place in an alien society that took over their country, long excluded them from participation, but today impatiently expects them to accept whatever place is offered them or rapidly find their own.

## Some reflections

One thing that I found striking in all the applications with which I dealt was the peaceful and law-abiding way in which Aboriginals pressed their claims, and their capacity to be understanding of their opponents. The only occasion on which the question of violence was raised was in relation to Boobera Lagoon. As I described in my report, the Aboriginals of the area had a long history of pressing their claims lawfully and constructively whenever the opportunity arose, and no one could have credibly predicted violence on their part. It was white residents who predicted that if a declaration were made prohibiting waterskiing, water-skiers would resort to violence and defy it, and that the white community would also react vindictively against Aboriginals, for example by refusing them employment. Two members of parliament hinted at the same thing when, in opposing protection, they expressed their fear that it might 'lead to a worsening of the already fragile relations'. The supposition in all these submissions was that the threat of white violence was a reason for refusing the Aboriginal claim, a view that I rejected, although I did recommend a strategy of community public relations to head it off.[14]

The reaction of the Aboriginal community was stoic. The submission on their behalf read:

Any racial violence which flows from the granting of the declarations will merely be a continuation of what they have had to tolerate since the beginning of European occupation. Concern about the possibility of racial violence should not sway the Minister away from making the declarations. To do so would be a grave injustice to Aboriginal people. It would be a continuation of what is already perceived to be a flawed system biased against Aboriginal people. It would be the law succumbing to intimidation from those prepared to threaten violence by the use of illegitimate force to obtain their ends.

This was a view with which I agreed, and one that, in my view, the state must be prepared to stand up for in negotiating the sacred in a multicultural community.

The Australian state on whose behalf I was acting is essentially secular. Although its Constitution was expressly adopted in humble reliance on the blessing of Almighty God,[15] it gave no powers or privileges to God or God's representatives or adherents and expressly forbade the Commonwealth from establishing any religion, imposing any religious observance, prohibiting the free exercise of any religion, or requiring any religious test for any Commonwealth office or public trust. As it happens, my personal outlook is secular, although I hope respectful and understanding of other views, but even if I had not been, it would have been my duty to act in a manner becoming the secular agent of a secular state. From this secular viewpoint, the beliefs of Aboriginal claimants, whether sacred in character or not, were not something to be judged as right or wrong, or as better or worse, or more or less credible, than other beliefs, but something to be respected, not merely as an expression of their liberal right to different views, but as part of their human identity. It may well be that it is easier for a secular state to negotiate the sacred, than it would be for one committed to a particular view of the sacred as the official and correct one.

# THE STOLEN GENERATIONS

*The following extract is a critical review of a booklet by Ron Brunton, Betraying the Victim: The Stolen Generations Report (1998, Institute of Public Affairs). Hal's evisceration of an old adversary is largely omitted here in favour of his own comments and criticisms of the Stolen Generations Report.*

## The achievement of the 'Stolen Generations' Report

*Bringing them Home,* the Report of the Human Rights and Equal Opportunity Commission into the removal of Aboriginal children from their families under past government policies, has had an enormous impact on the Australian public. Many non-Indigenous people became aware for the first time of the terrible individual suffering and community terror and destabilisation that accompanied the deliberate separation of Aboriginal children from their families over much of this century.

Unforgettable images have touched the hearts of many Australians. Children rushing to hide when they heard a car. Grandmothers running after trains carrying deeply loved children away to sob their hearts out, unconsoled, in stark, severely disciplined dormitories. A teenage girl told to wash out her mouth when she pleaded with a matron not to send her to a placement where she had suffered sexual interference, and then reviled when she returned pregnant. Little children taught to shun and scorn their own families, and the very identity that their skin and features indelibly stamped on them. Mothers assured their children would be returned, and helpless when they disappeared forever. Children told their parents had rejected them, or had died, only to discover decades later that they had a parent, recently dead, who had never ceased to grieve for them.

Members of the inquiry channelled their limited time and resources into the task of allowing as many as possible to tell their stories. Anyone who has seen how difficult it is for those who suffered to unburden themselves of their experiences, and how healing it can be when they do so, will appreciate the value of this work. Making these experiences available to the Australian public in the simple, unvarnished, first-person language of those who suffered, but without breaching their privacy, has been a tremendous contribution to interracial understanding.

Australians have come in their thousands to sign the Sorry Book, to join the Sea of Hands, and with new understanding to support reconciliation and the protection of native title. No criticism of other aspects of the Report can take away the importance of this achievement.

## Criticising the Report

The tremendous emotional impact of the Report, the fact that it is an attempt to tell a story that Australia long repressed, and that it is a call to the nation to redress a great wrong, all make criticism of the Report difficult and suspect. Yet precisely because it is such an important step in coming to terms with the past, and in achieving reconciliation, it is important that it be subject to fair-minded criticism. It is not the last word on a difficult and painful subject, but a foundation on which scholars can build, a foundation which ensures that the voices of those who suffered can never again be ignored.

In particular, the Report is not a definitive and rounded treatment of the protection and assimilation eras, and could not have been, given the Inquiry's limited time and resources. Ordinary experience tells us, as indeed the Report itself occasionally hints, that the problems perceived by administrators, the motives which determined their responses, the changing content and practical effects of their policies and practices over the years, and the differences between jurisdictions, were more complex and significant than the Report allows ...

## Genocide

In 1948, the United Nations adopted the Genocide Convention, which was the first clear recognition that forcibly transferring children of one national, ethnic, racial or religious group to another group with the intent to destroy the former group as such, in whole or in part, was genocide and a crime against humanity. The Report quotes some of the well-known statements by administrators of earlier periods to which this definition can be retrospectively fitted, but none that I can find from the period after its adoption. This leads me to wonder how the Inquiry found that the crime was being committed in Australia at least until the 1960s and arguably until the 1980s.[16]

The Report simply asserts that '[T]he Inquiry's process of consultation and research has revealed that the predominant aim of Indigenous child removals was the absorption or assimilation of the children into the wider, non-Indigenous, community so that their unique cultural values and ethnic identities would disappear, giving way to models of Western culture'.[17] This is a most unsatisfactory way of dealing with an issue which, as the Inquiry recognised, was central to its terms of reference. It is the more serious as the alleged predominant aim was not stated in legislation and could only lie in the acts and intentions of individuals who, so far as one can tell from the Report, were being judged without notice or hearing to be guilty of a crime against humanity.

A quite unnecessary legal ruling has led the Inquiry into pointless controversy. The enormity of what was done speaks for itself through the lips of those to whom it was done, and the lips of self-righteous administrators of the past whose ideas would today be seen as genocidal. As Commissioner Johnston said when he declined to make an unnecessary finding of genocide in the Royal Commission into Aboriginal Deaths in Custody, what matters is what Australia now does to redress the wrongs which the failed policies wrought upon Aboriginal people.[18]

## Reasons for removals

The Report's broadband finding of genocide is also made problematic by its failure to distinguish between separations for different purposes. Virtually all lasting separations where parents did not have free choice are lumped together as 'forcible separations', whether they were for the purpose of ensuring that children would grow up physically or culturally cut off from an Aboriginal community, to remove them from an environment where their safety or health was considered in jeopardy, to secure them a secondary education, or to take them into custody under the processes of the criminal justice system.

For some purposes the reasons are of little importance. If a small child is forced to grow up cut off from family and community, in an emotionally barren environment in which its racial background is despised, told that its parents are dead or uninterested in it, and treated as having no destiny except as unskilled or domestic labour for the superior white race, its childhood will be misery and it will be at risk of lasting psychic disturbance. This will be true whether the child is removed for genocidal motives, because its fair skin in a blacks' camp is an embarrassment to white society, because it is considered neglected, or because it lives far from a hospital or school. On the other hand, if one intends to make judgments about responsibility, reasons may be highly important.

As a practical matter, there was no realistic possibility that the Inquiry, resourced as it was, could make reliable distinctions. To cross-examine a person who is publicly baring their agony for the first time as to whether their mother was a worthless person would have been cruel, and irrelevant to their suffering and psychic deprivation. To find out the reasons for removal given in official files, and check the accuracy of those files against the testimony of living witnesses, would have been theoretically possible in those cases where records still existed and could be related to individuals, many of whom had been denied knowledge of their ancestry. Brunton claims the Inquiry should have done this and holds up the Royal Commission into Aboriginal Deaths in Custody as an example. The Royal Commission sat for four years at a cost of $30 million, with up to five full-time Commissioners assisted by many counsel and staff, and supplied with files by cooperative state governments which had joined in commissioning the Inquiry. In that time, it investigated the lives and deaths of about 100 Aborigines who died in custody. The Inquiry, by contrast, lasted for about 18 months, with a budget of $1.5 million, no full-time members and no counsel assisting, and was confronted with the stories of over 1500 lives. The tasks of the two inquiries were of course completely different, and any comparison between them is absurd. Yet Brunton makes it. It is ironic that when the Royal Commission's reports seemed to be gaining public sympathy, Brunton produced for the IPA a booklet denigrating them.

Seven years later, when he needs a stick to beat *Bringing them Home,* Brunton holds up the reports of the Royal Commission as models of what the Inquiry should have done.

It would simply have been impossible for the Inquiry to check the individual stories ... with the time and resources available. For the Report's picture of the suffering of the removed children and its psychic effects, the lack of checking is not very important. On the other hand, as I have already argued, the failure to investigate individual circumstances makes problematic any finding that the removals were all carried out with intent to destroy a group, as such ...

## FINDING THE FUTURE: INDIGENOUS AUSTRALIANS IN THE 21ST CENTURY

*In this paper, delivered as the Inaugural Nulloo Yumbah Lecture at the University of Central Queensland, Rockhampton, in 2002, Hal provides an enlightening history of Australia's Indigenous policies and provides guidance on the way forward. This includes acknowledging the real problems in some Indigenous communities and insisting on those communities taking responsibility for their future. Here, his approach shows the strong influence of his challenging engagement with Noel Pearson's work.*

Vice-Chancellor, members of the Darumbal people on whose land we meet, members of the University, the Mayor and citizens of Rockhampton, and guests. I am deeply honoured by your invitation to me, a southerner and a white person, to give the first of these ongoing lectures, which are intended to have a focus on reconciliation, and will be given in yearly rotation by an Indigenous and a non-Indigenous speaker. This leaves me more comfortable to speak in the only way I can – as a

Delivered as the Inaugural Nulloo Yumbah Lecture at the University of Central Queensland, Rockhampton (1 May 2002).

whitefella – knowing that next time I will be balanced by a black voice. What may seem tonight a monologue by a whitefella will hopefully then be seen as the opening of a conversation between black and white voices, one of the many conversations this country must have if it is to achieve that mutual understanding that must precede any formal reconciliation. I speak, however, not as advocate or representative of the group into which I was born, but as one seeking an outcome in which all who live in Australia will be able to find satisfying futures.

It would be easy to give a warm and fuzzy speech in favour of reconciliation, or a cynical one questioning its meaning and value, or even a neutral one analysing its possibilities and parameters. Or I could recycle the well-worn statistics of Aboriginal disadvantage and how they infringe the human rights of Indigenous people, a recital now so ritualistic that it is more likely to arouse a self-righteous glow of recognition than feelings of horror. In either event, I could receive your polite applause and go home unscathed. But what a cowardly evasion that would be, when we all know of the anguish, the suffering, the sense of bewilderment that is so widespread in Aboriginal communities; when I know that the very community whose members are here tonight are mourning the loss of yet another young person who has taken her own life, and are searching for some way forward. I can't provide solutions to such problems, but perhaps if we publicly acknowledge them in a spirit of friendship, share the sorrow and discuss some of the explanations and remedies that have been suggested, it may be easier to see the next step forward.

I know that some may accuse me of blaming the victims, and of intruding where a white man has no business to be. I understand why people feel this way. I know how the long history of racism and marginalisation, and cruel policies imposed by arrogant people who thought they knew best, have made wounds so sensitive to outside gaze. It is hard to talk of these painful matters without risking giving hurt. I can only say to my Aboriginal listeners that I speak as a long-time friend of Aboriginal people who knows what history has done to them, and does not think he knows best, and that I know something of your sorrow, having myself lost a close and dear Aboriginal friend to a drug overdose. I have no greater wish than that Aboriginal people may find a dignified and satisfying place in an Australia of which I can be a proud citizen, and in which my grandchildren may live with theirs in mutual respect and trust.

One thing I believe we must not do is just pass by and pretend that we do not see. All of us, as citizens of Australia, as members of the Australian community, as fellow human beings living in the same land, must be concerned about the extent of suffering, the loss of life and the ongoing denial of opportunity to lead rewarding lives for successive generations in many Aboriginal communities. For whites to turn our backs and ignore these devastating problems would be to add another great act of rejection of our common humanity to the many that have shamed our history. Aboriginals were rejected as white settlement simply took their land and destroyed their societies and way of life, as whites simply waited for them to die out, as they were segregated in the name of protection, as their ties to their children were overridden, as they were pressed to abandon their languages and beliefs and identity, as they were left out of the Constitution, as they were left outside the economy to become chronically welfare dependent. Surely the time has come to draw a line and insist that Aboriginal people be truly included in the Australian Commonwealth, among the people for whom we truly care as our fellow citizens.

## A progressive consensus

Whitlam's categorical rejection in 1972 of assimilation in favour of what came to be known as self-determination was accompanied by the outlawing of racial discrimination, very large increases in expenditure to address Aboriginal disadvantage, and a commitment to land rights.[19] Although his government was short-lived, the momentum he established carried on in essentially bipartisan policies for nearly 25 years.[20]

The consensus continued because it was progressive but not radical, sympathetic but not judgmental. It assumed that goodwill and expertise could produce solutions to Aboriginal disadvantage and made no greater ideological demands on the public than sympathy for the underdog and a rejection of racial discrimination. Even in the rural areas of substantial

Aboriginal population, where racism was most overt, the money that Aboriginal welfare policies brought into towns tempered opposition to them.

The 1991 National Report of the Royal Commission into Aboriginal Deaths in Custody (RCIADIC) was written in the spirit of, and substantially endorsed, the bipartisan consensus, calling for renewed and increased efforts by government, and a much greater commitment to self-determination. However, RCIADIC was to be the swansong of the consensus, which was already crumbling … Bipartisanship … was further ruptured with the election in 1996 of the Howard Government, whose policy of 'practical reconciliation' essentially aims to treat Aboriginals as disadvantaged citizens in a unified nation, who should be brought up to community levels in the statistics, primarily by health, education, housing and employment programs. It has little sympathy for any policies involving recognition of Aboriginals as a distinct people.

Although substantial expenditure to remedy Aboriginal disadvantage has continued, and ATSIC and native title remain,[21] there has been quite bitter conflict between Aboriginal people and the national government over a number of issues.[22] However, a large section of public opinion, which had responded sympathetically to the reports of RCIADIC, was deeply moved by accounts of child removal in the *Bringing them Home* report,[23] and hundreds of thousands of people marched over bridges in a symbolic expression of support for reconciliation.[24]

## The collapse of confidence

For nearly a quarter of a century, there had been little public questioning of the consensus, and a widespread acquiescence in the substantial government expenditure involved. But this was based on an assumption that it would achieve its objectives, and the internationally embarrassing statistical gap between black and white Australia would, at least, substantially diminish within a reasonable time.[25] Reassurance that progress was being made came to the public from the only side of Aboriginal society that most white people saw – the outstanding Aboriginal leaders that emerged on the national scene and the impressive achievements of Aboriginals in literature, the arts, sport and the professions.

For many white Australians it has come as a shock in recent times to learn that in the general Aboriginal population the gap has not narrowed, few of the social indicators have improved, and some have got worse. Life expectancy and incarceration rates, for example, are vastly unfavourable compared to the mainstream community. Even more chilling have been the frequent accounts of dysfunctional Aboriginal communities, with widespread alcohol and drug abuse; petrol, paint and glue sniffing; chronic welfare dependency; family breakdown; neglect of children; youth suicide; violence; and physical and sexual abuse of women and children. While remote communities appear to be most severely affected, most communities suffer these problems in some degree, and most families have some harrowing stories to tell. Many of these accounts come from distressed members of the communities themselves, often people who are desperately seeking ways to stem the tide of disorder. They touch raw nerves in a white public wrestling with its own unresolved problems of drug abuse, youth suicide, domestic violence and sexual abuse.

This picture has only recently become part of the public knowledge that sympathetic whites can acknowledge without feeling guilty of racism or assimilationism or of giving comfort to the enemy, a change made possible particularly by the work of Noel Pearson. However, it is not a new story. Blacks have been understandably reluctant to tell it, but one who did so 25 years ago was Kevin Gilbert.[26] It has also been rare for anthropologists to speak frankly, but one who did was John von Sturmer.[27] In 1990, Marcia Langton reported with brutal honesty as head of the RCIADIC Northern Territory Aboriginal Issues Unit.[28] In 1999, [Colin] Tatz gave a pessimistic account.[29] In 1991, Lowitja O'Donoghue spoke of 'alcoholism, child abuse, domestic violence and early death' as features of many communities.[30]

It is important that these problems do not found a new stereotype for a very diverse Indigenous people. There is great variation within and between communities. We should keep in mind, for example, not only the large group of distinguished Indigenous people who have contributed much to Australian life in recent years, but the many less well-known people in the communities who have successfully struggled to maintain a decent way of life for themselves and their families, and who not infrequently take courageous stands against those who subvert community life. History has left communities with all the depressing statistics of drunkenness, drugs, violence and delinquency, alongside the things statisticians don't measure – courage, humour, caring, and constant struggles to improve the situation – Aboriginal life 'in all its hardships and all its many glories'.[31]

But one thing I have learnt is that you cannot stop the world and get off to go looking for a better one. You can't go back to the past; you can't even stay in the present; you can only go forward to a future that you have only a tiny bit of power to shape. Hopefully if we can work together, combining our little bits of power, Indigenous people striving to find an acceptable future for themselves, the rest of us making reasonable room for them, and negotiating the conflicts in a spirit of reconciliation, we can make Australia, not our ideal future, but a bit more satisfying for all of us than it might otherwise have been.

# 11

# WILDERNESS VALUES: CONSERVATION AND THE ENVIRONMENT

*It is no coincidence that Hal Wootten ends his iconic 'Living in the law' speech[1] by instructing students and young lawyers not to forget climate change nor that the two portraits painted of Hal have him in the countryside. The natural world was indispensable to his life. From childhood, he loved forests and hiking and birds, and completed a diploma in ornithology from Charles Sturt University in his 80s. He farmed and bred quarter horses. His love of the Australian countryside was deepened by his connections with Indigenous communities from whom he learnt a different way to relate to the land.*

*These passions led him to becoming President of the Australian Conservation Foundation (ACF). He was, as he says in a speech extracted below, no token president. Among much else, he wrote several articles about conservation and Indigenous interests, including the impact of mining and the effect of the Mabo decision.[2]*

*The three sections of this chapter illustrate the diversity of his commitment. In the first, he provides a philosophy of environmentalism. In a sharp shift of gear in the second, he addresses political issues in a devastating critique of then Commonwealth Shadow Minister for the Environment, Alexander Downer, whose insulting and misleading depiction of the ACF led Hal to an uncharacteristic public expression of anger (which he later regretted as a discourteous loss of control). In the third, he defines the role that lawyers can take in protecting the environment.*

# WILDERNESS, VALUES AND THE
# SEARCH WITHIN OURSELVES

A few days before World Environment Day I was walking up King Street, ruminating on a speech I was to give, when I realised that I had just passed a shop window with a magnificent coloured photograph of a rainforest. I went back and saw that across the picture were printed the words: *'Wilderness has the power to soothe, to calm, to restore and recreate'*.

I looked up to see what environmentally enlightened organisation was preaching this message to the citizens of NSW, a state which had recently decided to save its remaining rainforests. Lo and behold, it was the Queensland Government Tourist Bureau. The whole window display was devoted to persuading the citizens of NSW to come to Queensland to enjoy the rainforest on the Lamington Plateau, whence, no doubt, they could look across at the rainforests of NSW, which, unlike those of Queensland, are being nominated by the state government for World Heritage listing. The main obstacle to the success of the NSW nomination is that international authorities are wanting to know why the Australian Government is nominating the forests of that state but not the even more precious wet tropical rainforests of Queensland. The full irony will be appreciated by those familiar with the campaign to save the Daintree and other North Queensland rainforests.

The timely text with which the Queensland Government so kindly provided me contains two assumptions. The first is that the normal conditions of life and work in our society leave us so stressed, frustrated and dissatisfied that we need a holiday in which we will be calmed, soothed, restored and recreated. The second is that wilderness has the power to do this for us. Common experience tells us that these assumptions are true. Why is this so?

One of the unlikely sources from which I learnt great truths was Humphrey Bogart. I have never forgotten a dramatic scene in *Key Largo*,[3] a film in which the lay-about Humphrey is trapped by a typhoon

---

in a remote Florida Hotel, complete with Lauren Bacall. Who should drop in but Edward G Robinson, whom those of my age will recall as the archetypal villain. He is a gangster from the Prohibition era returning from Cuba with his gang to make a comeback. As the typhoon increases in fury, tension grows in the hotel. A woman becomes hysterical and the gangsters threatening. At a critical moment, under the drawn guns of the gangsters, Humphrey walks up to Robinson, stares him in the eye, and says: 'I know what you want. You want more'. There is silence, then Robinson says: 'Yeah, yeah, that's good. I want more.' Devastatingly, Humphrey replies: 'Will you ever have enough?'

In the 35 or so years since then, with the aid of advertising and political promises, most of us have become more and more like Edward G Robinson. We are stressed, frustrated and dissatisfied because we want more and we can never have enough. There is nothing that can satisfy us. We just want something new to acquire, use up and throw away. Imagine if you were to wake up one morning and find everything you had ever thrown away piled up on the front lawn! Mentally compare it with a midden that represents several hundred years of debris from a whole Aboriginal tribe. They, of course, before they met us, lived in the wilderness all the time and didn't need to go to Queensland to be calmed, soothed, restored and recreated …

There is always someone who wants more and experts to tell us we can't do without it. More, that is of material goods and services, not more justice, more beauty, more happiness, more love, more untouched wilderness, for these are satisfying things that do not figure in the Gross National Product by which we measure our progress and welfare. They do not generate the economic growth on which everything is now said to depend. It is our duty to generate more material wealth, we are told, because the only way to help the poor is for the rich to get richer, so that more can trickle down to them.[4] It may even be necessary, apparently, to destroy the environment in order to amass the riches that alone will enable it to be saved.

This comforting doctrine has only recently become respectable political morality. I doubt that when I was a child any public figure would have denied the teaching of Christianity, shared by all the great religions, that wealth is an obstacle, not an avenue, to the good life. We all knew that when the rich young ruler asked Christ what he must do to inherit eternal life, he was not told to get richer so as to improve the trickle-down effect, but to sell all that he had and distribute to the poor, thereby gaining treasure in heaven. It was the young ruler's sorrowfulness on hearing this advice that led Christ to comment that it is easier for a camel to pass through the eye of a needle than for a rich man to enter the kingdom of God. It is true that not many public figures did distribute their riches to the poor, but they conceded their adherence to wealth as a human weakness rather than as a cross they had to bear for the benefit of the poor.

While these views have only recently become generally respectable, they … came in … with the Industrial Revolution. In the thousands of years before then, no great philosopher equated wealth with virtue or selfishness with the public good. Only then was the basis laid for the current orthodoxy that a free market in which each pursues his or her self-interest is the best way to protect everything, from the poor to the environment.

But another shift in traditional thinking was necessary before concern for the environment could be put aside. For long people had spoken and thought of Mother Nature and Mother Earth, and one could scarcely rape one's mother. In the 17th century, Descartes came to the rescue. He promised to make mankind 'masters and possessors of nature' by means of his reductionist philosophy which dominated science until its bankruptcy became obvious in the last few decades, and which left no room for values. The late EF Schumacher, best known to conservationists for *Small is Beautiful,* has described in another brilliantly simple book, *A Guide for the Perplexed,* how what he calls 'the science for understanding' was replaced by the 'science for manipulation'.[5] 'The old science', he writes, 'looked upon nature as God's handiwork and man's mother; the new science tends to look upon it as an adversary to be conquered or a quarry to be exploited'.[6]

We in the conservation movement must go on fighting our holding battles to save what we can from the wreckage around us. We must fight to preserve special places, to protect endangered species, to keep needed habitats, to end pollution that threatens ourselves and our fellow creatures. We must fight to have the great resource base used in a permanently sustainable way – the rich top soil that is so often washed away; the fragile arid lands that can stand so little; the overgrazed pastures; the forests so long in maturing; the vegetation that controls flooding, drought and salinity; the rivers, estuaries and ocean that can yield so much or so little. We must fight for the integrity of the air we breathe and the water we drink. We must fight to preserve the upper atmosphere that so shelters the Earth that it alone of the planets is a haven for life. We must fight to limit the explosion of human population so that mankind does not spread across the Earth like locusts in an all destructive and ultimately suicidal plague. We must fight to end the childish tinkering by so-called great powers with nuclear weapons and technology that could render the Earth uninhabitable.

It is essential that all these battles be fought day by day. But let us not delude ourselves that a victory on any single issue can of itself be final. Let us indeed realise that we are not just fighting a series of unrelated issues of individual enemies of the environment, but something more fundamental and pervasive – a whole set of social and personal values embedded in our culture. These values are 'ours' as well as 'theirs', and if we are to change the world, we must start by changing ourselves. Let no one tell you that we are going against human nature or against the foundations of our society. History and anthropology give the lie to such assertions. We are seeking to change a set of values that crept into Western culture with the Industrial Revolution and have since spread across the world, obscuring the ancient wisdom that taught people to live in harmony with each other and with the natural world.

Finally, to complete the exposition of my text, why is it that wilderness has the power to sooth, to calm, to restore and recreate those who live in the world of more? It is no use asking for more in the wilderness. You can't consume wilderness. There are no shops and no advertisements. All the material wealth you have in the wilderness is what you can carry on your back, and you soon learn, as did the Aborigines many millennia ago, that the less you have on your back, the better. The only riches you can enjoy in the wilderness are the riches of the spirit, and through history people have gone to the wilderness to discover the spiritual riches within themselves. Wilderness is a place where we cannot escape the fundamental truth that what matters is not what we have, but what we are.

# THE AUSTRALIAN CONSERVATION FOUNDATION AND THE ELECTION

*Hal gave this speech to an ACF meeting at the Seymour Centre, Sydney, 30 June 1987, which was attended by politicians of all parties, including Alexander Downer. The federal election was held on 11 July 1987, with the incumbent Australian Labor Party government under Prime Minister Bob Hawke returned to power.*

The Australian Conservation Foundation and the Wilderness Society are conducting a campaign to put conservation on the map as an election issue. The campaign focuses on our last chance to save the forests, not because this is the only conservation issue – there are many – but because it is one of the most critically urgent and it is one on which the policies of the major parties stand in starkest contrast and on which there is a choice of major progress or disastrous regression as a result of this election. Given the policies of the parties, the logic of such a campaign points inexorably to seeking a return of the Labor government with all its faults ... The Council of the ACF has expressly decided to advocate a vote along these lines. Why has this happened? Mr Downer[7] has given his explanation – not tonight when there is someone to answer him, but he and others have spread it widely as part of a campaign to smear and discredit ACF. I quote his press release of 15 June: 'The ACF has been hijacked by left-wing political activists and is not a genuine environmental body.'

---

Unpublished speech, delivered 30 June 1987 at the Seymour Centre, Sydney.

Well, here I am Mr Downer, your left-wing political activist hijacker.
I have been unanimously elected President by the last two Councils of
ACF. I have been an active not a token President. I have been personally
responsible for the major changes in ACF in the last three years …

I usually leave speaking on behalf of ACF to Phillip Toyne[8] because
he does it much better than I. I have come tonight specifically to give
the lie to Mr Downer's allegations about the hijacking of ACF. I deeply
resent his latter-day McCarthyist smear. While Mr Downer was in
short pants, I spent years fighting real left-wing hijacking of trade
unions, an experience which impressed me with the importance of
proper democratic procedures both in the state itself and in voluntary
associations. Over my lifetime, I have worked to strengthen these
procedures in many ways, here and overseas, through the Law Council
of Australia, LAWASIA, the Aboriginal Legal Service, the Law
Reform Commission of NSW, and as founding Dean and Professor
of Law at the University of New South Wales. I spent ten years as a
Supreme Court judge on the appointment of a Liberal government. On
retirement, I worked as Chairman of the Press Council of Australia
to defend the liberal notion of freedom of the press against erosion by
government regulation and private monopoly, including its hijacking
by Mr Murdoch with the connivance of Government and Opposition.[9]
Finally, I became President of the ACF because I believed that there is
no future for any of us – left, right or centre – unless we learn to love and
cherish our environment.

So you may understand why I feel such resentment at these cheap
and untruthful smears by the latest novice recruit to Mr Howard's ever-
changing shadow Cabinet.[10] ACF is a highly constitutional body governed
by a Council of 35 members elected every two years by secret ballot …
Its members come from many backgrounds. They have one thing in
common – a deep concern for the environment in all its aspects. It takes
up as wide a range of issues as its resources permit, not just 'boutique'
issues as Mr Downer in his Philistinism has called the destruction of
our last virgin forests in Tasmania and in North Queensland, but issues
such as soil conservation, arid lands, hazardous wastes and Antarctica.
We would be able to do much more on long-term issues if our resources

were not continually strained in fighting the destruction of our last precious natural areas.

ACF is not in any way unique in its attitude to the election. It stands four square with The Wilderness Society (TWS) and even with such a normally conservative body as the Nature Conservation Council of NSW, a mainstream body by any definition, which has strongly adopted a similar policy. We are all reluctant recruits to electoral politics, but have been driven there, and into our present stance, by the Opposition. It is not that the Labor Party has a good overall environmental policy – I agree with many of the criticisms made of it tonight by Mr Downer and others. It is only the barbaric policy of the Opposition that makes it look good.

What happened about the election was this. Early in the year, Phillip Toyne called on the major parties to consider their environmental policies and warned of the possible effects of the environmental vote. The results are instructive. Phillip and Jonathan West of TWS had three personal interviews with the Prime Minister, and obtained not just promises but significant action on Shelburne Bay, Kakadu, the Tasmanian forests and the Daintree.

In contrast, Mr Howard rejected three requests for an interview, referring us to his then shadow Minister, a Queensland National Party Senator who first attracted environmental attention by informing Mr Murphy of Murphyores Inc Pty Ltd that he would be able to resume sand-mining on Fraser Island under a Coalition Government. He developed what has become a consistent theme of Opposition policy, that the Commonwealth's powers over exports and foreign affairs would not be used for environmental ends. This means that an Opposition victory would mean not only the end of any chance of saving the Queensland rainforests and the Tasmanian forests, but that the Franklin, Kakadu, Fraser Island and Shelburne Bay are all at risk ...

Notwithstanding all this, Phillip Toyne with my support advised ACF Councillors not to endorse any party but to confine ACF's activities to publicising and criticising the party policies. We didn't like being in the business of endorsing any party. It was Mr Howard who ensured the overwhelming defeat of our recommendation. On the day Council was to vote, he announced his tax policy. The Department of Arts, Heritage and Environment would be abolished – not incorporated into a more senior department as Mr Downer has sought to suggest tonight, but 'abolished' as a cost-cutting measure and any 'residual functions' transferred to other departments ... ACF received the supreme accolade of being singled out from all other organisations. As one of the few specific ways of saving $9 billion which Mr Howard was able to reveal, he announced the abolition of ACF's grant of $145 000.

Coupled with all the other things, it became clear ... that Mr Howard had virtually declared war on the Australian environment. Getting past the waffle has been difficult – and I have admired Mr Downer's capacity to waffle tonight, as well as his capacity to reinterpret his leader's policies – but it now seems clear that under Liberal policy Joh[11] can sand mine Fraser Island, Moreton Bay and Shelburne Bay, and log the Daintree to his heart's content ... Robin Gray[12] can build the Franklin Dam and log the Lemonthyme and Southern Forests. National estate areas generally can be logged and mined. Much of Kakadu can be mined ...

Mr Downer likes to exaggerate the record of the Fraser Government, in whose achievements he claims some part. It was the Whitlam Government which passed the Great Barrier Reef Marine Park Authority Act but it lost office before it could be implemented. In seven years – even with the benefit of Mr Downer working for it – the Fraser Government brought only 14 per cent of the Reef into the Park. In the 1983 election Labor promised to proclaim the rest of the Park and within seven months had 98.5 per cent of the Reef within the Park ...

We in the environment movement have no love for party politics. We draw our members from all parties and wish to work with all parties. We look forward to and work for the day when all parties will reflect a common outlook that humans must walk gently on the Earth, taking from it our reasonable needs in a sustainable way and treating with love and respect the earth itself and the other life forms with which we share it. If we are to survive, that day must come. But as well as working for it, we must ensure that in the meantime the Earth is not impoverished by short-sighted destruction that would mean that those who come after us would never know the majesty of Australia's eucalypts or the incredible complexity and beauty of our ancient tropical rainforests.

Whatever you do, don't vote against the forests.

# THE EARTH'S LAWYERS

*This is the Preface to Murray Hogarth,* Law of the Land: Rise of the Environmental Defenders. *Hal was Patron of the Environmental Defenders Office for many years. His admiration for the EDO is made clear here.*

In Sydney in 1985, a small group of people met to realise a bold dream – that a system of law that over a millennium had been geared primarily to protect private property and individual freedom should be regularly used to protect the commons of mankind against the depredations of those very interests. It was by no means the first time or the first place that the potential of law to advance environmental values had been recognised. Conservation organisations of various kinds have existed for a long time and have shown a remarkable growth in numbers and influence since the middle of the 20th century. From time to time, they have been able to employ, or recruit on a *pro bono* basis, lawyers to assist them in their campaigns.

What was remarkable about the 1985 gathering was that it was not a meeting of potential environmental clients seeking lawyers to represent them, but a meeting of lawyers who were themselves environmentalists and wanted to establish a legal service that would be on call to protect the environment, and indeed might even at times be seeking lay clients with the courage and fortitude to take up the role of litigant. The organisation that resulted, originally the Environmental Defenders Office, now officially shortened to its nickname, the EDO, remains as it was conceived a quarter of a century ago, a lawyers' organisation ...

---

Preface to Murray Hogarth, *Law of the Land: Rise of the Environmental Defenders* (Environmental Defenders Office, 2015).

The fact that the EDO has remained a lawyers' organisation means that it is not simply an instrument of environmental campaigners but works within the framework of professional independence captured in the motto of the NSW Bar Association 'Servants of all yet of none.' Unlike a member of the NSW Bar, however, the EDO is not subject to the cab rank rule that would require it to respond to any who seek its services; it must be highly selective among potential clients and issues, in order to make the most effective use of its limited resources as it pursues its mission 'to promote the public interest and improve environmental outcomes through the informed use of the law'.

The result is that none of the work undertaken by the EDO is routine, in pursuit of selfish interests, or at the behest of the powerful, a contrast with many other forms of legal practice that leads many young lawyers to prefer it to more lucrative openings elsewhere. The fact that enthusiastic recruits of excellent quality are always available, that leading barristers can always be found to accept its briefs for modest fees or on a *pro bono* basis, that graduates from its ranks have been appointed to high office, and that it is treated with respect by its professional opponents and the judiciary is, in my view, a tribute not only to the reputation it has established but also to a widespread ethos among local lawyers that respects professional excellence and integrity, public service and social empathy. As one who had a role in the re-envisioning of legal education 40 years ago, this state of affairs gives me great satisfaction.

This book traces, during the relatively short life of the EDO, truly remarkable changes in the nature of perceived environmental problems, in the horizons of concern, and in the range of possible legal reactions. Whereas the first EDO solicitor expressed frustration over the domination of his practice by disputes over the location and management of quarries, his successors today may be concerned with forestry issues in Melanesia, with international conventions on a variety of issues, the development of universal human rights, and problems like climate change that know no boundaries and threaten the very basis of life on the planet. Their pursuit of improved environmental outcomes may lead them into such disparate fields of law as defamation; trade practices; wrongful interference with economic relations; intellectual property; the disclosure obligations of superannuation funds; restructures, schemes of arrangement and reporting obligations under corporations law; free trade agreements; and public passenger transport, to name a few.

Litigation is but one tool. Research, submissions, lobbying, and public education are increasingly important. As the old warhorse Michael Mobbs said: 'Legal reformers have to first fight to get law changes, then fight to have them enforced, then fight to keep them when they start to work.'[13] The issues of standing, orders for costs, and the extent of judicial review, for example, are hardy perennials.

As President of the Australian Conservation Foundation, I was asked to support a move for the amalgamation of environmental organisations. My view was and remains that the variety of organisations is a great strength of the environmental movement; everyone who cares about an issue can find an organisation, compatible company and methods that suit them, whether they want to lie in front of bulldozers, engage in specialised research or wear suits to Canberra or the IUCN (the International Union for Conservation).

The EDO is the perfect example of the niche organisation, which could never have flourished so successfully without its independence. Like Shakespeare's veterans of Agincourt, its staff and alumni are a happy few, not covetous for gold, who stand tip toe and strip their sleeves and show their scars when the EDO is mentioned.[14] Murray Hogarth has caught their voices and celebrated their achievements. I join him in saluting them and wishing them more successes in a struggle that will never end while there is life and law on the planet we share.

# ACKNOWLEDGEMENTS

Every effort has been made to contact all copyright holders, and we gratefully acknowledge the permissions granted to reproduce the material contained in this book. We will be pleased to amend in any future editions any errors or omissions brought to our attention.

For permission to reproduce photographs of Hal, we gratefully acknowledge Professor Gillian Cowlishaw, Peter Solness, Richard Wootten and the University of New South Wales.

We acknowledge these publishers for permission to reproduce copyright materials:

- ANU Press for 'Resolving Disputes over Sacred Sites' in chapter 10
- Australian Academy of the Humanities for 'Conflicting Imperatives' in chapter 6
- *Australian Indigenous Law Review* for 'Foreword' in chapter 9
- Aboriginal Studies Press for the Australian Institute of Aboriginal and Torres Strait Islander Studies for 'Mabo at Twenty' in chapter 9
- *Australian Journal of Anthropology* for 'Mabo and the Lawyers' in chapter 9
- *Indigenous Law Bulletin* for 'Reflections on the 20th Anniversary of the Royal Commission into Aboriginal Deaths in Custody' in chapter 8; 'A Cheer for the Mabo Nudgers' in chapter 9; 'Ron Brunton & Bringing Them Home' in chapter 10
- *UNSW Law Journal* for 'Living in the Law' in chapter 3; 'Occasional Address' in chapter 4; 'Aborigines and Police' in chapter 8; 'Occasional Address' in chapter 4; 'Tribute to Robert William Bellear' in chapter 7.

# SELECTED PUBLICATIONS BY HAL WOOTTEN

## Articles and books

'Land Tenure in the Colonies: A Review Article' (1947) 2 *South Pacific* 26–28

'The Orr Dismissal and the Universities' (1957) 1(2) *Quadrant* 25–29

'The Orr Case: A Rejoinder' (with JR Kerr) (1958) 4(11) *The Free Spirit* 13

'Re-opening the Orr Case' (with JR Kerr) (1958) 4(10) *The Free Spirit* 3–5

'Review: Harold Gatty, *Nature is Your Guide*' (1958) 2(4) *Quadrant* 94–95

'The Orr Case: A Further Rejoinder' (with JR Kerr) (1959) 5(1) *The Free Spirit* 22–23

'The Community's Interest in Trade Unions' in John Wilkes and SE Benson (eds), *Trade Unions in Australia* (Angus & Robertson, 1959) 89–126

'The Stuart Case' (1959) 5(2) *The Free Spirit* 1–3

'An Indigenous Legal Profession for New Guinea: A Pressing Problem' (1964) 1(2) *Australian Bar Gazette* 3–6.

'Another Congo in New Guinea: What Happened to the University of Port Moresby?' 86(4423) *The Bulletin* (28 November 1964) 17–20

'Review of "The Cargo Cult"' (1965) 87(4436) *The Bulletin* (6 March 1965) 51

'The World's Most Generous Colonisers But still the Prisoners of Race ...' (1965) 87(4435) *The Bulletin* (27 February 1965) 41–43

'The Law Association for Asia and the Western Pacific: An Experiment in Regional Cooperation' (1968) 7(2) *Washburn Law Journal* 211–38

'New Guinea and the Outside World' in John Wilkes (ed.), *New Guinea ... Future Indefinite?* (Angus & Robertson, 1968) 65–100

'The Role of the Tribunals' (1970) 12(2) *Journal of Industrial Relations* 130–44

'Dean's Letter to New Students' in *Faculty of Law: 1971 Handbook* (UNSW, 1971) 5–8

'Dean's Letter to New Students' in *Faculty of Law: 1972 Handbook* (UNSW, 1972) 5–9

'The Aboriginal Legal Service' in *Social Service: Aboriginal People in the Greater Sydney Area* (Council of Social Service of New South Wales, 1972)

'Bureaucracy and Individual Liberty' in John Wilkes (eds), *Parliament, Bureaucracy, Citizens: Who Runs Australia?* (Australian Institute of Political Science, 1972) 205–37

'Creativity in the Law' (1972) 4(3) *Australian Journal of Forensic Sciences* 107–20

'Aboriginal Legal Services' in G Nettheim (ed.), *Aborigines, Human Rights and the Law* (ANZ Book Company/International Commission of Jurists, 1974) 59–67

'The New South Wales Aboriginal Legal Service' in Lorna Lippman (ed.),
     *Aborigines in the 70s* (Centre for Research into Aboriginal Affairs, Monash
     University, 1974) 157
'Commentary' on 'JE Isaac, Lawyers and Industrial Relations' in D Hambly and
     J Goldring (eds), *Australian Lawyers and Social Change* (Law Book Company,
     1976) 349–60
'Occasional address given by the Honourable Justice Wootten, Foundation
     Professor and Dean of the Faculty of Law, University of New South Wales,
     at the first conferring of degrees for the faculty, April 1976' (1976) 1(3)
     *University of New South Wales Law Journal* 189–92
'Environment is New, Rapid Growth Area of the Law' (1985) 20(6) *Australian
     Law News* 20–21
'The Future of the Conservation Movement' (1985) 13(3) *Habitat* 25–27
'Mining Law and the Environment' *Habitat* (1985) 13(4) 35–38
'Wilderness Values and the Search within Ourselves' (1985) 13(4) *Habitat* 2–3
'World Rainforest Shrinks: What Will History Say of Us?' (1985) 13(2) *Habitat*
     2–3
'The Australian Heritage Commission Act and the Natural Environment:
     A Conservation Viewpoint' (1986) 14(1) *Habitat* 7–9
'The Australian Press Council' (1986) 9(1) *University of New South Wales Law
     Journal* 17–26
'How a National Timber Policy Could Save Australia's Forests' (1986) 14(3)
     *Habitat* 18–23
'The Meaning of Mountains: A Personal View' in *Australia's Alpine Areas:
     Management for Conservation* (National Parks Association of the Australian
     Capital Territory, 1986)
'Conservation and Resource Development: Are they Mutually Exclusive?'
     (Seminar Paper, 'Exploring for Minerals – The Community's Right to
     Know', Chamber of Mines, Metals and Extractive Industries (NSW) and
     the Australian Mining Industry Council, 20 October 1987)
'Conservation Objectives' in John Dargavel and Gordon Sheldon (eds), *Prospects
     for Australian Hardwood Forests* (Centre for Resource and Environmental
     Studies, ANU, 1987)
'Elections and Environmental Politics: The Search for Consensus' (1987) 15(5)
     *Habitat* 7–10
'99 Reasons: Royal Commission into Black Deaths in Custody' (1991) 2(3) *Polemic*
     124–28
'Deaths in Custody' (1991) 2(3) *Current Issues in Criminal Justice* 57–68
'20th Anniversary of the UNSW Law School' (1992) 2 *UNSW Law School
     Bulletin* 4
'Beyond Vocational Purposes: The University and its Curriculum' (1992) 14(2)
     *Higher Education Research and Development Society of Australasia News* 3–5

'Aboriginal People and the Criminal Justice System' in Chris Cunneen (ed.),
    *Aboriginal Perspectives on Criminal Justice* (Institute of Criminology, 1992) 49
'Aborigines and Police' (1993) 16(1) *University of New South Wales Law Journal*
    265–301
'The Alice Springs Dam and Sacred Sites' (1993) 65(4) *The Australian Quarterly* 8–22
'A Cheer for the Mabo Nudgers' (1993) 3(62) *Aboriginal Law Bulletin* 2
'Environmental Dispute Resolution' (1993) 15(1) *Adelaide Law Review* 33–78
'Green and Black after Mabo' (1993) 21(4) *Habitat* 18–21
'The High Court, Native Title and National Parks' (1993) 25(3) *Conservation News* 8
'Mabo and National Parks' (1993) *Wild* 20 (October–December) 50
'Putting Mabo in Perspective' (1993) 1(2) *Evatt Papers* 55
'The Alice Springs Dam and Sacred Sites' in Murray Goot and Tim Rowse (eds),
    *Make a Better Offer: The Politics of Mabo* (Pluto, 1994) 8–22
'The Mabo Decision and National Parks' in S Woenne-Green et al. (eds), *Competing
    Interests: Aboriginal Participation in National Parks and Conservation Reservations
    in Australia* (Australian Conservation Foundation, 1994) 306–74
'*Mabo*: Issues and Challenges' (1994) 1(4) *The Judicial Review* 303–65
'The End of Dispossession? Anthropologists and Lawyers in the Native Title
    Process' in J Finlayson and D Smith (eds), *Native Title* (Centre for Aboriginal
    Economic Policy Research, 1995) 101–18
'Mabo and the Lawyers' (1995) 6(3) *Australian Journal of Anthropology* 116–33
'Occasional Address on Being Awarded LLD at UNSW' (1995) 18(2) *University of
    New South Wales Law Journal* 232–36
'Policy Issues in Policing Aboriginal People' in Barbara Etter and Michael Palmer
    (eds), *Police Leadership in Australasia* (Federation Press, 1995) 170–207
'Consequential Impacts of the Recognition of Native Title on Land Management'
    in Gary D Meyers (ed.), *Implementing the Native Title Act: First Steps* (National
    Native Title Tribunal, 1996)
'The Rights and Recognition of Indigenous People – Consequential Land
    Management Impacts on the Environment, and on the Recognition of Native
    Title' in Gary D Meyers (ed.), *Implementing the Native Title Act: First Steps*
    (National Native Title Tribunal, 1996) 60–73
'Some Thoughts on Native Title and Doing Business' in Gary D Meyers (ed.),
    *Implementing the Native Title Act: First Steps* (National Native Title Tribunal,
    1996) 47
'Mediating between Aboriginal Communities and Industry' in Gary D Meyers
    (ed.), *Implementing the Native Title Act: The Next Step* (National Native Title
    Tribunal, 1997) 161–82
'Negotiation, Mediation and Third Party Decision in the Age of Native Title'
    in Gary D Meyers (ed.), *Implementing the Native Title Act: The Next Step*
    (National Native Title Tribunal, 1997) 190

'Paper' in Noel Pearson and Karin Calley (eds), *The Wik Summit Papers 21–24 January 1997* (Cape York Land Council, 1997) 118–22

'Ron Brunton & Bringing Them Home' (1998) 4(12) *Indigenous Law Bulletin* 4–8

'Towards a More Workable Native Title Act' in Gary D Meyers (ed.), *In the Wake of Wik* (National Native Title Tribunal, 1999) 100–110

'Review Article: Indigenous Futures: Choice and Development for Aboriginal and Islander Australia' (2002) 2 *Australian Aboriginal Studies* 78–82

'Book Review: The Stuart Case by Ken Inglis' (2003) 5(24) *Indigenous Law Bulletin* 22–23

'Conflicting Imperatives: Pursuing Truth in the Courts' in Iain McCalman and Ann McGrath (eds), *Proof and Truth: The Humanist as Expert* (Australian Academy of the Humanities, 2003) 15–50

'Self-Determination after ATSIC' (2004) 23(2) *Dialogue: Academy of the Social Sciences* 16–25

'Tribute to Bob Bellear' (2005) 28(1) *University of New South Wales Law Journal* vii–viii

'Resolving Disputes' in Elizabeth Burns Coleman and Kevin White (eds), *Negotiating the Sacred: Blasphemy and Sacrilege in a Multicultural Society* (ANU Press, 2008) 191–203

'Living in the Law' (2009) 32(1) *University of New South Wales Law Journal* 198–212

'Finding a Life in the Law', The 2010 Sir Ninian Stephen Lecture, Newcastle Law School

'Foreword' (2011) 15(1) *Australian Indigenous Law Review* 1–6

'Reflections on the 20th Anniversary of the Royal Commission into Aboriginal Deaths in Custody' (2011) 7(27) *Indigenous Law Bulletin* 3–8

'Mabo at Twenty: A Personal Retrospective' in Toni Bauman and Lydia Glick (eds), *The Limits of Change: Mabo and Native Title Twenty Years On* (AIATSIS, 2012) 431–44

'Much Too Promised Land', *Inside Story* (Carlton, Victoria, 16 February 2012) <insidestory.org.au/much-too-promised-land>

'The Earth's Lawyers', Preface to Murray Hogarth, *Law of the Land: Rise of the Environmental Defenders* (Environmental Defenders Office 2015)

'Where Were the Aborigines?', *Inside Story* (Carlton, Victoria, 19 December 2016) <insidestory.org.au/where-were-the-aborigines>

### Interviews

'Interview: Commissioner Wootten' (1989) 1(36) *Aboriginal Law Bulletin* 8–9

'Hal Wootten interviewed by Ken Inglis in the Law in Australian Society Oral

History Project' (National Library of Australia, 1996–97)

'Hal Wootten interviewed by Jon Ritchie in the Australians in Papua New Guinea 1942–75 Oral History Project' (National Library of Australia, 2008)

Bill Bunbury, *It's not the Money it's the Land: Aboriginal Stockmen and the Equal Wages Case* (Fremantle Arts Centre Press, 2002) 67–104

Peter Thompson, 'Wisdom Interviews: Hal Wootten QC', *Big Ideas* (ABC Radio National, 1 May 2005) <https://www.abc.net.au/listen/programs/bigideas/wisdom-interviews-hal-wootten-qc/3446536>

Anne Susskind, 'The Little Nudges that Change the World' (2008) 46(11) *Law Society Journal* 24–26

Sue Georgevits, 'Interview with Emeritus Professor Hal Wootten' (UNSW Library Oral History Program, 23 February 2009 and 16 September 2010)

Aboriginal Legal Service, 'Hal Wootten in The Story Project: 40 years of the ALS' (YouTube, 18 July 2013) <https://www.youtube.com/watch?v=uhbe4ldByEA>

## Major reports and submissions

'Professional Legal Education for Papua and New Guinea' (Report to the Law Council of Australia, 1962)

'The Establishment of a Law School' (Paper prepared in support of submissions to the Professorial Board and University Council concerning the curriculum of the Law School, UNSW, 1970)

'Legal Education in the LAWASIA Region' (LAWASIA, 1971)

'Discrimination against Aborigines by or under Commonwealth and State Laws' (Statement to Standing Committee on Constitutional and Legal Affairs of the Australian Senate, in Official Hansard Report of Proceedings of the Committee, 18 August 1972)

'Legal Education in a Changing World' (Report of the Committee on Legal Education in the Developing Countries, 1975)

Report of Committee of Review of New South Wales Institute of Technology (NSWIT, 1983)

Publications of the Law Reform Commission of New South Wales under the chairmanship of JH Wootten:

  *The Legal Profession: General Regulation* (Discussion Paper No 1, Inquiry into the Legal Profession, 1979)

  *The Legal Profession: Complaints, Discipline and Professional Standards* (Discussion Paper No 2 of the Inquiry into the Legal Profession, 1979)

Reports as Royal Commissioner into Aboriginal Deaths in Custody (all at <https://www.austlii.edu.au/au/other/IndigLRes/rciadic>:

  Report of the Inquiry into the Death of Malcolm Charles Smith (1989)

Report of the Inquiry into the Death of Thomas William Murray (1989)

Report of the Inquiry into the Death of Mark Wayne Revell (1989)

Report of the Inquiry into the Death of James Archibald Moore (1990)

Report of the Inquiry into the Death of Arthur Moffatt (1990)

Report of the Inquiry into the Death of Harrison Moore (1990)

Report of the Inquiry into the Death of Clarence Alec Nean (1990)

Report on Preliminary Investigation into the Death of Paul Pryor (1990)

Report of the Inquiry into the Death of Thomas Carr (1990)

Report of the Inquiry into the Death of Paul Lawrence Kearney (1990)

Report of the Inquiry into the Death of Bruce Thomas Leslie (1990)

Report of the Inquiry into the Death of Peter Wayne Williams (1990)

Report of the Inquiry into the Death of Glenn Allan Clark (1990)

Report of the Inquiry into the Death of Maxwell Roy Saunders (1990)

Report of the Inquiry into the Death of Lloyd James Boney (1991)

Report of the Inquiry into the Death of Shane Kenneth Atkinson (1991)

Report of the Inquiry into the Death of Mark Anthony Quayle (1991)

Report of the Inquiry into the Death of David John Gundy (1991)

Regional Report of Inquiry in New South Wales, Victoria and Tasmania
(1991)

'The Commonwealth and the Mabo Case' (A paper dated 23 October 1992
discussing the appropriate Commonwealth response to the *Mabo* decision,
forwarded to the Prime Minister, members of Federal Cabinet, and
Aboriginal and industry organisations)

*Significant Aboriginal Sites in Area of Proposed Junction Waterhole Dam, Alice
Springs,* Report to Minister for Aboriginal Affairs under s 10(4) of the
*Aboriginal and Torres Strait Islander Heritage Protection Act 1984* (Cth)
(Department of Aboriginal Affairs, 1992)

*Significant Aboriginal Sites in Area of Iron Princess Mine, Iron Knob, South Australia,*
Report to Minister for Aboriginal Affairs under s 10(4) of the *Aboriginal
and Torres Strait Islander Heritage Protection Act 1984* (Cth) (Department of
Aboriginal Affairs, 1993)

*Significant Aboriginal Sites in Area of Boobera Lagoon,* Report to Minister for
Aboriginal Affairs under s 10(4) of the *Aboriginal and Torres Strait Islander
Heritage Protection Act 1984* (Cth) (Department of Aboriginal Affairs, 1996)

Submission to the Senate Legal and Constitutional Legislation Committee's
Inquiry into the provisions of the Australian Human Rights Commission
Legislation Bill 2003

# NOTES

## Foreword

1    Hal Wootten, 'Conflicting Imperatives: Pursuing Truth in the Courts' in Iain McCalman and Ann McGrath (eds), *Proof & Truth: The Humanist as Expert* (Australian Academy of the Humanities, 2003) 36–37. See chapter 5 (Eds).

## Chapter 1: Introducing Hal

1    Peter Thompson, *Big Ideas,* ABC, May 2005 <https://www.abc.net.au/listen/programs/bigideas/wisdom-interviews-hal-wootten-qc/3446536>.

2    Richard A Posner (ed.), *The Essential Holmes: Selections from the Letters, Speeches, Judicial Opinions, and Other Writings of Oliver Wendell Holmes, Jr.* (University of Chicago Press, 1992) ix–xxxi, ix, xi. See also Stephen Budiansky, *Oliver Wendell Holmes: A Life in War, Law, and Ideas* (WW Norton, 2019).

3    Posner, *Essential Holmes*, xvi.

4    Oliver Wendell Holmes, *The Common Law* (Little, Brown, 1881) 1.

5    Anthony Blackshield, 'Julius Stone (1907–1985)', *Australian Dictionary of Biography* <adb.anu.edu.au/biography/stone-julius-15728>; Leonie Star, *Julius Stone: An Intellectual Life* (Oxford University Press, 1992).

6    Julius Stone, *The Province and Function of Law* (Harvard University Press, 1950).

7    Peter Edwards, 'Sir John Robert Kerr (1914–1991)', *Australian Dictionary of Biography* <adb.anu.edu.au/biography/kerr-sir-john-robert-23431>.

8    Jeremy Beckett and Geoffrey Gray, 'Hogbin, Herbert Ian Priestley (1904–1989)', *Australian Dictionary of Biography,* <adb.anu.edu.au/biography/hogbin-herbert-ian-priestley-12644>.

9    See Brian Costar, Peter Love and Paul Strangio (eds), *The Great Labor Schism* (Scribe Publications, 2005).

10   David Hough, 'Chaney, Frederick Michael 1941–' *The Biographical Dictionary of the Australian Senate, Vol. 4, 1983–2002* (Department of the Senate, Canberra, 2017) 484–90.

11   Thompson, *Big Ideas.*

12   Beckett and Gray, 'Hogbin'.

13   James Davis, ed., *Choice and Change: Essays in Honour of Lucy Mair* (Routledge, 1974).

14   David Wetherell, 'Wedgwood, Camilla Hildegarde (1901–1955)', *Australian Dictionary of Biography,* <adb.anu.edu.au/biography/wedgwood-camilla-hildegarde-11992/text21503>.

15    KS Inglis, 'Rowley, Charles Dunford (1906–1985)', *Australian Dictionary of Biography*, <adb.anu.edu.au/biography/rowley-charles-dunford-14191/text25203>.

16    Peter Pierce, 'McAuley, James Phillip (1917–1976)', *Australian Dictionary of Biography,* <adb.anu.edu.au/biography/mcauley-james-phillip-10896/text19347>.

17    Patricia Grimshaw, 'Cowlishaw, Gillian', *The Encyclopaedia of Women and Leadership in Twentieth Century Australia*, <www.womenaustralia.info/leaders/biogs/WLE0674b.htm>.

18    Shulman is an Israeli Indologist and a founding member of the Israeli–Palestinian peace movement Ta'ayush who has written numerous books on the Israel–Palestine relationship and on resistance to the illegal settlements in the West Bank, notably including *Dark Hope* (University of Chicago Press, 2007), *Freedom and Despair: Notes from the South Hebron Hills* (University of Chicago Press, 2018) and *The Bitter Landscapes of Palestine* with Margaret Olin (Intellect, 2024).

19    Margalit is an Israeli philosopher whose many works on the human condition and the Palestinian question include *The Decent Society* (Harvard University Press, 1996), *The Ethics of Memory* (Harvard University Press, 2000), and *Occidentalism: The West in the Eyes of its Enemies* with Ian Buruma (Penguin, 2004).

20    Shehadeh is a Palestinian lawyer who co-founded Al-Haq, a leading human rights organisation. He is the author of many books on Palestine, from *The Third Way* (Quartet, 1992) to *What Does Israel Fear From Palestine?* (Profile Books, 2024).

21    Archibald Percival Wavell, *Other Men's Flowers: An Anthology of Poetry* (Jonathan Cape, 1944).

22    An Australian popular poet: see Ian F McLaren, *Australian Dictionary of Biography*, 'Clarence Michael James Dennis' (1876–1938), <adb.anu.edu.au/biography/dennis-clarence-michael-james-5957>.

23    An American humourist. See Thomas Fensch, *The Man Who Was Walter Mitty* (Sharons Books, 2001).

24    'The Bear Who Let It Alone', *New Yorker* (29 April 1939).

### Chapter 2: Principles, vision and action

1    A shorter version of this chapter was published as 'Why, and Why Not?', *Inside Story* (Carlton, 17 September 2021), <insidestory.org.au/why-and-why-not>.

2    For Kerr's relationship with Hal, see chapter 1 (Eds).

3    Neville Wran was Premier of NSW 1976–86; Frank Walker was Attorney-General of NSW in the Wran Government 1976–83 and the state's first Minister for Aboriginal Affairs 1981–84, before a career in federal

politics 1990–96 and afterwards in the NSW judiciary; Paul Landa was also a Minister in the Wran Government, including for Planning and Environment, before succeeding Walker as Attorney-General in 1983 (Eds).

## Chapter 3: Living greatly in the law

1   For Holmes's influence on Hal, see chapter 1 (Eds).
2   The lectures and Hal's responses are available at 'The Hal Wootten Lecture', University of NSW, <www.unsw.edu.au/law-justice/news-events/events/annual-hal-wootten-lecture> (Eds).
3   Hal Wootten, 'Response to Lecture Delivered by Julian Burnside AO QC' (Speech, Hal Wootten Lecture, UNSW, 30 March 2015).
4   Archibald Percival Wavell, *Other Men's Flowers: An Anthology of Poetry* (Jonathan Cape, 1944).
5   *R v Knowles; Ex parte Somersett* (1772) 20 Howell's State Tr. 1; *Somerset v Stewart* 1 Lofft 499; 98 ER 499.
6   Lord Diplock, 'Speech to the 16th Legal Convention of the Law Council of Australia' (1971) 45(9) *Australian Law Journal* 450–51, 451. This was a time when, Hal commented acidly, no Australian law conference was complete without a visiting English law lord. Diplock was speaking of nudges long before the idea was popularised by Richard Thaler and Cass Sunstein, *Nudge* (Yale University Press 2008). Both Hal and Diplock overestimated the significance of Mansfield's nudge: see James Oldham, 'New Light on Mansfield and Slavery' (1988) 27(1) *Journal of British Studies* 45–68 (Eds).
7   William Henley, 'Invictus' in William Henley, *A Book of Verses* (David Nutt, 1888) 56–57, 57.
8   William Shakespeare, *Hamlet*, Act 1, Scene 3.
9   On Williams, Stone and their conflict, see Anthony Blackshield, 'Julius Stone (1907–1985)', *Australian Dictionary of Biography,* <adb.anu.edu.au/biography/stone.julius-15728/text26916> (Eds).
10  When Hal applied for a lectureship at the University of Tasmania, Williams took his revenge for Hal's support for Julius Stone by blackballing him in a reference (Personal Communication, from Hal to David Dixon, 21 June 2018).
11  For Kerr's relationship with Hal, see chapter 1 (Eds).
12  Julius Stone, *The Province and Function of Law* (Harvard University Press, 1950).
13  Harold Laski, *The Danger of Being a Gentleman* (Routledge, 1939). Laski's essay was a biting critique of the English ruling class. Although Hal was not explicit, he was drawing attention to the antisemitism that Stone encountered: see Blackshield, 'Julius Stone'. See also Hal's reference to 'beyond the pale' in this paragraph (Eds).
14  Oliver Wendell Holmes, 'The Profession of the Law' in Sheldon M Novick

(ed.), *The Collected Works of Justice Holmes* (University of Chicago Press, 1995) vol 3, 471.

15   Herbert Wechsler, 'Toward Neutral Principles of Constitutional Law' (1959) 73(1) *Harvard Law Review* 1–35, 35.

16   'Some there are who are nothing else than a passage for food and augmentors of excrement and fillers of privies, because through them no other things in the world, nor any good effects are produced, since nothing but full privies results from them.' Jean Paul Richter (ed.), *The Notebooks of Leonardo da Vinci* (1888) 1179 (Eds).

17   See Oliver Wendell Holmes, 'The Path of the Law' (1897) 10(8) *Harvard Law Review* 457–78, 459–61.

18   In *Buck v Bell*, 274 U.S. 200 (1927), Holmes upheld a state law on sterilisation of people 'afflicted with hereditary forms of insanity that are recurrent, idiocy, imbecility, feeble-mindedness or epilepsy': see Adam Cohen, *Imbeciles: The Supreme Court, American Eugenics, and the Sterilization of Carrie Buck* (Penguin, 2016). Budiansky points out that belief in eugenics in the 1920s was common and respectable: *Oliver Wendell Holmes*, 14–15, 428–31 (Eds).

19   Oliver Wendell Holmes, 'Speech to the Bar Association of Boston' in *Speeches* (Little, Brown, 1913) 85, quoting Ecclesiastes, 9:10.

20   'O wad some Pow'r the giftie gie us / To see oursels as ithers see us!'. Robert Burns, 'To a Louse' (1786).

21   John Masefield, 'Consecration' in *Salt-Water Ballads* (Grant Richards, 1902) 1–2.

22   A statement by the leaders of the USA and UK in 1941 on the principles to be followed in post-war reconstruction. It was a step towards the formation of the United Nations. See Douglas Brinkley and David R Facey-Crowther (eds), *The Atlantic Charter* (Palgrave Macmillan, 1994) (Eds).

23   The 1951 referendum on a proposal of the Menzies government to amend the Commonwealth Constitution to authorise banning of the Australian Communist Party failed (Eds).

24   Hal's writing on industrial law included: 'The Community's Interest in Trade Unions' in John Wilkes and SE Benson (eds), *Trade Unions in Australia* (Angus & Robertson, 1959) 89–126; 'The Role of the Tribunals' (1970) 12(2) *Journal of Industrial Relations* 130–44; and 'Commentary' on JE Isaac, 'Lawyers and Industrial Relations' in AD Hambly and JL Goldring (eds), *Australian Lawyers and Social Change* (The Law Book Company, 1976) 349–60 (Eds).

25   On the Papua New Guinea Local Officers' Award case, see Troy Bramston, *Bob Hawke: Demons and Destiny* (Penguin, 2022) ch 8, and Commonwealth, *Parliamentary Debates*, Senate, 21 September 1967, 848–72 (Eds).

26   'Another Congo in New Guinea: What Happened to the University of Port Moresby?' 86(4423) *The Bulletin* (28 November 1964) 17–20; Letter, 'New

Guinea, Money, the World Bank Blueprint' 87(4446) *The Bulletin* 17 (15 May 1965); 'The World's Most Generous Colonisers But Still the Prisoners of Race ...' 87(4435) *The Bulletin* 41–43 (27 February 1965).

27 Hal Wootten 'Where Were the Aborigines?' *Inside Story* (19 December 2016) <insidestory.org.au/where-were-the-aborigines>. See also Bill Bunbury, *It's Not the Money it's the Land: Aboriginal Stockmen and the Equal Wages Case* (Fremantle Arts Centre Press, 2002). This includes extensive quotations from an interview with Hal about the case (Eds).

28 *Australasian Meat Industry Employees Union v Meat and Allied Trades Federation of Australia* (1969) 127 CAR 1142.

29 'People' (1979) 50(12) *Pacific Islands Monthly* 27–29, 29.

30 Stephen Wilks, 'James Robert (Jim) McClelland (1915–1999)', *Australian Dictionary of Biography* <adb.anu.edu.au/biography/mcclelland-james-robert-jim-32753/text40720>.

31 Brian Costar, Peter Love and Paul Strangio (eds), *The Great Labor Schism* (Scribe Publications, 2005).

32 Henry Bournes Higgins, *A New Province for Law & Order: Being a Review, by its late President for Fourteen Years, of the Australian Court of Conciliation and Arbitration* (Dawsons, 1968).

33 Edmund Burke, *On Conciliation with America* (1775).

34 Hal was Chancellor of the NSW Institute of Technology 1980–88, overseeing its development into the University of Technology, Sydney, an appointment that he much enjoyed (Eds).

35 David Marr, *Barwick* (Allen & Unwin, 1980) ch 13.

36 Hal Wootten, 'The Orr Dismissal and the Universities' (1957) 1(2) *Quadrant*, 25–29; Hal Wootten and John Kerr, 'Re-opening the Orr Case' (1958) 4(10) *The Free Spirit* 3–5; Hal Wootten and John Kerr, 'The Orr Case: A Rejoinder' (1958) 4(11) *The Free Spirit* 13; Hal Wootten and John Kerr, 'The Orr Case: A Further Rejoinder' (1959) 5(1) *The Free Spirit* 22–23. See also Cassandra Pybus, *Gross Moral Turpitude: The Orr Case Reconsidered* (Heinemann, 1993).

37 Hal Wootten, 'Current Comment: The Stuart Case' (1959) 5(2) *The Free Spirit* 1–3; Hal Wootten 'Book Review – The Stuart Case' (2003) 5(24) *Indigenous Law Bulletin* 22–23.

38 JH Wootten, 'The Law Association for Asia and the Western Pacific: An Experiment in Regional Cooperation' (1968) 7(2) *Washburn Law Journal* 211–38.

39 The Bible, Mark 8:36.

40 To, respectively, the NSW State Industrial Commission and the Commonwealth Arbitration Commission (Eds).

41 See chapter 6 (Eds).

42 Philip Knightley, *The Vestey Affair* (The Book Service, 1981).

43  See chapter 3 (Eds).

44  Bret Walker, 'Lawyers and Money' (Speech, St James Ethics Centre Lawyers' Lecture Series, Sydney, 18 October 2005).

45  Oliver Wendel Holmes, 'The Profession of the Law' in Posner, *The Essential Holmes*, 218. Sancho Panza is the peasant recruited by Don Quixote to be his squire in Miguel de Cervantes' novel, *Don Quixote* (1605–15) (Eds).

46  US Secretary of Defense 2001–06, much criticised for his role in the 'War on Terror' (Eds).

47  Jean-Dominique Bauby, *The Diving Bell and the Butterfly* (Éditions Robert Laffont, 1997).

48  See chapter 4 (Eds).

49  The Global Financial Crisis of 2007–08 saw financial institutions, which had insisted 'the market rules', bailed out by governments (Eds).

50  Henley, 'Invictus', 57.

51  See note 2, above.

52  David Marr and Marian Wilkinson, *Dark Victory* (Allen & Unwin, 2004).

53  An asylum seeker, Reza Barati, was murdered by a guard in 2014 in a detention camp on Manus, the island on which Hal had such formative experiences in the late 1940s (Eds).

## Chapter 4: A new law school

1  Peter Thompson, *Big Ideas* (ABC, 1 May 2005) <www.abc.net.au/listen/programs/bigideas/wisdom-interviews-hal-wootten-qc/3446536>.

2  Personal communication from Hal to David Dixon (21 June 2018). Unfortunately, a copy has not survived (Eds).

3  See chapter 3 (Eds).

4  On the circumstances of his appointment, see Marion Dixon, *Thirty Up* (UNSW Law School, 2001) 1–3 (Eds).

5  For more detailed retrospective, see Interview with Emeritus Professor Hal Wootten (Sue Georgevits, UNSW Library Oral History Program in UNSW Archives, 23 February 2009 and 16 September 2010) (Eds).

6  Emeritus Professor David Brown gave a warning against the 'teleology of the founding vision' in his Address to UNSW Law's Thirtieth Anniversary Dinner (Eds).

7  In the 1972 Handbook, Hal commented, 'We have not changed our objectives … The wonderful response of our first year of students has enabled us to go a very long way towards achieving those objectives. We look to you, the new students of 1972, to join in the challenge and excitement of this unfinished task'. 'Faculty of Law: 1972 Handbook' (UNSW, 1972) 5 <legacy.handbook.unsw.edu.au/archive/historical/UNSWLawHandbook1972.pdf> (Eds).

8  All the original academics were men. The first woman to be appointed was

Pat Hyndman, followed quickly by Mary Jane Mossman and Jane Levine (Personal Correspondence, from Mary Jane Mossman to David Dixon, 6 September 2024) (Eds).

9    In the version of this letter in 1972, a more focused review of teaching was noted: 'you will soon hear of TERC which is studying the development of the Law Faculty as a piece of educational research, and at the time helping us develop and improve our teaching methods' (Eds).

10   The 1973 Handbook noted that 'student representatives on Faculty also serve on School's Examinations Committees and other Committees of the School and of the Faculty. Meetings of the Faculty are open to all Law students'. Faculty of Law, '1973 Handbook' (UNSW, 1973) 8 <legacy.handbook.unsw. edu.au/archive/historical/UNSWLawHandbook1973.pdf?> (Eds).

11   The 'huts' were part of the mythology of the early years – as David Dixon found out when the demolition of the last of them unfortunately coincided with a visit to campus by a group of the 'Originals' (Eds).

12   Professor Martin Krygier is the Gordon Samuels Professor of Law and Social Theory at UNSW (Eds).

13   Philip Selznick, *Leadership in Administration: A Sociological Interpretation* (Harper & Row, 1957) 17. See Martin Krygier, *Philip Selznick: Ideals in the World* (Stanford University Press, 2012) 76 (Eds).

14   Here, Hal refers to the way in which the Socratic method was applied at some US law schools as questions to supposedly *tabula rasa* students from intimidating professors who knew the (only acceptable) answers. The fictional Professor Kingsfield in John Jay Osborn's *The Paper Chase* (Houghton Mifflin, 1971) is the classic example: he tells his students, 'You come in here with a skull full of mush. You leave thinking like a lawyer' (Eds).

15   Richard W Effland, 'On the Retirement (So-Called) of Willard H. Pedrick' (1982) 4 *Arizona State Law Journal* 805–806. Pedrick had visited Australian law schools. In turn, Hal visited several US law schools while also collecting material for the new Law Library with Rob Brian, the librarian who was a vital member of Hal's team (Eds).

16   The 'very creative man' was John Kerr (see chapter 1). Later acolytes of Gough Whitlam at UNSW may have been surprised by Kerr's influence on their law school (Eds).

17   Professor Sir Rupert Myers KBE, AO was UNSW Vice-Chancellor 1969–81 (Eds).

18   The original academics were Professors Hal Wootten, Garth Nettheim, and Curt Garbesi; Senior Lecturers Tony Blackshield and Bob Hayes; and Lecturer Richard Chisholm: see Dixon, *Thirty Up*, 5–10 (Eds).

19   Professor Katz was Director of the UNSW Tertiary Education Research Centre (TERC) (Eds).

20  Daniel Rezneck, 'In Memoriam: Paul A. Freund Remembered' (1993) 62 *The American Scholar* 277–80.

21  This was Patricia O'Shane: see Nikki Henningham, 'O'Shane, Pat', *Encyclopedia of Women & Leadership in Twentieth-Century Australia* <www.womenaustralia.info/leaders/biogs/WLE0771b.htm> (Eds).

22  See chapter 7 (Eds).

23  Professor Martin Krygier, *Between Fear and Hope* (ABC Books, 1997).

24  Professor Graham Greenleaf, cofounder of AustLII, the Australasian Legal Information Institute (Eds).

25  Sir Gerard Brennan, '25th Anniversary of the University of New South Wales Law School' (1997) 20(1) *University of New South Wales Law Journal* 210–14.

26  David Hicks was an Australian detained by the United States at Guantanamo Bay between 2002 and 2007. See Leigh Sales, *Detainee 002 – The Case of David Hicks* (Melbourne University Press, 2007) (Eds).

27  UNSW Chancellor David Gonski AC graduated from UNSW with a Bachelor of Commerce in 1976 and a Bachelor of Laws (with the University Medal) in 1977 (Eds).

28  Hal here refers to one of his favourites – King Harry's St Crispin's Day speech to his comrades at the Battle of Agincourt in *Henry V*, Act IV, Scene III (Eds).

29  The name 'Originals' is claimed for themselves by the very first student cohort when the Faculty commenced teaching in 1971 (Eds).

30  Padraic McGuinness (1938–2008) was an Australian journalist and commentator. He edited *Quadrant* from 1997 to shortly before his death (Eds).

31  OW Holmes, 'Memorial Day' in Posner (ed.), *The Essential Holmes* 80–87, 86.

32  UNSW Law & Justice was ranked 1st in Australia and 12th in the world in 2025 by QS: see QS Top Universities, *QS World University Rankings by Subject 2025: Law & Legal Studies* (14 March 2025) <www.topuniversities.com/university-subject-rankings/law-legal-studies> (Eds).

33  See chapter 1 (Eds).

### Chapter 5: In an ancient land: Palestine and Israel

1   David Shulman, *Dark Hope: Working for Peace in Israel and Palestine* (University of Chicago Press, 2007).

2   For opposing views of the wall, see 'Saving Lives: Israel's anti-terrorist fence – Answers to Questions (January 2004)', *Israel Ministry of Foreign Affairs* (1 January 2004) <www.gov.il/en/pages/saving-lives-israel-s-anti-terrorist-fence-answers-to-questions-jan-2004> and 'Explainer: Israel's West Bank Wall', *Institute for Middle East Understanding* (3 July 2024) <imeu.org/article/israels-west-bank-wall>; 'The Separation Barrier', *B'Tselem* (11 November 2017). <www.btselem.org/separation_barrier>; Eyal Weizman, Hollow Land: Israel's Architecture of Occupation (Verso, 2007) ch 6. In 2004, the International Court of Justice gave an advisory opinion that the wall was

illegal under international humanitarian law and human rights instruments: *Legal Consequences of the Construction of a Wall in the Occupied Palestinian Territory* (Advisory Opinion) [2004] ICJ Rep 2004 136 <web.archive.org/web/20100706021237/http://www.icj-cij.org/docket/files/131/1671.pdf> (Eds).

3   Despite the Bedouin being Israeli citizens, their villages are unrecognised by the Israeli state, which refuses to supply services, frequently disrupts them by home demolitions and evictions, and seeks to replace them with Jewish Israeli citizens: see Human Rights Watch, *Off the Map: Land and Housing Rights Violations in Israel's Unrecognized Bedouin Villages* (Human Rights Watch, 2008) (Eds).

4   Communal agricultural communities: see Yuval Achouch, 'The Rise and Decline of the Kibbutz Movement in Israel' in PR Kumaraswamy (eds), *The Palgrave International Handbook of Israel* (Palgrave Macmillan, 2023) 978–81 (Eds).

5   The territory of Israel defined not by international law and agreement, but by the Old Testament (Eds).

6   Hal commented on a Palestinian who drove a bulldozer down a busy Jerusalem street until he was shot dead. 'He had no particular target except the traffic and pedestrians that chanced to be there, but three people were killed and 45 injured. This was not a skilfully devised terrorist operation, but a reckless rampage by a person who for some reason had snapped' (Eds).

7   Raja Shehadeh, *The Third Way: A Journal of Life in the West Bank* (Quartet, 1982). Shehadeh was the founder of Al Haq, see below (Eds).

8   See Prineas's 2006 photographs in Toine van Teeffelen, with Victoria Biggs and the Sumud Story House in Bethlehem, *The Spirit of Sumud: Soul of the Palestinian People* at <assets.super.so/d05895a3-5ecd-4d1e-9871-f435a8278885/files/45fd71b5-ea0a-48fb-8a84-6cbd427e7273/Sumud_Soul_Of_The_Palestinian_People.pdf>.

9   While Yasser Arafat, chairman of the Palestinian Authority 1994–2004, is often blamed for the failure of the Camp David summit convened by President Bill Clinton, for a different evaluation of the competing Israeli and Palestinian narratives around the summit see Jeremy Pressman, 'Visions in Collision: What Happened at Camp David and Taba' (2003) 28(2) *International Security* 5–43 (Eds).

10  The founder of political Zionism: see Derek Penslar, *Theodor Herzl* (Yale University Press, 2020) (Eds).

11  Uri Avnery, 'A Maddened Cow', *ZNetwork* (6 July 2002) <znetwork.org/znetarticle/a-maddened-cow-by-uri-avnery>.

12  See further Ian Black, *Enemies and Neighbours* (Allen Lane, 2017) 237, 341, 349, 352, 441–44 (Eds).

13  Avishai Margalit, 'A Moral Witness to the "Intricate Machine"', *New York Review of Books* (6 December 2007). On the significant role of exclusive roads, see Black, *Enemies and Neighbours* 237, 239, 352, 441 (Eds).

14  In 2012, Jabarin visited UNSW at Hal's invitation (Eds).

15  Lynn Welchman, *Al-Haq: A Global History of the First Palestinian Human Rights Organization* (University of California Press, 2021) (Eds).

16  <www.alhaq.org>.

17  <www.btselem.org/about_btselem>.

18  <www.ta'ayush.org>.

19  Quoted by David Kretzmer, *The Occupation of Justice: The Supreme Court of Israel and the Occupied Territories* (SUNY Press, 2002) 24. The 2012 appointment to the Court of Justice Noam Sohlberg, who lives in a settlement in the West Bank, did nothing for Palestinian confidence in the institution: see Uri Misgave, 'The Israeli Justice Who Violates International Law Every Time He Comes Home', *Haaretz* (Tel Aviv, 10 June 2016). Justice Sohlberg is in line to be Chief Justice in 2028 (Eds).

20  David Kretzmer, *The Occupation of Justice: The Supreme Court of Israel and the Occupied Territories* (SUNY Press, 2002).

21  See, eg, Raja Shehadeh, *Palestinian Walks: Notes on a Vanishing Landscape* (Profile Books, 2008); *Strangers in the House: Coming of Age in Occupied Palestine* (Penguin, 2013); *Occupation Diaries* (Profile Books, 2023); *What Does Israel Fear from Palestine?* (Penguin, 2024).

22  See DK Fieldhouse, *Western Imperialism in the Middle East* (Oxford University Press, 2008) ch 5. In the post–World War I settlement, Britain took responsibility for Palestine, seeing it as a vital imperial foothold in the Middle East. Fieldhouse concludes that 'Palestine was the greatest failure in the whole history of British imperial rule'. Preparations for self-government were derisory. In 1948, British forces were simply withdrawn, setting the stage for the inevitable conflict between Jewish settlers and Palestinian residents which culminated in the Nakba (Eds).

23  Referring to the time at which Hal was writing, being 2008–14 (Eds).

24  The geography is usefully explained by Matt Garrow, 'Understanding the History of the Israeli–Palestinian Conflict in Five Charts', *The Conversation* (Melbourne, 26 October 2023). For a detailed report, see B'Tselem, 'State Business: Israel's Misappropriation of Land in the West Bank through Settler Violence', *B'Tselem* (November 2021), and also a series of reports by Al-Haq available on their website (Eds).

25  Idith Zertal, Akiva Eldar and Vivian Sohn, *Lords of the Land: The War over Israel's Settlements in the Occupied Territories, 1967–2007* (Nation Books, 2007) 7–8.

26  Nir Hefez and Gadi Bloom, *Ariel Sharon* (Random House, 2006) 108; Zertal et al., *Lords of the Land* 60.

27  The significance of the reference should be clear from this description: 'Bantustans (also known as "homelands") were a cornerstone of the "grand apartheid" policy of the 1960s and 1970s, justified by the apartheid government as benevolent "separate development." The Promotion of Bantu Self-Government Act of 1959 … abolished indirect representation of blacks in Pretoria and divided Africans into ten ethnically discrete groups, each assigned a traditional "homeland." [These] homelands constituted only 13% of the land – for approximately 75% of the population. The Bantu Homelands Citizenship Act of 1970 declared that all Africans were citizens of "homelands," rather than of South Africa itself – a step toward the government's ultimate goal of having no African citizens of South Africa. Between 1976 and 1981, four homelands – Transkei, Venda, Bophuthatswana, and Ciskei – were declared "independent" by Pretoria, and eight million Africans lost their South African citizenship. None of the homelands was recognized by any other country' <overcomingapartheid.msu.edu/multimedia.php?kid=163–582–19>. When Apartheid fell, the bantustans were reintegrated into Mandela's democratic South Africa.

28  Zertal et al., *Lords of the Land* 422–23.

29  <www.peacenow.org.il/site/en/peace.asp?pi=61&fld=495&docid=3159>.

30  What David Shulman calls 'the Gazafication of what is left of the Palestinian West Bank': Shulman, 'Heading towards a Second Nakba', *New York Review of Books* (19 October 2023) (Eds).

31  Avnery, 'A Maddened Cow'.

32  Tanya Reinhart, *Israel/Palestine: How to End the War of 1948* (Seven Stories Press, 2nd ed, 2005) 221.

33  'East Jerusalem', *B'Tselem* (11 November 2017) <www.btselem.org/jerusalem>.

34  See David Shulman, 'On Being Unfree: Fences, Roadblocks, and the Iron Cage of Palestine' (2008) 20(2) *Mānoa* 13–32; Black, *Enemies and Neighbours*, 237, 239, 352, 441.

35  A decade later, the number was over 700 000: see <www.aljazeera.com/news/2024/9/16/ten-maps-to-understand-the-occupied-west-bank>; <www.un.org/unispal/document/human-rights-council-hears-that-700000-israeli-settlers-are-living-illegally-in-the-occupied-west-bank-meeting-summary-excerpts> (Eds).

36  An uprising against Israeli occupation of the OPT 2000–05, during which time some 1000 Israelis and 4700 Palestinians were killed. See Wendy Pearlman, *Violence and Nonviolence and the Palestinian National Movement* (Cambridge University Press, 2011) ch 6 (Eds).

37  Hal Wootten, 'Much Too Promised Land', *Inside Story* (Carlton, Victoria, 16 February 2012) <insidestory.org.au/much-too-promised-land>.

38   Hal died before the establishment of a new organisation, the Australian
     Jewish Council: see <www.jewishcouncil.com.au>. The AJC says of its role:
     'We are proud Jewish people in Australia with diverse histories, traditions
     and politics. We are committed to the values of tikkun olam (repairing the
     world), calling out injustice, challenging assumptions and promoting debate.
     We reject the assertion that Jews and the State of Israel are one and the same,
     or that all Jewish people support, without criticism, the actions of the Israeli
     government and military' (Eds).
39   David Dixon (Dean of UNSW Law, 2006–16).

## Chapter 6: Judges, lawyers, evidence

1    (1982) 7 ACLR 202. Hal decided that a civil plaintiff is not automatically
     prevented from pursuing their case merely because to do so might result
     in the defendant having to disclose their likely defence to any existing or
     potential criminal proceedings. Hal outlined the factors that should be taken
     into account in exercising the relevant discretion, including whether there is
     a real danger of injustice if the defendant is required to reveal their criminal
     defence in the civil proceedings.
2    David Lusty, 'Coercive Powers and Criminal Justice: Lawfully Compelled
     Self-Incrimination and the Use of Compelled Evidence' (Forthcoming PhD
     Thesis, UNSW).
3    See Damien Freeman, 'Roderick Pitt (Roddy) Meagher 1932–2011' *Australian
     Financial Review* (Sydney, 8 July 2011) 29. In an unpublished letter to the
     *Sydney Morning Herald*, Meagher and colleagues suggested that, rather than
     the Legal Professional Council mooted by the Law Reform Commission,
     there should be a 'a praesidium of 365 black trade unionists': 100(5160)
     *The Bulletin* (15 May 1979) 50. On this dispute, see 'Struggling with the
     Modern World', *Justinian* (February 1980) (Eds).
4    Hal's paper was published in Iain McCalman and Ann McGrath (eds),
     *Proof & Truth: The Humanist as Expert* (Australian Academy of the
     Humanities, 2003).
5    From the symposium program.
6    I follow the symposium description in using the term 'humanist' to refer
     to scholars in the humanities. Both the areas and the concept of humanities
     are conventionally and historically defined. Although anthropologists are
     more commonly regarded as social scientists, much of their intellectual work
     overlaps with recognised areas of the humanities, and I include them in my
     discussion because they have been heavily involved, along with historians,
     linguists and archaeologists, as expert witnesses in litigation arising out of
     Indigenous claims.
7    See, for example, the definition in Geoffrey Millerson, *The Qualifying
     Associations* (Routledge, 1964).

8   Oliver Wendell Holmes, 'The Path of Law' (1897) 10(8) *Harvard Law Review* 457–78. On Holmes, and Hal's reliance on him, see chapter 1 (Eds).

9   At least since Socrates, scholars have been blamed for the supposedly pernicious effects of their ideas, as when books are burnt, postmodernists blamed for undermining commitment to truth, and liberals for moral permissiveness. However, that is a different problem. At times some anthropologists have had an itch to take responsibility for a sector of community problems, viz the administration of colonised or indigenous people, and individuals have accepted such a role, but the discipline as a whole has resisted the temptation and the responsibility this would bring: see Gillian Cowlishaw, 'Helping Anthropologists: Cultural Continuity in the Construction of Aboriginalists' (1990) 13(2) *Canberra Anthropology* 1–28. Since anthropologists have become frequently involved as expert witnesses in land claims, there have been proposals to establish a professional body to certify the qualifications of its members.

10  I trust I will not be considered naïve for making this assumption about humanists and downplaying what seem to me sometimes excessive (although not groundless) concerns expressed about a widespread 'betrayal of scholarship', or abandonment of the quest for truth, in the humanities, social sciences and legal scholarship.

11  However, in Australian experience it is not uncommon for governments to be forced to grant extensions of the terms of reference when it becomes apparent that related issues on which there is public interest in knowing the truth lie outside the terms of reference. The Commission of Inquiry into Possible Illegal Activities and Associated Police Misconduct (the 'Fitzgerald Inquiry': 1987–89) into Queensland Police corruption is one of the more famous examples (as is the Royal Commission into Aboriginal Deaths in Custody (RCIADIC)).

12  This has led some scholars to describe the official processes of adjudication as a form of social ordering rather than mere dispute settlement: Lon L Fuller, 'The Forms and Limits of Adjudication' in Kenneth I Winston (ed.), *The Principles of Social Order: Selected Essays of Lon L Fuller* (Hart Publishing, 2001) 79–139.

13  This formulation draws on Fuller, 'The Forms and Limits ...'.

14  *Wilson v Minister for Aboriginal and Torres Strait Islander Affairs* (1996) 189 CLR 1.

15  *Universal Declaration of Human Rights*, GA Res 217A (III), UN GAOR, UN Doc A/810 (10 December 1948) art 10. Fact-finding processes, for example as to alleged breaches of human rights, are increasingly part of the armoury of international organisations and they too recognise that a fundamental requirement is a fair procedure: Henry J Steiner and Philip Alston, *International Human Rights in Context: Law, Politics, Morals* (Clarendon Press, 1996).

16  *Australian Broadcasting Tribunal v Bond* (1990) 170 CLR 321, 367 (Deane J).

17  It was at one time common to make a sharp contrast between the 'adversarial' common law procedure and the 'inquisitorial' continental or civil law. A Royal Commission, especially one involving allegations against individuals, often blends adversarial and inquisitorial features. Parties are given leave to appear adversarially to protect their interests, but the Commission is assisted by independent counsel who oversees investigation on behalf of the Commission and takes the leading role in the presentation of evidence.

18  John Lukacs, *Churchill: Visionary. Statesman. Historian* (Scribe Publications, 2002) 21.

19  Patrick Sullivan, 'Don't Educate the Judge: Court Experts and Court Expertise in the Social Disciplines' (Conference Paper, AIATSIS Native Title Conference, 4 September 2002).

20  Uniform Evidence Act s 140.

21  *Pearse v Pearse* (1846) 63 ER 950, 957.

22  Carlo Ginzburg, 'Checking the Evidence: The Judge and the Historian' in James Chandler, Arnold I Davidson and Harry Harootunian (eds), *Questions of Evidence: Proof, Practice and Persuasion across the Disciplines* (University of Chicago, 1994) 290–303, 294.

23  Tony Honore, 'The Primacy of Oral Evidence?' in Colin Tapper (ed.), *Crime, Proof and Punishment* (Butterworths, 1981) 172–92. It would appear that in this respect the experience of the legal process is much longer and deeper than that of historiography, of which one of its practitioners has written: 'It is only fair to admit that the criticism of oral testimonies has not reached the sophistication of the critique of documents, which historians have been practising for centuries' (Peter Burke, 'Overture: the New History, its Past and its Future' in Peter Burke (ed.), *New Perspectives on Historical Writing* (Polity Press, 1991) 1–23). Yet in discussion of recent litigation over native title and stolen children, historians have suggested that the courts give an unwarranted priority to documents over oral history and could learn from historians how to use them together. If so, well and good, but it may be that historians can also learn from law and anthropology about the shallowness and factual unreliability of tradition in pre-literate societies. See, for example, John Toohey, *Report by the Aboriginal Land Commissioner, Mr Justice Toohey, to the Minister for Aboriginal Affairs and to the Administrator of the Northern Territory*, quoting WEH Stanner, *On Aboriginal Religion* (Sydney University Press, 1966/2014). The suggestion of a supposed favouring of documentary evidence is based mainly on the decisions of Justice Olney in *Members of the Yorta Yorta Aboriginal Community v Victoria* [1998] FCA 1606 and Justice O'Loughlin in *Cubillo and Gunner v Commonwealth of Australia* [2000] FCA 1084. The decisions in those Federal Court cases, unfavourable to Indigenous interests, caused great disappointment and in my view attracted much ill-

founded and unfair criticisms of the judges, based on a misreading of their reasons or a misunderstanding of their functions. It is an easy reaction to shoot the messenger of unpalatable news, but in my view, which I develop later, the real problem in each case was not the shortcomings of the judges but the fact that the historical grievances of Indigenous people have been relegated to the courts, instead of being confronted as the political problems they are.

24  This consideration was important to the majority judges of the Full Federal Court (Justices Branson and Katz) who were unwilling to uphold the appeal against Justice Olney in *Members of the Yorta Yorta Aboriginal Community v State of Victoria* [2001] FCA 45.

25  Thomas E Scrutton, 'The Work of the Commercial Courts' (1921) 1 *The Cambridge Law Journal* 6–20, 8.

26  Jerome Frank, *Courts on Trial: Myth and Reality in American Justice* (Princeton University Press, 1950) 448. Frank was a leading legal realist: see Julius Paul, 'Jerome Frank's Contributions to the Philosophy of American Legal Realism' (1958) 11(3) *Vanderbilt Law Review* 753–82 (Eds).

27  JM Kelly, *A Short History of Western Legal Thought* (Oxford University Press, 1992) 367.

28  The novelist Somerset Maugham, who was the brother of a Lord Chancellor, wrote that he wished, when listening to judges moralising with unction in the criminal courts, that every judge should keep beside him on the bench a packet of toilet paper to remind him that he was a man like other men (William Somerset Maugham, *The Summing Up* (William Heinemann, 1938) 55). Lawyers like to tell the apocryphal story of a group of Victorian judges considering a draft petition to the Queen. In the prolix language of the day, it began 'Conscious as we are of our manifold defects ...'. One judge objected that he wasn't conscious of any defects. After some discussion they agreed that the petition should commence 'Conscious as we are of the manifold defects of each other ...'.

29  This is particularly true of appointment from a separate Bar and is an argument invoked for confining judicial appointments to barristers.

30  For an example involving humanist witnesses in native title, see *De Rose v State of South Australia* [2002] FCA 1342 (O'Loughlin J).

31  Speaking of the responsibility this places on a judge, the United States Supreme Court said:

> The scientific project is advanced by broad and wide-ranging consideration of a multitude of hypotheses, for those that are incorrect will eventually be shown to be so, and that itself is an advance. Conjectures that are probably wrong are of little use, however, in the project of reaching a quick, final, and binding legal judgment – often of great consequence – about a particular set of events in the past. We

recognize that, in practice, a gatekeeping role for the judge, no matter how flexible, inevitably on occasion will prevent the jury from learning of authentic insights and innovations. That, nevertheless, is the balance that is struck by Rules of Evidence designed not for the exhaustive search for cosmic understanding but for the particularized resolution of legal disputes. (*Daubert v Merrell Dow Pharmaceuticals*, 509 US 579, 597 (1993)).

Once expert evidence is admitted and acted on by a jury, it will be very difficult to overturn the decision on the ground that the weight of expert evidence was to a different effect: *Government Transport v Adamcik* (1961) 106 CLR 292.

32   *Buckley v Rice Thomas* (1554) 1 Plowd 118; 75 ER 182, 191.

33   Ian Freckelton, Prasuna Reddy and Hugh Selby, *Australian Judicial Perspectives on Expert Evidence: An Empirical Study* (Australian Institute of Judicial Administration, 1999); Ian Freckelton, Prasuna Reddy and Hugh Selby, *Australian Magistrates' Perspectives on Expert Evidence: A Comparative Study* (Australian Institute of Judicial Administration, 2001).

34   Although the concern of courts about the impartiality of witnesses has historically arisen from experience with doctors, scientists and technologists, the anthropologists who have more recently entered the courts have a particular problem. Their specialised knowledge of a particular community results from research that requires the building of confidence and trust, and inevitably results in relationships of friendship and obligation, and expectations that the anthropologist will act as community advocate with the outside world. Moreover, the mysteriousness of native title to lawyers has often led to anthropologists being called on to play a major role in preparing the applicant's case. For an introduction to the extensive literature on anthropologists, see Edwin N Wilmsen (ed.), *We are Here: Politics of Aboriginal Land Tenure* (University of California Press, 1989).

35   *Buckley v Rice Thomas*. Today such problems would probably be resolved by reference to dictionaries or authoritative texts, not then available.

36   Carol AG Jones, *Expert Witnesses: Science, Medicine, and the Practice of Law* (Clarendon Press, 1994).

37   An exception to the general welcome has been what seems to me an idiosyncratic decision by Justice Young. In *Bellevue Crescent Pty Ltd v Marland Holdings* [1998] NSWSC 68, the judge drew a distinction between 'the facts of history' and 'social history' saying that while courts may obtain the basal facts such as when a particular war broke out or other matters of record from reputable histories, analyses as to why certain things happened and generally how people behaved is not a matter which can be proved by the evidence of people who were not there but have ascertained the historical facts and then have analysed them to work out a conclusion. He argued that

the knowledge of an historian does not fit within s 79 of the *Uniform Evidence Act* 'because it is, first of all, based on the hearsay material of the past and then the opinion is not wholly or substantially based upon that knowledge but, rather, is an analysis'.

I find this unconvincing. Much expert knowledge in other disciplines is based on reports of the investigations of others and is hearsay but nonetheless is accepted as 'specialised knowledge based on the person's study'. 'Analysis' of knowledge is surely simply a means by which the expert forms an opinion based on the knowledge.

38   EH Carr, *What is History?* (Palgrave, 1961/2001).

39   Keith Windschuttle, *The Fabrication of Australian History: Volume 1, Van Diemen's Land 1803–1847* (Macleay Press, 2002); Lyndall Ryan, 'No Historian Enjoys a Monopoly Over the Truth', *The Australian* (Sydney, 17 December 2002). The other prominent target of Windschuttle's criticism responded differently, seeing the need for the criticisms to be tested by scholarly work: see Henry Reynolds, 'Historians at War', *The Weekend Australian* (Sydney, 14 December 2002).

40   Hal Wootten, 'The End of Dispossession? Anthropologists and Lawyers in the Native Title Process' in J Finlayson and DE Smith (eds), *Native Title: Emerging Issues for Research, Policy and Practice* (Centre for Aboriginal Economic Policy Research, 1995) 101–18.

41   *Chapman v Luminis Pty Ltd (No 4)* [2001] FCA 1106 [296]. In fairness to Justice von Doussa, it should be noted that he observed that 'professional people are required by their professional standards to act honestly and not knowingly or recklessly to misrepresent the facts or mislead'. His remarks were made in the context of deciding that an anthropologist preparing a report for a client did not owe a duty of care to a third party. However that may be, the report in this case was for presentation to a rapporteur appointed by the Minister under the *Aboriginal and Torres Strait Islander Heritage Protection Act 1984* (Cth), who would in turn pass the report to the Minister who would decide whether to make a declaration under the Act. It is surely to be expected that the Minister would assume professional integrity rather than mere advocacy on the part of the anthropologist, a role that the anthropologist herself repudiated. An appeal by the developers against the decision that the anthropologist owed them no duty of care has been abandoned.

42   Francesca Merlan, 'An Assessment of von Doussa on Anthropology' (2001) <www.researchgate.net/publication/237208198>. In expressing my admiration for her rejection of the advocacy role which von Doussa considered to be in accord with community expectation, I am not intending to comment on the particular facts involved in the case. For an earlier exhortation to anthropologists to maintain their independence, see Wootten, 'The End of Dispossession'.

43    Andrew Ligertwood, *Australian Evidence* (Butterworths, 3rd ed, 1998) 6.

44    William Twining, *Rethinking Evidence* (Basil Blackwell, 1990).

45    Twining, *Rethinking Evidence* 76.

46    Robert P George, 'What is Law? A Century of Arguments' [2001] (Spring)
      *First Things* 23–29.

47    Isaiah Berlin, *The Crooked Timber of Humanity: Chapters in the History
      of Ideas*, ed Henry Hardy (John Murray, 1990).

48    See, eg, Ann McGrath, 'History and Land Rights' in McCalman and
      McGrath (eds), *Proof and Truth: The Humanist as Expert* (Australian
      Academy of the Humanities, 2003) 233–48.

49    Ron Hagen, 'Anthropologists, Historians and Native Title' (Conference
      Paper, Australian Historical Association Conference, 6–10 July 1988).
      Published works of apparent authority may be directly referred to by courts,
      or used to challenge or support the views of experts who are called.

50    RJ Evans, *Telling Lies about Hitler* (Verso, 2002). Evans' experience was
      admittedly unusual in the time and financial resources available to pursue
      the truth, in the fact that the dispute was between historians and about the
      proper practice of historians, and in the fact that he was cross-examined by
      the plaintiff, David Irving, rather than a barrister.

51    RJ Evans, 'History, Memory and the Law' (2002) 41(3) *History and Theory*,
      326–45.

52    To its credit, the Federal Court has made valiant efforts to adapt to the
      challenge: see Michael Black, 'Developments in Practice and Procedure
      in Native Title Cases' (2002) 13(1) *Public Law Review* 16–25.

53    Nicholas Evans, 'Country and the Word: Linguistic Evidence in the Croker
      Island claim' in John Henderson and David Nash (eds), *Language in Native
      Title* (Aboriginal Studies Press, 2002) 53–100.

54    *Mabo v Queensland (No 2)* (1992) 175 CLR 1.

55    Hal Wootten, 'Native Title in a Long Perspective: A View from the Eighties'
      (Native Title Representative Bodies Conference, Geraldton, September
      2002). This paper is extracted in chapter 9 (Eds).

56    This analysis puts me at odds with some lawyers writing from the perspective
      of critical legal theory for whose commitment to the pursuit of Indigenous
      justice I have the greatest respect. Whereas I see 'native title' as a bona
      fide attempt by the *Mabo* court to find a legal basis for recognising that on
      acquisition Australia was not *terra nullius* but owned by the Indigenous
      inhabitants, and for giving what limited legal recognition was feasible to
      what remained of that ownership, Ritter sees it as the political construct of
      an instrument of a colonialist state invented 'as a kind of reward that is given
      to Indigenous communities that are deemed "worthy"'. Whereas I see the
      historiography forced on a reluctant Justice Olney in the *Yorta Yorta* case as
      a bona fide and reasonable attempt by a sympathetic but 'black letter' lawyer

to apply the *Mabo* decision to a situation of severe social disruption, Ritter and Flanagan see it as something embraced to 'legitimate' his prior political decision that the *Yorta Yorta* should not have native title: David Ritter and Frances Flanagan, 'Stunted Growth: The Historiography of Native Title Litigation in the Decade since Mabo' (2003) 11 *Public History Review* 21–40. It is obvious that, as Ritter says, Justice Olney and Justice Lee, who decided the *Ward* case in the Kimberley favourably to Aboriginal claimants, are 'different people'. For all I know they may be as different as, say, [Justices] Dyson Heydon and Michael Kirby on the High Court, and put very different weight on the range of factors that judges may legitimately allow to influence their decisions. Nevertheless, I think the different outcomes in the *Ward* and *Yorta Yorta* cases had far more to do with the different histories of the Kimberley and Victoria than the personalities of the judges and cannot reasonably be represented as the political allocation of rewards between the 'worthy' and the 'unworthy'. It is precisely because the courts cannot and do not deliver political justice that they are an inappropriate forum for dealing with historical injustices. I am in full sympathy with native title lawyers who may wish to take the advice of Ritter and Flanagan and recast their roles so that 'rather than just seeking determinations of legal rights, it is the project of the native title lawyer to redress power disparity': David Ritter and Frances Flanagan, 'Lawyers and Rats: Critical Legal Theory and Native Title' in Sandy Toussaint (ed.), *Crossing Boundaries* (Melbourne University Press, 2003) 128–42. However, I think the constructive way to do this is to take the struggle to the political arena where it belongs, not to 'unmask' and further politicise the courts, which for all their shortcomings remain the best guarantor of a rule of law that is a necessary support for all democratic struggles: cf Gillian Cowlishaw, 'Policing the Races' (1994) 36 *Social Analysis: The International Journal of Anthropology* 71–92; Edward Palmer Thompson, *Whigs and Hunters* (Allen Lane, 1975). This is not to say that litigation may not be a legitimate and powerful tool in the pursuit of political justice, as it provides a forum for exposing to the public gaze the grievance of parties, the facts relating to them, and the limits of redress available through judicial process. Moreover, despite its restricted character, native title can yield real benefits for some communities.

57    A submission by the Law Council of Australia to the Australian Law Reform Commission in support of the retention of the adversarial system in the ordinary courts unintentionally emphasises how inappropriate it is for the historic Indigenous issues. One of the merits attributed to the adversarial system was that it 'was in accord with an individualistic, rights-based society', whereas the term 'inquisitorial' refers to 'a proceeding in which a neutral judicial officer carries out an investigation to discover facts, the discovery of which will serve some identifiable public purpose. There is no dispute

per se': Australian Law Reform Commission, *Managing Justice: A Review of the Federal Civil Justice System* (Report No 89, February 2000) ('Managing Justice') [120], [123].

58    Notoriously, governments present sums spent on resisting Aboriginal claims in the public account totals supposedly spent for the benefit of Aboriginals. Those who have seen examples of the Commonwealth's vigorous defences to Indigenous claims will be interested to know that it puts itself forward generally as a 'model litigant'. In praising the working of the adversarial system, the Australian Law Reform Commission noted that 'The government's own approach to disputes, dispute prevention, resolution and litigation is highly influential' (Managing Justice, [164]).

59    Linguistic difficulties alone, including the often-unrecognised fact that there are many different versions of 'English', are enough to make many findings in native title cases problematic. In the Wellesley Island case, when a trained linguist (Nicholas Evans) acted as interpreter he was forced to point out that questions he was being asked to put could not even be asked in the witness's language, yet similar questions had been allowed over objection to witnesses from the same language group with limited English.

60    The most constructive outcomes occur when parties manage to turn their back on court processes and negotiate Indigenous Land Use Agreements.

61    The operation of the Tribunal has given rise to considerable discussion of the process of seeking truth and the role of historians: see, eg, William Oliver, 'The Future Behind Us' in Andrew Sharp and Paul McHugh (eds), *Histories, Power and Loss* (Bridget Williams Books, 2001) 9–29.

**Chapter 7: Access to law: Papua New Guinea and the Aboriginal Legal Service**

1    Hal Wootten, 'Another Congo in New Guinea: What Happened to the University of Port Moresby?' 86(4423) *The Bulletin* (28 November 1964) 17–20, 17.

2    Hal was Secretary General of LAWASIA from 1967 to 1973. His successor, David Geddes, commented that the 'significance of Professor Wootten's contribution to the development of LAWASIA and, through this development, to the strengthening of the rule of law in the region, has been incalculable': 7 *Victorian Bar News* (September 1973). On the creation and role of LAWASIA, see JH Wootten, 'The Law Association for Asia and the Western Pacific – An Experiment in Regional Cooperation' (1968) 7(2) *Washburn Law Journal* 211–38 (Eds).

3    Hal chaired the Law Council's Committee on PNG affairs 1963–66 and was a member of a Law Council committee on legal education in PNG (see below). He had first-hand knowledge of PNG. Disillusioned by work in a Sydney solicitor's office, he went in 1946 to teach law at the Australian School of Pacific Administration, which trained 'field staff, magistrates, patrol officers

and so on for New Guinea, for the resumption of civil administration. [Part] of the picture of ASOPA was that it was to work towards preparing Papua-New Guinea for independence, as part of the world-wide decolonisation process': 'Wisdom Interviews: Hal Wootten QC', *Big Ideas* (ABC Radio National, 1 May 2005). In 1947, Hal went to PNG, living in a remote village on Manus for six months, preparing to undertake a PhD in anthropology and/or to work as a patrol officer. In 1965, Hal appeared in a case about pay for PNG's civil servants which is discussed in chapter 3. In 1968, he published a substantial paper about the prospects for PNG's independence: see Hal Wootten, 'New Guinea and the Outside World' in John Wilkes (ed.), *New Guinea … Future Indefinite?* (Angus & Robertson, 1968) 65–100. In 1980, he was appointed Chief Justice of PNG but did not take up the position because of a change of government (Eds).

4    'Few Australians now recall that Papua was the first territory of the Federation (1906), predating the Northern Territory (1911), and New Guinea (1921). Few remember that until 1975 Papua and New Guinea shared the same constitutional status with the Northern Territory (and the other Australian territories), or that from 1948 to 1975 Papuans held Australian citizenship.' Helen Gardner, Jonathan Ritchie and Brad Underhill, '"The Moat of Oblivion": Australia and the Forgetting of Papua New Guinea' (2024) 55(2) *Australian Historical Studies* 233–54, 233–34 (Eds).

5    Hal was a member of this sub-committee (Eds).

6    The sub-committee's submission is reprinted as Appendix III in *The Report of the Commission on Higher Education in Papua and New Guinea* (Report, 1964) (Eds).

7    As noted above, the PNG University School of Law was established in 1965 (Eds).

8    Peter Thompson, *Big Ideas* (ABC, 1 May 2005) <www.abc.net.au/listen/programs/bigideas/wisdom-interviews-hal-wootten-qc/3446536>.

9    Aboriginal Legal Service, 'Hal Wootten in The Story Project: 40 Years of the ALS' (YouTube, 18 July 2013) <www.youtube.com/watch?v=uhbe4ldByEA>. For more information on The Story Project, see <redfernoralhistory.org/Organisations/AboriginalLegalService/tabid/210/Default.aspx>. Other videos in the series are available on YouTube: <www.youtube.com/playlist?list=PLxTqByWNqE9vArVn6aHEBgPpXUqj3kr9C> (Eds).

10    Hal Wootten, 'The Aboriginal Legal Service' (Unpublished Speech, 2005). He went on to cite Henry V's St Crispin's Day speech from the eve of the Battle of Agincourt: William Shakespeare, *Henry V* (1599) Act 4, Scene 3, 18–67 (Eds).

11    Thompson, *Big Ideas*.

12    Wootten, 'The Aboriginal Legal Service'.

13  Thompson, *Big Ideas*.

14  Ibid.

15  For example, Faith Bandler, Tom Williams and Trudy Longbottom (Eds).

16  For example, Paul Coe, Gary Foley and Gary Williams (Eds).

17  He credited Aunty Shirl and Chicka Dixon with making this bridge (Eds).

18  ALS, 'Hal Wootten in The Story Project'.

19  Ibid.

20  Tony Stephens, 'Pomp Replaced with Wit and Pragmatism', *Sydney Morning Herald* (Sydney, 13 December 2007).

21  Wootten, 'The Aboriginal Legal Service'.

22  Ibid.

23  Michael Sturma, 'Policing the Criminal Frontier in Mid-Nineteenth Century Australia, Britain and America' in Mark Finnane (ed.), *Policing in Australia: Historical Perspectives* (UNSW Press, 1987) 16.

24  Ibid. 26.

25  CD Rowley, *The Destruction of Aboriginal Society* (ANU Press, 1970) 153.

26  Ibid. 155.

27  An African-American revolutionary movement, active in the USA 1966–82 (Eds).

28  CD Rowley, *Outcasts in White Australia* (ANU Press, 1972) 367–68.

29  See 'Our People: Eddy Neumann', *Eddy Neuman Lawyers* <www.eddyneumann.com.au/eddy-neumann.html> (Eds).

30  For a photographic record, see 'Our History: 50+ Years of Resistance, Resilience and Solidarity', *Aboriginal Legal Service (NSW/ACT) Limited* <www.alsnswact.org.au/history> (Eds).

31  In 2019, Hal attended UNSW Law's celebration of its 100th Indigenous graduate: see UNSW Law, 'Celebrating 100 Indigenous UNSW Law Graduates' (YouTube, 4 April 2019) <www.youtube.com/watch?v=IDYJZYSkg30> (Eds).

32  The Empress Hotel was located at 87 Regent Street, near Redfern Station. From the 1950s through to the 1970s, it was one of the few pubs in Sydney where Aboriginal people were permitted to drink: Catie Gilchrist, 'The Empress Hotel, Redfern', *The Dictionary of Sydney* (2015) <dictionaryofsydney.org/entry/the_empress_hotel_redfern> (Eds).

33  This refers to a moment in Jenny Brockie's classic documentary *Cop it Sweet* (ABC, 1991). The incident Hal refers to concerns a police officer pointing out the attention given to a young Aboriginal man for driving a red Ford Laser. The long final sequence illustrates these tensions best when an officer arrests an Aboriginal man for expressing in 'offensive language' his dislike of police 'studying the Block'. What follows is two men playing out historically structured roles in a futile process of arrest and detention. Filmed 20 years after the ALS was established, the film showed not only a little-

changed policing style, but also a valuable picture of street-life in Redfern before gentrification. For analysis of the reaction to the film, see Janet Chan, *Changing Police Culture* (Cambridge University Press, 1997) ch 8 (Eds).

34 This was Norman Allen, subsequently the subject of corruption allegations: see David Hickie, *The Prince and the Premier* (HarperCollins, 1985) (Eds).

35 The same logic was evident in *Cop it Sweet*. In the NSW Police Annual Reports from 1970–73, the only mention of Aboriginal people referred to the employment of three Aboriginal 'trackers' (Eds).

36 Ron Brunton, *Black Suffering, White Guilt?* (Institute for Public Affairs, 1993).

37 CJ Malcolm, 'Opening Address' in RH Bartlett (ed.), *Resource Development and Aboriginal Land Rights in Australia* (Centre for Commercial and Resources Law, 1993) 5.

38 For a specific example, see JH Wootten, *Report of the Inquiry into the Death of Marie Quayle* (Royal Commission into Aboriginal Deaths in Custody, 1991) 119.

39 John Avery, *Police, Force or Service?* (Butterworths, 1981) 41.

40 Ibid. 41.

41 Ibid. 41.

42 Ibid. 58–59.

43 Ibid. 65.

44 Aboriginal Legal Service, *Annual Report 1971–72* (Report, 1972).

45 The RCIADIC recommended that such notification should be compulsory (Recommendation 224). This was implemented in NSW in the Law Enforcement (Powers and Responsibilities) Regulation 2005 (NSW) s 37 (Eds).

46 In 1971, the all-white South African rugby team's tour of Australia was disrupted by anti-apartheid demonstrators. On Aboriginal people's involvement, see Sarah Garnham, 'Gary Foley Reflects on the 1971 Springbok Tour protests', *Red Flag* (Melbourne, 8 August 1971) <redflag.org.au/article/gary-foley-reflects-1971-springbok-tour-protests> (Eds).

47 Brunton, *Black Suffering, White Guilt*.

48 For example, Sergeant Feltham in Echuca: JH Wootten, *Report of the Inquiry into the Death of James Archibald Moore* (Royal Commission into Aboriginal Deaths in Custody, 1990).

49 Hal's concentration on civil cases was not coincidental. He was initially going to be appointed to the Court of Appeal (which, inter alia, hears appeals in criminal and police matters). The NSW Police, via the Minister of Police, objected to this, citing Hal's involvement in the ALS. He was instead appointed to the Supreme Court, dealing with politically safer equity matters: Personal Communication, from Hal Wootten to David Dixon, 21 June 2017 (Eds).

50    Avery, *Police, Force or Service?* 2.
51    Ibid. 1–5, 86.
52    This paper was published in 1993. Much has changed since then: see below (Eds).
53    Avery, *Police, Force or Service* 86.
54    In NSW, the change from 'Force' to 'Service' was made in 1990. But its reversal only 16 years later signified the marginalisation of the kind of policing championed by Avery, even though it was recommended as an essential part of the reform agenda of the Royal Commission into the NSW Police Service 1995–97. In 2006, the Service was renamed the NSW Police Force: see Janet Chan and David Dixon, 'The Politics of Police Reform: Ten Years after the Royal Commission into the New South Wales Police Service' (2007) 7(4) *Criminology & Criminal Justice* 443–68. This reflected the dominance of 'crime control' policing which spawned the apparently relentless rise in the numbers of Aboriginal people in gaol and the rejection of the key recommendations of another Royal Commission, that into Aboriginal Deaths in Custody: see chapter 8 (Eds).
55    See Gordon Briscoe, *Racial Folly: A Twentieth Century Family* (ANU Press, 2010).
56    'Kanaka' is now regarded as an offensive term for the South Sea Islanders who were brought, sometimes involuntarily, to work in Australian sugar fields as indentured labourers. See Alex McKinnon, 'Blackbirds: Australia's Hidden Slave Trade History', *The Monthly* (Melbourne, July 2019) <www.themonthly.com.au/issue/2019/july/1561989600/alex-mckinnon/blackbirds-australia-s-hidden-slave-trade-history> (Eds).

### Chapter 8: The Royal Commission into Aboriginal Deaths in Custody

1    Those of Shane Atkinson, Lloyd Boney, Peter Campbell, Thomas Carr, Glenn Clarke, Harrison Day, David Gundy, Paul Kearny, Bruce Leslie, Arthur Moffatt, James Moore, Thomas Murray, Clarence Nean, Mark Quayle, Mark Revell, Max Saunders, Malcolm Smith and Peter Williams. Hal's reports on their deaths are available at <austlii.edu.au/au/other/IndigLRes/rciadic> (Eds).
2    JH Wootten, Royal Commission into Aboriginal Deaths in Custody (Regional Report of Inquiry in New South Wales, Victoria and Tasmania, 1991).
3    Hal's individual reports total 1363 pages, while the Regional Report is another 248 (Eds).
4    In his Regional Report, Hal noted: 'To give some idea of just how big the task has been, the documentary evidence assembled in the case of David Gundy, excluding the witnesses' statements taken by Royal Commission staff, totalled just on 8,500 pages. Even so the hearing covered 38 days and produced 3,928 pages of transcript. This was the largest case as far as preparation and hearing

were concerned, but there were several others which were not far behind'
(24). For all the RCIADIC reports, see <austlii.edu.au/au/other/IndigLRes/
rciadic> (Eds).

5    CD Rowley, *The Destruction of Aboriginal Society* (ANU Press, 1970) 2.
6    The Commission explained process corruption as 'the kind of corruption
     whereby unnecessary physical force is applied, police powers are abused,
     evidence is fabricated or tampered with, or confessions are obtained by
     improper means. It is often directed at those members of the community who
     are least likely or least able to complain, and is justified by police on the basis
     of procuring the conviction of persons suspected of criminal or anti-social
     conduct, or in order to exercise control over sections of the community',
     Royal Commission into the NSW Police Service (*Final Report*, May 1997)
     vol 1: *Corruption* 26. See David Dixon (ed.), *A Culture of Corruption* (Hawkins
     Press, 1999) (Eds).
7    Personal correspondence from Hal to Martin Krygier (3 September 1997).
8    This term was coined by WEH Stanner and popularised in his 'The
     Australian Dreaming' (1968 Boyer Lectures, ABC, 1972). Other coinages are
     my own.
9    Elliott Johnston, Royal Commission into Aboriginal Deaths in Custody
     (*Report of the Inquiry into the Death of John Peter Pat*, 1991).
10   Royal Commission into Aboriginal Deaths in Custody (*National Report*, 1991)
     vol 5, app A (see amendment to National Commissioner's terms of reference
     of 6 May 1988).
11   The documentary, *Who Killed Malcom Smith?* (Film Australia, 1992) and
     the Tiddas' song 'Malcolm Smith', see Tiddas – Topic, 'Malcolm Smith'
     (YouTube, 15 September 2018) <www.youtube.com/watch?v=pANO
     sshMsqw>.
12   Gary Johns, *Aboriginal Self-Determination: The Whiteman's Dream* (Connor
     Court, 2011).
13   Don Weatherburn and Jessie Holmes, 'Re-thinking Indigenous Over-
     representation in Prison' (2010) 45(4) *Australian Journal of Social Issues* 559–76.
14   Ibid.; Noel Pearson, 'Lessons from Palm Island', *The Australian* (Sydney,
     7 October 2006); Noel Pearson, *Up from the Mission: Selected Writings*
     (Black Inc, 2009).
15   Hal Wootten, 'Reflections on the 20th Anniversary of the Royal Commission
     into Aboriginal Deaths in Custody' (2011) 7(27) *Indigenous Law Bulletin* 3–8.
16   *Mabo v Queensland (No 2)* (1992) 175 CLR 1. See also chapter 9 (Eds).
17   RCIADIC vol 2, ch 15; vol 4, ch 32.
18   Ibid. vol 4, 275–79; vol 5, 130–31. As to personal responsibility, see vol 2, 322.
19   Ibid. vol 1, 151.

20   For an extraordinary case of lack of care of a prisoner, see Deaths in Custody
     Watch Committee WA, *Ward Campaign for Justice*
     <http://www.deathsincustody.org.au/ward>. For a controversial police
     investigation, see 'CMC Review of the Queensland Police Service's Palm Island
     Review' (Report, Crime and Misconduct Commission, Queensland, June 2010).

21   Aboriginal and Torres Strait Islander Social Justice Commissioner, *Second
     Report*, 1994.

22   Tess Lea, 'When Looking for Anarchy, Look to the State: Fantasies of
     Regulation in Forcing Disorder within the Australian Indigenous Estate'
     (2012) 32(2) *Critique of Anthropology* 109–24.

23   Stephen Gray, *The Northern Territory Intervention* (Castan Centre for Human
     Rights, 2020).

24   Pearson, *Up from the Mission*.

25   RCIADIC, vol 1, 15–16.

26   Ibid. vol 1, 16–19.

27   Maria Lane distinguished the 'open society population' and the 'embedded
     welfare population'. See discussion in Noel Pearson, 'Radical Hope: Education
     and Equality in Australia' (2009) 35 *Quarterly Essay* 1.

28   Recent debate has centred on remote bounded communities: see Diane Austin-
     Broos, *A Different Inequality* (Allen & Unwin, 2011). However, many of the
     same problems remain in the embedded welfare community in cities and
     country towns: see Gillian Cowlishaw, *The City's Outback* (UNSW Press,
     2009).

29   Pierre Clastres, *Society Against the State: Essays in Political Anthropology*
     (Zone Books, 1989).

30   This application of Christopher Lasch's phrase to remote Aboriginal
     communities is from Gillian Cowlishaw, 'Crime and Governance through
     Culture' (Conference Paper, Crime, Justice and Social Democracy Conference,
     Queensland University of Technology, 27 September 2011).

31   Stanner, *Australian Dreaming*.

32   Jon Altman, 'What Future for Remote Indigenous Australia? Economic
     Hybridity and the Neoliberal Turn' in Jon Altman and Melinda Hinkson
     (eds), *Culture Crisis: Anthropology and Politics in Aboriginal Australia* (UNSW
     Press, 2010) 259.

33   Pearson, *Up from the Mission*.

34   RCIADIC vol 1, 16.

35   See also 'Aborigines and Police' (1993) 16(1) *University of New South Wales
     Law Journal* 265–301, 276–301; 'The RCIADC and Aboriginal Education'
     (Address, AGM of the NSW Education Consultative Group at Richmond,
     NSW, 28 October 1991); 'The RCIADC' (Conference Paper, Martung Upah
     Conference of the Australia Council of Churches, 9 December 1993).

**Chapter 9: *Mabo*, native title and squandered opportunities**

1   *Mabo v Queensland [No 2]* (1992) 175 CLR 1 ('*Mabo*').
2   *Mabo* (Brennan J) 29.
3   Hal Wootten, 'Occasional Address' (1995) 18(1) *University of New South Wales Law Journal* 232–36, 234.
4   'Mabo at Twenty' in Toni Bauman and Lyria Glick (eds), *The Limits of Change: Mabo and Native Title Twenty Years On* (AIATSIS, 2012) 431–44, 435.
5   Hal Wootten, 'Response to Lecture delivered by Sir Gerard Brennan' (Speech, Hal Wootten Lecture, UNSW, 23 August 2012) <www.unsw.edu.au/law-justice/news-events/events/annual-hal-wootten-lecture>.
6   Hal Wootten, 'Mabo: Issues and Challenges' (1994) 1(4) *The Judicial Review* 303–65.
7   Hal Wootten, 'Mabo and the Lawyers' (1995) 6(3) *Australian Journal of Anthropology* 116–33, 117–21.
8   'The End of Dispossession? Anthropologists and Lawyers in the Native Title Process' in J Finlayson and D Smith (eds), *Native Title* (Centre for Aboriginal Economic Policy Research, 1995) 101–18, 109.
9   Wootten, 'Mabo: Issues and Challenges' 309–11.
10  Ibid. 303–4.
11  Hal's first publication may have been 'Land Tenure in the Colonies' (1947) 2(2) *South Pacific* 25–28 (Eds).
12  *Mabo* 110.
13  *Dietrich v The Queen* (1992) 177 CLR 292, [5].
14  Wootten, 'Mabo and the Lawyers' 130–31.
15  *Milirrpum v Nabalco* (1971) 17 FLR 141, known as the Gove case because the land in question was the Gove peninsula in the Northern Territory. Hal explained that this decision had not been appealed because of its likely reception by the High Court at that time: 'Had an unsuccessful appeal been made, the possibility of overturning *terra nullius* may well have been buried, perhaps beyond resurrection. So, the issue had to wait another 20 years, until the work of many little nudgers found six receptive judges on the Mason Court'. From 'Response to Brennan' (Eds).
16  *Milirrpum v Nabalco* (1971) 17 FLR 141.
17  Noel Pearson, 'From Remnant Title to Social Justice' (1995) 6(3) *Australian Journal of Anthropology* 95–100.
18  H Wootten, 'The Mabo Decision and National Parks' in S Woenne-Green et al. (eds), *Competing Interests: Aboriginal participation in National Parks and Conservation Reservations in Australia* (Australian Conservation Foundation, 1994) 306–74. Wootten was President of the ACF, 1985–89, a role he found rewarding and interesting: see chapter 11 (Eds).

19 H Wootten, 'The Commonwealth and the *Mabo* Case' (23 October 1992) (unpublished).

20 MW Hunt, 'The Legal Implications of Mabo for Resource Development' in R Bartlett (ed.), *Resource Development and Aboriginal Land Rights in Australia* (Centre for Commercial and Resources Law, 1994).

21 The Minister in the Aboriginal Affairs portfolio at the time was Robert Tickner. Phillip Toyne had been recruited by Hal as Director of the ACF, a position he held 1986–92. (Eds).

22 *Fejo v Northern Territory* (1998) 195 CLR 96; *Western Australia v Ward* (2002) 213 CLR 1.

23 Katy Barnett, 'Western Australia v Ward: One Step Forward and Two Steps Back: Native Title and the Bundle of Rights Analysis' (2000) 24(2) *Melbourne University Law Review* 462–77.

24 Premier of Western Australia, 1993–2001. Hal commented on the 'chilling blatancy and hypocrisy of the Western Australian Government's attempt to convert native title by legislation from a legal right to a discretionary Ministerial handout': 'The End of Dispossession?' 102 (Eds).

25 Prime Minister of Australia, 1991–96.

26 See <pmtranscripts.pmc.gov.au/sites/default/files/original/00008765.pdf>.

27 A conservative constitutional law association: see Dominic Kelly, *Political Troglodytes and Economic Lunatics* (Black Inc, 1997) 54–72 (Eds).

28 B Hassall, 'Mabo and Federalism: The Prospect of an Indigenous People's Treaty', *Proceedings of the Samuel Griffith Society* (Melbourne, 1993) vol 2.

29 HM Morgan, 'Mabo Reconsidered' (The Joe and Enid Lyons Memorial Lecture, Australian National University, 12 October 1992); see also HM Morgan, 'Mabo and Australia's Future' (1993) 37(12) *Quadrant*, 63–67 (Eds). Morgan's campaigning drew Paul Keating's caustic attention: 'Mr Morgan has always painted himself as a thoughtful thinker on the right. He has never been thoughtful, and he has never been a thinker. What we have here is just bigotry. It is the voice of ignorance, the voice of hysteria and the voice of the 19th century' (quoted, Kelly, *Political Troglodytes* 69) (Eds).

30 Elsewhere, Hal commented acidly: 'Most legal recipients would have registered surprise that there was still a living lawyer who believed that judges simply apply and interpret the law, and do not bring values to its development. After all, the common law was not found under a raspberry bush or in a judge's navel, but was an artifact of the judges who have kept it growing vigorously for nearly a millennium' ('Mabo and the Lawyers' 117) (Eds).

31 'Mining Chief Lashes Mabo', *Sydney Morning Herald* (Sydney, 1 July 1993).

32 'Comments May Cost Bosch Role as Adviser', *Sydney Morning Herald* (Sydney, 9 August 1993).

33 'Blacks Centuries Behind Us: Perron', *Sydney Morning Herald* (Sydney, 7 July 1993).

34  Geoffrey Blainey, 'Land Rights for All', *The Age* (Melbourne, 10 November 1993) 15.
35  G Cowlishaw, 'Did the Earth Move for You? The Anti-Mabo Debate' (1995) 6(3) *Australian Journal of Anthropology* 43–63.
36  President of the National Native Title Tribunal 1994–98 and later Chief Justice of the High Court of Australia 2008–17 (Eds).
37  *Members of the Yorta Yorta Aboriginal Community v Victoria* (2002) 214 CLR 422.
38  *De Rose v State of South Australia [No 2]* (2005) 145 FCR 290.
39  *Western Australia v Ward* (2002) 213 CLR 1 ('*Ward*').
40  *Wilson v Minister for Aboriginal and Torres Strait Islander Affairs* (1996) 189 CLR 1.
41  *Commonwealth v Yarmirr* (2001) 208 CLR 1; H Wootten, 'Conflicting Imperatives: Finding Truth in the Courts' in I McCalman and A McGrath (eds), *Proof and Truth: The Humanist as Expert* (The Australian Academy of the Humanities, 2004). See chapter 6 (Eds).
42  EG Whitlam, 'Speech at the Opening of a National Seminar on Aboriginal Arts' (Speech, Canberra, 21 May 1973) <pmtranscripts.pmc.gov.au/release/transcript-2932>.
43  *Ward*.
44  Ibid. 561.
45  Ibid. 561.
46  Ibid. 561.
47  Kevin Gilbert, *Living Black: Blacks Talk to Kevin Gilbert* (Penguin, 1978) 305.
48  The Bible, Proverbs 29, 18.
49  *Wik Peoples v Queensland [1996]* 187 CLR 1.

## Chapter 10: Sacred sites, the Stolen Generations and looking forward

1  For a summary of the affair, see the beginning of the judgment of Justice von Doussa of the Federal Court in *Chapman v Luminis (No 4)* [2001] FCA 1106; 123 FCR 62, which ended the litigation. For an overview, see Margaret Simmons, *The Meeting of the Waters: The Hindmarsh Bridge Affair* (Hachette, 2003) (Eds).
2  See also Hal Wootten, 'The Alice Springs Dam and Sacred Sites' in Murray Goot and Tim Rowse (eds), *Make a Better Offer: The Politics of Mabo* (Pluto, 1994) 8–22 (Eds).
3  For example, in the Northern Territory, the *Native and Historical Objects and Areas Preservation Ordinance 1955* was enacted to protect 'prescribed objects'. A prescribed object was defined as 'an object relating to the Aboriginal natives of Australia which is of ethnological or anthropological interest or value' (s 3). Six years later the Ordinance was amended to prohibit interference with 'any place used by Australian Aboriginal natives

as a ceremonial, burial, or initiation ground' (s 9H). Another 17 years went by before there was an attempt in the Territory to give general legislative protection to sites of significance according to Aboriginal tradition (*Aboriginal Sacred Sites Ordinance 1978*). The first legislation in Western Australia vested control of sites in the Western Australian Museum (*Aboriginal Heritage Act 1972*).

4   There are no doubt levels of generalisation at which one might speak of *an* Aboriginal culture, but in pre-invasion Australia there were many distinct Aboriginal groups, and thereafter dispossession, contact with different aspects of Western society, education, opportunity and many other pressures for cultural change and adaptation have operated, and continue to operate, differentially on groups and individuals.

5   *Aboriginal Land Rights (Northern Territory) Act 1976* (Cth), *Aboriginal Sacred Sites Ordinance 1978* (NT). The former Act remains in force; the latter is superseded by the *Northern Territory Aboriginal Sacred Sites Act 1989*, which continues to use the same definition. Other examples of legislative broadening of the concept included 'sites and items of sacred, ceremonial, mythological or historic significance to the Aboriginal people' (*Aboriginal Heritage Act 1979* (SA)) and places and objects 'which are or have been of sacred, ritual or spiritual or ceremonial significance to persons of Aboriginal descent' (*Aboriginal Heritage Act 1972* (WA).

6   'Aboriginal' is defined as 'a member of the Aboriginal race of Australia, and includes a descendant of the Indigenous inhabitants of the Torres Strait Islands'.

7   *Significant Aboriginal Sites in Area of Boobera Lagoon*, Report to Minister for Aboriginal Affairs under s 10(4) of the *Aboriginal and Torres Strait Islander Heritage Protection Act 1984* (Cth) (Department of Aboriginal Affairs, 1996).

8   *Commonwealth v Tasmania* (1983) 158 CLR 1 ('Tasmanian Dam case').

9   Hon Hal Wootten QC AC, *Report to the Minister for Aboriginal Affairs Re: Boobera Lagoon* (Department of Aboriginal Affairs, 1996).

10   See chapter 6 (Eds).

11   In October 1995, following unfortunate events in the Hindmarsh Island Bridge application, the then Labor Minister for Aboriginal and Torres Strait Islander Affairs asked Elizabeth Evatt AC to report on the operation of the Act. In her *Review of the Aboriginal and Torres Strait Islander Heritage Protection Act 1984* (August 1996) she made a number of recommendations to amend the Act. In December 1996, the government having changed, the new Liberal Minister announced the government's intention to make wide-ranging changes to the Act 'designed to prevent another Hindmarsh Island saga'. Very few of the Evatt recommendations were reflected in the government's subsequently issued proposals, which were considered by the Parliamentary Joint Committee on Native Title and the Aboriginal

and Torres Strait Islander Land Fund but remained contentious, and no legislation has resulted.

12    *Significant Aboriginal sites in area of proposed Junction Waterhole Dam, Alice Springs: report to the Minister for Aboriginal Affairs under s 10(4) of the Aboriginal and Torres Strait Islander Heritage Protection Act 1984* (Department of Aboriginal Affairs, 1992).

13    Lowitja O'Donohue described Senator Herron as 'a Minister without influence or purpose': *The Australian* (Sydney, 17 November 1997) 10.

14    My recommended strategy was not adopted. Instead, as I have already noted, opposition was deflected by applying $5 million of funds allotted for Aboriginal heritage protection to provide an alternative site for the water-skiers.

15    Australian Constitution preamble para 1.

16    *Bringing them Home Report* (National Inquiry into the Separation of Aboriginal and Torres Strait Islander Children from Their Families, 1997) 273–75.

17    Ibid. 272–73.

18    E Johnston, Royal Commission into Aboriginal Deaths in Custody (*National Report*, 1991) vol 5, 34.

19    Until 1967 the separate states had been entirely responsible for Aboriginal policy. In 1967, following a successful referendum and constitutional amendment that granted the federal government new powers, the Holt Government had established an Office of Aboriginal Affairs (OAA) with Barrie Dexter the head and HC 'Nugget' Coombs and WEH Stanner as advisers. Prime Minister Gough Whitlam established the National Aboriginal Consultative Council and the Department of Aboriginal Affairs in 1972 (Eds).

20    This is not to deny that there have been differences in emphasis, sometimes expressed in the substitution of another term for self-determination, eg self-management, self-sufficiency or self-reliance.

21    ATSIC – The Aboriginal and Torres Strait Islander Commission – was abolished soon after this lecture. Although Hal saw ATSIC as an inappropriate white style of institution for Aboriginal people, he was very critical of the reasons for the abolition. See Hal Wootten, 'Self-determination after ATSIC' (2004) 23(2) *Dialogue* 16–24 (Eds).

22    Notably the failure to give a national apology for the removal of children as recommended in the *Bringing Them Home Report* (1997); the amendment of the Native Title Act after the High Court *Wik* decision; Aboriginal heritage issues; the funding and functions of ATSIC; and the refusal to override the Northern Territory's mandatory sentencing laws. Although the Liberal Party responded to Pauline Hanson's populist challenge to the consensus at the 1996 election by withdrawing her endorsement, her continued electoral

success revealed a latent hostility to the consensus among a section of the population that has continued to affect the attitude of the major parties.

23    Hal's work in RCIADIC was influential in drawing attention to the removal of Aboriginal children from their families and its consequences, not least in his report on Malcolm Smith's death (see chapter 8). His response to *Bringing Them Home* was equivocal: he welcomed the report and defended it against familiar detractors like Brunton, but he also identified its shortcomings, due in considerable part to the underfunding of the inquiry. See Hal Wootten, 'Ron Brunton & Bringing Them Home' (Eds).

24    On 28 May 2000, about 250 000 people participated in a 'Walk for Reconciliation' across the Sydney Harbour Bridge, one of the largest public demonstrations in Australia's history. Related events were held in other cities and towns across the country in the weeks afterward (Eds).

25    When the Department of Aboriginal Affairs was established in 1972, it was thought that it would be able to achieve its objectives in ten years: Lois O'Donoghue, 'Ending the Despair: The 1991 Sir Robert Garran Oration' (1992) 51(2) *Australian Journal of Public Administration* 214–22, 216.

26    Kevin Gilbert, *Because a White Man'll Never Do It* (Angus & Robertson, 1973) 148–64, 175–76; *Living Black* (Allen Lane, 1977).

27    John von Sturmer, *Talking with Aborigines* (Australian Institute of Aboriginal Studies, 1989).

28    *Too Much Sorry Business: The Submission of the Northern Territory Aboriginal Issues Unit of RCIADIC to Commissioner Elliott Johnston* (Royal Commission into Aboriginal Deaths in Custody, 1990).

29    Colin Tatz, *Genocide in Australia* (Aboriginal Studies Press, 1999).

30    O'Donoghue, 'Ending the Despair' 222.

31    Sally Dingo, *Dingo: The Story of Our Mob* (Random House, 1997).

## Chapter 11: Wilderness values, conservation and the environment

1    See chapter 3 (Eds).

2    For example, 'Mining Law and the Environment' (1985) 13(4) *Habitat* 35–38; 'Green and Black after Mabo' (1993) 21 (4) *Habitat* 18–21; 'The Mabo Decision and National Parks' in Susan Woenne-Green et al. (eds), *Competing Interests: Aboriginal Participation in National Parks and Conservation Reservations* (Australian Conservation Foundation, 1994) 306–74 (Eds).

3    *Key Largo* is a 1948 American film noir crime-drama directed by John Huston (Eds).

4    'Trickle down economics', promoted by Ronald Reagan in the USA and Margaret Thatcher in the UK, hypothesised that government policies favouring the rich (notably, tax cuts) would indirectly benefit the poor. The result was the opposite – a widening gap between rich and poor (Eds).

5    EF Schumacher, *A Guide for the Perplexed* (Jonathan Cape, 1977) 66.

6     Ibid. 66–67.

7     Alexander Downer was Shadow Minister for the Environment at the time. He later went on to be Leader of the Opposition (1994–95), Minister for Foreign Affairs (1996–2007) and High Commissioner to the United Kingdom (2014–18). Post-politics activities have included consulting for Woodside Energy and advising British strategic intelligence firm Hakluyt & Company (Eds).

8     Phillip Toyne was a leading environmental and Aboriginal rights campaigner who was the executive director of the ACF (1986–92). In this role, he worked with Rick Farley, the head of the National Farmers Federation, and the two organisations established Landcare in 1989, with the support of the Hawke Government (Eds).

9     As Chairman of the Australian Press Council, Hal gave a detailed overview of its purpose and functions in JH Wootten, 'The Australian Press Council' (1986) 9(1) *University of New South Wales Law Journal* 17–26. He resigned from the role later that year in protest after the Council voted not to object to the government's acquiescence in the takeover of the Herald & Weekly Times newspaper company by Rupert Murdoch (Eds).

10    John Howard was then Leader of the Opposition, and later Prime Minister 1996–2007 (Eds).

11    Sir Johannes Bjelke-Petersen was the National Party Premier of Queensland (1968–87). See Evan Whitton, *The Hillbilly Dictator* (ABC Books, 1989) (Eds).

12    Premier of Tasmania (1982–89) (Eds).

13    Michael Mobbs is an environmental lawyer and activist: see *Sustainable House: Living for Our Futures* (Choice Books, 1998).

14    Hal here again refers to one of his favourites – King Harry's St Crispin's Day speech to his comrades at the battle of Agincourt in *Henry V*, Act IV, Scene III.

# INDEX

www.ingramcontent.com/pod-product-compliance
Lightning Source LLC
Chambersburg PA
CBHW050236220326
41598CB00044B/7408